Exploring Psychology in Language Learning and Teaching

Published in this series
Oxford Handbooks for Language Teachers

Exploring Psychology in Language Learning and Teaching

Marion Williams, Sarah Mercer, and Stephen Ryan

OXFORD

UNIVERSITY PRESS

OXFORD
UNIVERSITY PRESS

ACKNOWLEDGEMENTS

The authors and publisher are grateful to those who have given permission to reproduce the following extracts and adaptations of copyright material: pp.53, 54 Extracts from *Towards an Understanding of Language Learner Self-Concept* by Sarah Mercer, Springer, 2011. Reproduced by permission of Springer; permission conveyed through Copyright Clearance Center, Inc. p.62 Extract from "The beliefs and practices of Thai English Language teachers" by Chamaipak Tayjasanant PhD thesis, 2001. Reproduced by permission. p.64 Extracts from "An investigation into the changes in student perceptions of and attitudes towards learning English as a second language in a Malaysian college" by S. Chee Choy, PhD thesis, 2003. Reproduced by permission. p.72 Table from "A theory of motivation for some classroom experiences" by Bernard Weiner, *Journal of Educational Psychology*, Volume 71 (1), 1979. © 1979 by the American Psychological Association. Reproduced with permission. p.86 Extracts from "Attitudes towards foreign language learning among secondary students in England" by Luba Atherton, PhD thesis, 2005. Reproduced by permission. p.90 Extracts from "Improving a college-level EFL writing class in Taiwan: From understanding students' writing anxiety to the implementation of a process-product approach" by Hanmin Tsai, EdD thesis, 2008. Reproduced by permission. pp.125–126, 135 Extracts from "A study of the strategies used by Hong Kong Chinese learners in learning English in an independent school environment in the United Kingdom" by Rita S. Y. Berry, PhD thesis, 1998. Reproduced by permission. pp.140,141 Figure from "Conceptualizing Willingness to Communicate in a L2: A Situational Model of L2 Confidence and Affiliation" by Peter D. MacIntyre, Zoltán Dörnyei, Richard Clément and Kimberly A. Noels, *The Modern Language Journal*, Volume 82 (4) 1998. Reproduced by permission of John Wiley and Sons.

Sources: p.13 *Motivation and Personality* by Abraham H. Maslow (Harper, 1954) p.24 Adapted from figure 2.3 in *Complexity and Education: Inquiries Into Learning, Teaching, and Research* by Brent Davis and Dennis Sumara (Routledge, 2006), which was adapted from *Engaging Minds: Learning and Teaching in a Complex World* by Brent Davis, Dennis Sumara and Rebecca Luce-Kapler (Routledge, 2000). p.74 "Learners' perceptions of their successes and failures in foreign language learning" by Marion Williams, Robert Burden, Gérard Poulet and Ian Maun, *The Language Learning Journal*, Volume 30 (1) 2004. p.83 "A neurobiological perspective on affect and methodology in second language learning" by John H. Schumann from *Affect in Language Learning* by Jane Arnold (ed.) (Cambridge University Press, 1999).

CONTENTS

ACKNOWLEDGEMENTS

We would like to thank our editors, Julia Bell and Sophie Rogers, for their support, guidance, enthusiasm, and encouragement. We would also like to thank our excellent editorial team, Anna Cowper and Alexandra Paramour, for their skilful and painstaking editing. We owe a big debt of thanks to Mark Fletcher for enhancing the book with his brilliant and very witty drawings. Thanks also go to the reviewers of our original submission for their supportive and constructive comments, which encouraged us to go ahead with this book.

INTRODUCTION

Why a book on psychology?

Language teachers are busy people. In addition to the day-to-day task of teaching, they need to keep up with developments in language teaching methodology. There are also a number of other disciplines that can usefully inform and even transform the practices of those working in the area of language learning and teaching; these include linguistics and the study of how the language functions, as well as the vast disciplines of educational and social psychology, which look at how people learn and the social interactions between people. However, the sheer enormity of these fields of psychology and their rapid pace of development makes it difficult for many teachers caught up in the daily work of teaching students to keep abreast of them.

A good language teacher already instinctively knows a considerable amount about psychology. The everyday classroom decisions that teachers make—such as the activities they use, how they organize and interact with the learners in their classes, and how they pace their lessons—are often informed by their understandings of psychological issues such as learner motivation, group dynamics, and emotions. In this book, we would like to suggest that developing a deeper understanding of psychology will help teachers to feel better equipped to teach with empathy and sensitivity to the needs, drives, and emotions of their learners. Such knowledge is invaluable in helping us to generate the best possible learning conditions in our language classrooms.

What this book is about

This book aims to provide an overview of some of the key areas of educational and social psychology that have particular insights to offer language teachers, and to draw out the implications for teachers' pedagogical practices. We are obviously unable to cover the whole discipline and so we have carefully selected areas that have particular relevance for language teachers. Our goal has been to make the book accessible to teachers with little or no previous knowledge of psychology and we have therefore tried to write it in a reader-friendly style, using concrete examples to help to make the concepts clear to readers who are unfamiliar with the field. We have aimed this book at language teachers, master's students, and doctoral students seeking an overview of the discipline. We also see teacher trainers as readers and they could use the activities provided in teacher training sessions. Additionally, the book will be of interest to those lecturing in other areas of applied linguistics who would like an overview of recent theorizing in the area.

How this book came about

The three of us have, for a long time, shared an interest in how educational psychology can help language teachers. We all hold the same deep conviction that a knowledge of psychological issues is important for those teaching language to learners who may lack confidence, question their ability, or be anxious about speaking in the foreign language. We have found that language learning experiences can be greatly enhanced when we attend to such issues as positive group dynamics, enhanced learner motivation, and a sense of well-being in class. Over the years, the three of us have collaborated on various publications in this area and this has proved to be a fruitful and fulfilling experience. Before this collaboration, in 1997, Williams and Burden published their book *Psychology for Language Teachers*, which was at the time one of the few books that aimed to explore the links between educational psychology and language teaching. With the rapid developments in educational psychology since then, we realized that it was now time to write a new book incorporating recent advances and theorizing in psychology, and so this book was conceived.

Organization of this book

We have divided the book into eight chapters. Each of the main chapters explores a separate concept from psychology. However, we would like to stress the importance of seeing the links and interconnections between the different concepts discussed. In Chapter 1, we present an overview of major psychological approaches and show how these have developed historically. This is intended to help readers see how these different perspectives have influenced language teaching methodologies, and to provide readers with a background against which to consider their own teaching practices. The chapter also serves as a framework for understanding the concepts addressed in the rest of the book. We start by briefly reviewing behaviourism and cognitive approaches to psychology, and then move on to look at humanistic and sociocultural approaches. After that, we consider ecological and complexity approaches, and discuss the implications of these for education broadly and language teaching specifically.

Chapter 2 considers the importance of groups of people, including cultural groups. It discusses how, as individuals, we are all situated within a number of different groups and contexts which influence how we think, feel, and behave. We have positioned this chapter at the beginning as all the other chapters need to be read with the social groups and contexts of individuals in mind. Chapter 3 then focuses on the individual and the many different facets of the self. It considers what is meant by various aspects of the self, such as identity and self-concept. We discuss how individuals can have many different understandings of their sense of self in different contexts and across time. It concludes by discussing ways in which we can seek to promote a healthy sense of self in our learners in respect to their language learning. In Chapter 4, we look at beliefs and how they influence the ways people approach learning. We explore some of the key beliefs learners have about learning a foreign language and we also discuss the value for teachers of understanding their own beliefs about the language learning process and how they impact upon learning. In Chapter 5, we examine the role of affect in language learning. Language learning is more than the mental acquisition of linguistic knowledge, and the various emotions learners experience are integral to the learning process. We consider the ways in which emotions can impede learning, but we also highlight the way they can enhance learning and the positive part they can play. Chapter 6 considers what is surely the most widely discussed psychological variable in foreign language learning: motivation. We look at how conceptualizations of motivation to learn a foreign language have changed over time and we stress the importance for teachers of developing their own understandings of the motivations of learners in their classrooms. In Chapter 7, we explore the ways in which learners can act and control their actions. We discuss the skills, strategies, and also the attitudes learners need to take control of their learning and thus learn effectively and autonomously. We also consider how learners regulate their own learning. Finally, Chapter 8 brings together the different aspects discussed to present a framework for looking at the psychology of language learning holistically.

Each chapter contains a set of activities for the reader to engage in. We consider these to be an integral part of the chapter. The aim of the activities is to encourage readers to explore the various concepts discussed and to reflect on the relevance of these for their own educational settings. In this way, we hope the activities will help readers to develop their own unique understandings of the issues discussed, and feel empowered and confident to make informed decisions about classroom issues that take account of the psychology involved. Most of all, we hope you enjoy reading this book and that you find something that is meaningful to you. We have enjoyed writing it. If it enriches your teaching in some way, we have achieved our purpose.

1

PSYCHOLOGY IN EDUCATION

Introduction

Imagine you are preparing to teach a class. The summer break is almost here, but you are already experiencing an early heatwave, and to make matters worse, noisy construction work has just begun outside your classroom. The students in the class recently took a high-stakes examination that is likely to have a significant effect on their futures, and you are aware that the stress associated with this examination has caused friction between some of the students in the class. To complicate the picture even further, there is some tension and excitement relating to the upcoming end-of-term social event. Personally, you have been looking forward to these classes after the examination. You have more freedom in what you can teach and you know that a group of students who are going abroad in the summer are keen to improve their language skills in the remaining few classes before they go away.

Such is the reality of day-to-day teaching. All of the conditions described in the opening paragraph are likely to have an impact on how you approach this class as a teacher. No single factor will account for your thoughts or actions. In the same way, the learners in that class will be affected in different and sometimes unpredictable ways by events within, but also beyond, the classroom setting. Teaching and learning any subject is a complex process that involves many different interactions between learners, teachers, the social environment, and the groups within the class, all of which are influenced by many other factors such as the time of day, the weather, or the class that took place beforehand. Everything learners bring to the classroom—including their beliefs, personalities, sense of self, and relationships with the people around them—will influence their actions in the class. Similarly, what teachers bring with them in these terms will impact on the way they behave and interact in class. In order to support their learners and empower them to succeed in their language learning endeavours, teachers need to understand how these multiple interacting factors affect learning. While most language teachers have knowledge of language and language teaching methodology, there are many other domains which can also inform our pedagogical decisions. One rich source of knowledge lies in the different branches of educational and social psychology, and it is to these that we turn in this book.

The discipline of psychology has seen a number of different approaches over the years and each one has had a significant impact on educational practices. In this chapter, we aim to provide an overview of some major psychological approaches and show how these have developed over the years. This will help readers to see how they have impacted at different times on different practices in education and, more specifically, in language teaching. It will also help readers to consider which psychological perspectives have influenced their own approaches to language teaching. As teachers, we constantly make decisions about what to do in our classes, and these decisions will be underpinned by our own views of what learning is all about. We will also outline some more recent approaches to psychology that are enabling us to look at educational processes in new ways and suggest how these might inform our practices as language teachers. This overview will provide an important foundation from which to understand aspects of psychology presented in other chapters, and we will refer back to this chapter at several points in the book.

Positivist approaches to learning

We will start with the **positivist approach** to psychology and look at the considerable influence this has had on education systems round the world, and in particular on language teaching. In the early part of the twentieth century, the discipline of psychology was seen strictly as a science and, as such, research in the field made use of rigorous scientific experimental methods. Experiments tended to be based on a scientific approach called **logical positivism**, which seeks to discover facts through carefully controlled experiments. The term 'control' in these experiments essentially means isolating a particular '**variable**' in order to study its effects. For example, in a chemistry experiment it is possible to observe the effects of, say, temperature on a particular substance by simply raising the temperature applied to that substance while all other conditions remain unchanged. It was this approach that dominated early studies of human behaviour. So researchers might attempt to study the effect of praise on student response, or the effect of different methods of correction on student achievement. In order to do so, they would, in the latter case, measure student proficiency using some form of language test before 'treating' the students with different methods of correction. At the end of the experiment, proficiency would be measured again using the same test, and differences in changes in proficiency would be attributed to the method of correction applied during the experiment. This is the scientific, experimental approach to psychology, based around the formation and testing of hypotheses in tightly controlled conditions.

Another important feature of the positivist approach in psychology was the belief that the human mind was not accessible to scientific investigation, and this was therefore not investigated. Research instead focused only on behaviour, which could be observed and recorded. This, in turn, led to a plethora of experiments on different types of animals, observing, for instance, how rats learned to run through mazes to find food, how pigeons could be trained to turn circles to the left, or how rats learned to pull levers to obtain food. It was thought that the results of such experiments would help us to understand the way humans learned and behaved and therefore how best to teach. Thus, many commonly accepted educational practices, such as the use of rewards and punishments, have been largely based on the findings from experiments with animals, as we shall see in the next section.

Behaviourism

Behaviourism is an approach to psychology which arises from the positivist tradition of enquiry, and has arguably been the most influential positivist theory within the field of education. Basically, behaviourist psychologists explain learning in terms of **conditioning**. The Russian psychologist Pavlov showed that animals would respond, for example by salivation, to a stimulus, for example food, and that this response could be triggered by a secondary stimulus, such as a bell ringing. Thus, when the bell sounded, the animal would salivate, linking the sound with food. This is known as conditioning.

Skinner (1987) extended the theory of behaviourism by explaining learning in terms of responding to a stimulus, and emphasized the importance of reinforcement. If the behaviour is reinforced—for instance, by being rewarded or punished—then the likelihood of that behaviour occurring again is increased or decreased. Thus, it was thought that any behaviour could be encouraged by reinforcing the required behaviour. Skinner (1957) even believed that language development could be explained in this way. He identified a number of principles of instruction, including breaking tasks down into small, sequential steps, and programming learning by providing positive reinforcement for each stage.

Behaviourist views have had a powerful influence on language teaching methodology. In many parts of the world, that influence lingers to this day, and it led to the widespread adoption of the **audiolingual method** of language teaching. In this method, a structure is first presented to students as a stimulus. The learners respond in some way—perhaps by repetition or substitution—and this behaviour is reinforced by the teacher indicating whether the response is right or wrong. An example of behaviourist teaching is the use of substitution drills, which can be completed correctly with no comprehension of what the words mean. Typically, a teacher presents a structure, asks students to repeat the sentence, and then substitutes other items within the sentence. Perhaps the most conspicuous manifestation of the influence of behaviourism within language education was the widespread use of language laboratories, which again presented language learning in terms of acquiring a set of correct habits or behaviours through repetition and substitution. A further defining characteristic of a behaviourist perspective on language learning is that errors are not acceptable, as they are seen as reinforcing bad habits.

Such an approach has obvious limitations. Firstly, learners are not cognitively engaged in the learning activity; they simply respond correctly to stimuli. In other words, they are not using their minds. There is no analysis of language, or engagement in discourse, or development of learning strategies, or choice of what to do. The outcome can be to turn something as potentially exciting as language learning into a dull chore, as many people who have spent hours with a set of headphones performing repetitive drills will testify. Secondly, such learning can be carried out with no attention to the meaning of the language used, as many drills can be performed without understanding what the words mean. In addition, there is no room for interaction or negotiation of meaning. Most significantly, in an audiolingual approach there is no scope for making mistakes, which is, in fact, a crucial part of the learning process.

Behaviourist approaches to learning have played a central role in educational systems round the world. One reason for this is that they can be highly attractive to institutions, teachers, parents, and even learners themselves. A behaviourist model of learning offers simplicity and certainty— the promise that someone is in control and that we know where we are going and how to get there. However, this is only to be achieved by simplifying what are highly complex processes, especially in a long-term, unpredictable endeavour such as learning a foreign language. In focusing only on observable behaviour, behaviourism does not allow for the sense that learners themselves make of the learning process, the cognitive processes that they use, or the feelings and emotions that are integral to learning. It was only when cognitive approaches to psychology began to be recognized that education, including language education, was able to take an entirely different direction.

Cognitive approaches to learning

Cognitive psychologists are basically interested in the way the mind works and the mental processes involved in learning. A **cognitive approach** to learning involves encouraging learners to use mental learning strategies to analyze, hypothesize, and deduce information so their minds are actively engaged in the learning process. In learning a language, a learner will use such strategies as analyzing language, seeing patterns, working out rules, and experimenting with using the language. Making mistakes is also seen as an important part of this process, as learners are able to notice the discrepancies between their own output and that of others. This allows them to develop by trying out new things with language. Such a view is in sharp contrast to the behaviourist approaches to learning discussed earlier, which focus only on observable behaviour rather than on what happens inside learners' minds and the personal sense they make of their learning. Typically, in a lesson informed by cognitive approaches, a teacher might ask learners to observe certain language structures in a text and analyze how they are used, or to listen to the way in which a speaker asks for information, disagrees with something, or expresses an opinion.

Cognitive psychology has, however, taken different routes which can be thought of as stretching along a continuum. At one end is **information processing**, whose advocates see the human mind as being like a complex machine working out rules and models. At the other end is **constructivism**, which is concerned with the ways in which individuals make their own sense of the world.

Information processing

Information processing is concerned with how we take in information and the various mental processes involved in learning. Recent developments in technology have facilitated huge advances in our knowledge of the workings of the human brain. There is a considerable amount of optimism that this progress will continue to a degree where we will one day be able to offer a satisfactory explanation of how the brain processes language.

One of the most productive areas of enquiry for researchers in investigating information processing has been the idea of **working memory**, the capacity to simultaneously store and process information. Research into working memory has become so dominant that there is a tendency for some to equate working memory with the brain's capacity to learn a language—in other words, the greater an individual's working memory capacity, the better the learner's ability to learn a language.

Activity 1.1

How does your memory work?

1 Read the following set of words to yourself once only. Now close your eyes and try to recall the words in the correct order. How many could you remember?

    girl   flag   wall   dance   play   heart

2 Now read the next set of words and do the same. How many could you remember this time? Which set of words was easier for you to remember? What explanation could you offer for this?

    weight   gate   late   mate   great   state

Most people, regardless of the mnemonic strategies they employ, find it easier to remember the first set of words and this is because all the words have different sounds. The second set of words is all based around the same vowel sound, making it more difficult for our working memory to process them. This is regarded by some as evidence of a phonological loop in our working memory, and this phonological loop is a key component in the best-known model of working memory (Baddeley, 2007). Put simply, our brains use sounds—or approximations of sounds—to process and temporarily store information. This clearly has huge implications for our understandings of the relationship between the human brain and language, and, ultimately, of how we learn language. The research into working memory also points to important implications for language learning. It suggests that it is productive for teachers to encourage learners to develop their memory skills through the use of different strategies, such as rehearsing, using mnemonics, forming mental images, or linking new information like a new word to something familiar. It also indicates that it is useful to engage learners in discussions about which strategies they use and encourage them to try out alternatives. (See also Chapter 7 for a discussion of learning strategies.)

Traditionally, information processing psychologists have inhabited a very different world from social and educational psychologists, with little interaction between the fields. However, in recent years, there has been a growing interest in exploring some of the connections, with research finding that working memory can play a significant role in how we regulate emotions, in our levels of interest, and in how we maintain **attention** (Hofmann, Schmeichel, Friese, & Baddeley, 2011). Attention is of particular interest to language teachers as it explains how individuals select what is important to attend to, filter out distractions, and concentrate their mental efforts. In his book *Teaching Children to Think*, Robert Fisher (1995) stresses that focusing attention is one of the most basic skills that children need to learn and one that should be encouraged. Language teachers could develop activities which guide learners to focus attention on the structure of the language, the use of words, or the way language is used in particular contexts.

Constructivism

An entirely different cognitive approach to psychology and education is constructivism, which is essentially about how individuals make personal sense of their worlds. To a constructivist, individuals are involved throughout their lives in 'constructing' their own personal understandings from their experiences. All individuals make their own sense of the world in a unique way that is different from the sense others make of it. For example, if you ask a class at the end of a lesson to tell you the main thing they learned, you are likely to get a different message from everyone.

An important early constructivist was Jean Piaget (1966, 1974), who was interested in the ways in which people develop their understandings as they mature from infants to adults. He identified the different stages children pass through in their thinking and learning. Infants, for example, explore the world through their basic senses. This is known as the **sensory-motor stage** of learning. Children progress through various stages to what Piaget calls **formal operational thinking** in adolescence, where they begin to use abstract reasoning to develop their understanding of the world. Piaget's work has important implications for

Constructivism

language teachers. Learners are actively involved in making sense of the language input they are given. As they are exposed to language, they seek to fit the new information into their existing knowledge, a process Piaget terms **assimilation**, and modify what they already know to accommodate this input, a process called **accommodation**.

Another key proponent of constructivism was Jerome Bruner. Influenced by Piaget's work on the development of children's thinking, Bruner believed that the development of cognitive abilities, rather than the acquisition of facts, is a central purpose of education. He saw the need to learn how to learn as essential and felt that learners should be challenged to be absorbed in problems. He stressed the importance of learners discovering principles and concepts for themselves, and highlighted the need for guesswork, intuitive thinking, an ability to take risks, a sense of curiosity, and also self-confidence (Bruner, 1960, 1966). Many of these ideas have influenced language teaching, for example, learning how to learn a language, discovering how the language works, and teaching problem-solving skills (Puchta & Williams, 2011).

Another pioneer of the constructivist movement was George Kelly (1955), whose **personal construct theory** has had profound implications for educators. Kelly saw people as actively trying to understand the world by making hypotheses, testing them out, and drawing conclusions, and then constructing personal understandings or theories about the world around them. These personal theories are known as constructs, and individuals' constructions of the world will be personal to them and different from those of other people.

Laurie Thomas and Sheila Harri-Augstein (1985) and Phillida Salmon (1988) have explored the applications of personal construct theory to our understanding of learning. They argue that learning is not concerned with absorbing information as whole chunks or with simply adding more information to our existing body of knowledge. Instead, what we do when we learn is 'map' new information onto our existing knowledge and, in the process, our understanding becomes reshaped to accommodate the new information. Worthwhile learning, therefore, does not involve merely taking in new facts. Learners need to be engaged in actively creating new personal understandings, and it is in this way that we develop our own perception of the world and are able to change and grow. Teachers need to remember that what they do in the classroom will be construed in different ways by different learners, depending on each individual's beliefs, past experiences, thoughts, feelings, and views of the world. Even if there is one syllabus, this will be interpreted by the teacher and the learners in individual ways.

A teacher who is informed—consciously or unconsciously—by a constructivist approach might start by getting her learners to think about what the topic means to them personally. She could, for instance, ask them to discuss what they already know about the topic and perhaps record it in a mind map. She would then provide opportunities for them to interact with new information and to personalize it by incorporating the new knowledge with their existing knowledge. She would also encourage the students to discuss what they think with each other and to reconstruct their own understandings.

As Salmon (1988) points out, it is important to bear in mind that although we each construct personal meanings, we also inhabit a social world where we develop shared understandings. The classroom is a place where shared understandings about the context and what is acceptable or unacceptable are constructed between the teacher and learners. Such a social constructivist perspective on language learning and teaching is explored in Williams and Burden's (1997) book *Psychology for Language Teachers*. (See also Chapter 2.)

Our discussion so far has shown how, in moving from behaviourism to cognitive approaches, psychologists began to place the learner's mind at the centre of the learning process. With constructivism, there was also greater recognition of the **agency** of learners—in other words, a feeling that they can have control over their actions, which we discuss in the next section (see also Chapter 7)—and the unique and personal ways in which learning can take place and be meaningful. However, cognitive approaches to learning, while focusing on the mind, do not take into account other attributes that learners bring to the learning process, such as feelings and emotions. In order to understand this broader view of learning and the ways in which emotions impact on learning, we turn next to another major psychological perspective, **humanism**.

Humanism

Humanistic approaches to education emerged in the 1960s and emphasize the importance of considering the whole person (**holistic learning**), the uniqueness of the individual, and the essential role of feelings and emotions in learning. As Mark Fletcher (2001) explains, learning involves 'body, mind, emotions and spirit' (p. 1), and we need to consider all of these if we are to understand and maximize learning. Among the psychologists who pioneered the principles of humanism are Abraham Maslow and Carl Rogers.

Maslow was interested in education as personal fulfilment. He identified what he termed a hierarchy of needs (Maslow, 1968, 1970). An individual's more basic needs, such as food, water, and warmth, are at the bottom of the hierarchy, followed by needs for safety, for interpersonal closeness, and for self-esteem. If these basic needs are satisfied, a person can fulfil needs further up the hierarchy: cognitive needs, aesthetic needs, and, finally, a need for **self-actualization**, where a person is completely fulfilled. (See Figure 1.1.) Maslow maintained that individuals will have difficulty meeting the higher-order needs if those lower in the hierarchy are not met. He believed that one of the main purposes of education is to enable learners to develop as individuals and to achieve self-actualization. Maslow's theories point to the importance of introducing classroom activities that help learners to realize their full potential. Teachers need to provide a secure environment which fosters a sense of belonging, where individuality is respected, where self-esteem can develop, and where learners are constantly challenged to fulfil their potential.

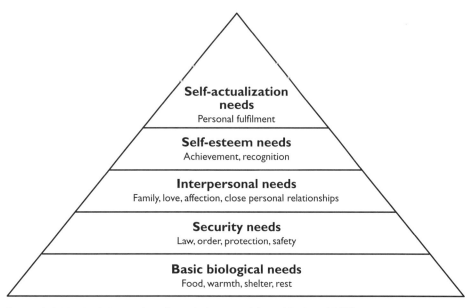

Figure 1.1 Maslow's hierarchy of needs (adapted from Maslow, 1987)

A basic assumption of humanism is that people have free will and act intentionally rather than their behaviour being determined by others. The concept of personal agency is important here. Agency, as we discuss in more detail in Chapter 7, is concerned with the individual's will and ability to take action to achieve goals. Linked to this notion is the belief that the aim of education is to develop autonomous learners capable of learning independently. As Rogers (1969) explains, learners need to initiate their own actions and learning must be personally relevant. Maslow (1954) argues that personal growth and fulfilment is a fundamental, innate human motive as we seek to achieve self-actualization and realize our full potential.

Central to a humanistic approach to learning is the notion that individuals are unique and learning should be as personalized as possible. Hamachek (1987) argues that every learning experience should help learners to develop a sense of their own identity and to achieve their personal goals. Thus, teachers should seek to understand their learners as unique individuals. This line of thinking was further developed in learner-centred approaches to language teaching, which place learners and their individuality at the centre of teaching decisions and curriculum design (see Nunan, 1988).

A humanistic approach has particular relevance for language education, where learning outcomes and success vary so much between individual learners. One of the great pioneers of a humanistic approach in the field of foreign language education, Earl Stevick, posed a riddle back in the 1970s (Underhill, 2013). He asked why it is that two completely different teaching methods, based on different theoretical frameworks about how languages are best learned, can lead to the same results through two different teachers. Teacher A, using Method A, can get comparable degrees of success to Teacher B, who may be working with a completely different method. This is because—as Stevick suggested and increasing numbers of scholars have come to recognize in recent years—there is 'no one best method' (Kumaravadivelu, 2006). In fact, what really makes the difference in the success of these different teaching approaches is most likely the result of what is going on inside the learners—their psychology—as well as between the learners and the teacher in terms of the interpersonal relationships in a particular classroom setting. As Stevick (1980) so aptly expressed it, 'success depends less on materials, techniques, and linguistic analyses, and more on what goes on inside and between people in the classroom' (p. 44). It is these inter- and intrapersonal processes that are regarded as crucial to success within a humanistic perspective.

Advocates of a humanistic approach to language education, such as Earl Stevick, Mario Rinvolucri, and Jane Arnold, have sought to find ways of taking account of learners' emotions and feelings in their learning. However, while Arnold and Brown (1999) emphasize the importance of considering emotions, they also stress that 'the affective side of learning is not in opposition to the cognitive one' (p. 1), and argue the case for uniting cognitive and affective domains in order to educate the whole person. A humanistic teacher might well start a class with an activity involving interacting, focusing on a partner, imagining what a partner feels, closing eyes and visualizing, exploring feelings, or building self-esteem. Interestingly, these humanistic principles resonate with many current concerns and several chapters of this book. In particular, Chapter 6 considers the important role of the emotions in learning.

Sociocultural perspectives

So far, we have looked at behaviourist views of learning—which see learning as occurring when an individual is conditioned, or shaped, to perform certain behaviours that are determined by others; cognitive approaches—which focus on the central role of the individual mind in learning; and humanistic perspectives—which acknowledge the importance of an individual's emotions and the holistic nature of learning. Although these represent radically different views of the human learning experience, one feature they share is that they all regard the individual as the principal unit of analysis. In contrast, sociocultural perspectives do not separate individuals from the context in which they are learning. A sociocultural view of human learning sees learning as essentially a social process, where the social world that the individual inhabits has an important impact on the development of that individual, while, in turn, the individual—through participation—is constantly influencing the social context.

Activity 1.2

Learners in a social world

Throughout this book we use the term 'language learner', often implying that there is such a thing as a typical language learner. However, people can learn languages for very different reasons, in very different circumstances, and in very different ways.

1 Read about the three language learners below.

Learner 1

A teenager is learning a language for the very simple reason that she has to. Everybody in full-time education in her country has to study this particular language. Therefore, every Tuesday and Thursday she attends a language class, as she has done for several years and will continue to do for at least another two years.

Learner 2

A recently divorced man in his late forties has moved to a new town where he hardly knows anybody. He has started to learn Chinese in the evenings, partly as a way to meet new people and partly because he is planning to treat himself to a big trip to China as a fiftieth birthday present. He enjoys the classes as he has a lot in common with some of the other students, who are mostly the same age as he is and share similar social backgrounds.

Learner 3

A recent immigrant in her late twenties is struggling with the language in her new home country, and she is especially worried about the consequences of this for her two young children. She has two part-time jobs and is required by the state to attend some free language classes held at weekends at her local community centre. She was hoping that the language classes might also help her make friends, but many other students are in a similar situation to herself and find it difficult to attend regularly.

2 Think about how the factors in these learners' personal backgrounds and learning environments may affect their goals, aspirations, and approaches to language learning.

3 Imagine you were teaching these individuals. In each case, what kind of measures could you take in order to create a classroom environment that would help the learner to set positive goals and aspirations, and facilitate that individual's learning of the language?

Countless personal and contextual factors can affect learning, and it is also impossible to predict the impact of any single factor. (Note the contrast between this view of learning and the controlled 'scientific' experiments described in the section on positivist thinking.) It is important to stress, however, that the relationship between the individual and the context is not unidirectional: as well as being shaped by the learning context, learners shape that context through their own participation in its events. For example, the efforts made by individual learners can affect the enthusiasm of their peers and of the teacher, which, in turn, influences the future commitment of those individual learners. Any context is continually shaped by interactions between individuals and the context, and a sociocultural perspective places these interactions at the centre of the learning experience. Fundamentally, all learning is embedded in social events and occurs as individuals interact with people and objects in their environment.

Current views of **sociocultural theory** draw mainly on the work of the Russian psychologist Lev Vygotsky (1978). They have been brought to the field of second language acquisition by a number of different writers, such as Donato (1994), Lantolf (2000), and Lantolf and Poehner (2008), giving us potentially new ways of looking at the language learning process. As Vygotsky developed his ideas in the 1920s and 1930s, in the aftermath of the Russian revolution, the publication of his work was suppressed by the authorities, who favoured a behaviourist approach to learning. It was not until the first translations of the writings of this remarkable psychologist became available in the1960s that the Western world was able to appreciate the contribution they made to our understandings of how people learn. From a sociocultural viewpoint, learning anything, including a language, occurs through social interaction between two or more participants. A child or unskilled person carries out an activity, often under the guidance of someone more skilled, and they engage in collaborative talk until the learner can carry out the activity without assistance. This supportive talk with teachers or peers, along with accompanying actions, is known as **scaffolding**, and it provides a support structure that helps the learner acquire new knowledge or skills.

Sociocultural theory provides helpful insights into the development of people's cognitive abilities and higher-order thinking skills. Cognitive functions are first developed socially through conversation and later become internalized and taken over by individuals into their own consciousness. As Mitchell and Myles (1998) explain, learning is first social and then becomes individual. Learning takes place in the area of knowledge or skill which is just above the learner's present level of ability, where that individual can function with the help of scaffolding. The distance between the present level of ability and a higher potential level that can be achieved with scaffolding is known as the **zone of proximal development (ZPD)**.

Another important aspect of Vygotsky's work is the concept of **tools**. As Lantolf (1994) explains, we use physical tools to organize and alter the world; these include hammers, diggers, axes, ploughs, oars, calculators, and computers. In the same way, humans use tools to organize and control mental processes, such as memory, learning, solving problems, or making decisions. These are known as **symbolic tools**. As an example, if we go to a supermarket to buy a number of different things, we need to remember what to buy. We could rehearse the items by reciting them repeatedly, or we could write the items in a list. Both are ways of using language as a tool to help our memory to function adequately. Language is a powerful symbolic tool; other examples are diagrams, mind maps, plans, mnemonic devices, maps, mathematical formulae, and notes. In learning a language, examples would be using a vocabulary notebook to organize new words, using mnemonics to remember words, and using mind maps to organize thoughts.

Children frequently verbalize their thoughts; they use this **private speech** to talk to themselves rather than to anyone else. They do this, for instance, when playing, painting a picture, putting things away, or solving a puzzle. Mitchell and Myles (1998) explain that, if viewed from a sociocultural perspective, this private speech is seen as evidence of children's developing ability to regulate their own behaviour.

This then becomes **inner speech**, which is when language is used to regulate inner thoughts without any external articulation. An autonomous individual has developed inner speech as a tool of thought. However, when tackling a new task, even skilled adults may use private talk to regulate their actions (Mitchell & Myles, 1998). Lantolf (2000) explains how, when learning to construct a wooden puzzle, young children first do so under the supervision of a parent. Gradually, they take control, as they begin to use the language that was used by the parent to regulate their own activity and instruct themselves in selecting the right piece and placing it in the puzzle.

Sociocultural perspectives have valuable messages for language teachers. Firstly, they point to the importance of scaffolding in the learning process; the teacher needs to play a part in helping the learner to move to the next level of ability. Second, they highlight the significance of learners talking to each other as they complete tasks, as this talk scaffolds the learning process. Communication is essential for learners to construct knowledge together, whether this is knowledge of grammar or knowledge of how the language is used. Learners therefore need to be able to talk about what they are doing to construct knowledge jointly before it becomes individual. They also need to discuss how they are learning so they can move towards regulating their learning. Finally, sociocultural theory highlights the influence of the context in the learning process and the importance of teachers understanding their learners' contexts and backgrounds in order to provide a classroom environment where interactions can take place and learners feel supported and valued.

Ecological and complexity perspectives

In more recent years, some strands of psychology have developed sociocultural thinking one step further into what are known as ecological perspectives on psychology or simply **ecological psychology**, as represented by the work of scholars such as James J. Gibson. Gibson (1979) stressed that individuals must be understood within the contexts of the environmental systems in which they live, work, and learn, such as the home, the school, the office, or a specific country. He argued that you cannot properly understand people and their psychology without also understanding the contexts within which they find themselves. (See Chapter 2.) Researchers using an ecological approach therefore look at people in real-world contexts to capture the complexity of their interactions with their settings. This is in contrast to the laboratory or experimental studies typical in behaviourist approaches, which sought to limit and reduce complexity for research purposes.

A particular concept that Gibson developed, and which has played a key role in understandings of education, is that of **affordances**. By this, he means that an object, such as a ruler, affords different opportunities to different people to do different things with it, and so its use depends on the individual's perception of the object. So, for example, one learner may use the ruler to underline an important passage in a book, whereas another may use it to cut paper in half, and another still may use it to squash a fly. All these 'action possibilities', or affordances, are inherent in the ruler, but the actual action it 'affords' emerges only from the interaction between the learner and the object. Thus, it is through each person's relationship to and interaction with an object that its purpose is determined. For language education, this suggests the importance of making learners aware of the latent potential that exists in tools, materials, and resources for learning (van Lier, 2004), but also the importance of understanding learners' own perceptions of and relationships with the objects and contexts of language learning and use. Let us think, for instance, of students learning Spanish as a foreign language. On the web, there are plenty of current TV news broadcasts from Spain. One learner may choose to watch these for the rich, idiomatic language they provide; another may watch them to attend to the pronunciation of the presenter; another may wish to learn about local Spanish culture; and yet another may simply be interested in watching the news for the news stories and overall listening practice.

A key scholar who brought discussions of ecological perspectives to foreign language learning is Leo van Lier (2004). He explains that 'the learner is immersed in an environment full of potential meanings. These meanings become available gradually as the learner acts and interacts within and with this environment' (van Lier, 2008, p. 246). He makes the point that the learners' interactions with and perceptions of their contexts are already, in fact, learning in action. He explains that we need to be looking at 'the active learner in her environment, not at the contents of her brain' (van Lier, 2008, pp. 246–7). He sees such a perspective as a way of thinking that ensures we keep in mind the interconnections between learners, their perceptions, actions, and contexts. This line of thinking is central to our approach in this book. Thus, when we discuss learners' psychology, we always try to consider how it varies according to individuals and their unique relationships to different contexts.

Such holistic views of learners situated within ecological systems link to another closely related development in psychology and other areas of the social sciences and education known as **systems thinking** or **complexity perspectives**. Basically, these perspectives suggest that we take a holistic view of whole systems and argue that 'the whole is more than the sum of its parts'. This means that you cannot meaningfully understand one part of a system without understanding the relationship of all the parts of the system together. A system could be, for example, a learner, a teacher, a classroom, a school, or even a national curriculum. Characteristically, a system is composed of multiple components and the context is usually an integral part of the system, rather than an element external to the system affecting it from the outside (Dörnyei & Ushioda, 2011). The focus in complexity perspectives is on the interconnectedness of all aspects of a system and the ways in which a system is dynamic and thus constantly undergoing changes both big and small.

In respect to foreign language learning, Diane Larsen-Freeman has been central in encouraging professionals in the field to think of various aspects of language learning, such as learners, classrooms, and indeed the language itself, as complex dynamic systems (Larsen-Freeman, 2012; Larsen-Freeman & Cameron, 2008). She has emphasized that such a view is vitally important in engaging with the real-world complexity that teachers face in their daily lives in actual classrooms. In this way, complexity perspectives can be seen as paying attention to and engaging more deeply with reality, and recognizing the 'messiness' of real classrooms, learners, and teachers.

At present, work from complexity perspectives in language learning is in its infancy and thus implications for practice have been somewhat limited so far. However, one of the insights provided by such a view is that there can be no recipes for pedagogy as there are no easily predictable cause-and-effect relationships between the various aspects of classroom life and learning. According to a complexity perspective, it is more appropriate to think in terms of contingencies—in other words, possible outcomes—acknowledging that each system, whether a learner, a teacher, a classroom, or a school, is unique in its complexity and that the system itself is in a constant state of flux. Complexity perspectives imply that we need to understand what happens in actual classrooms rather than in neat experimental settings. Insights about real situations will then help us to make principled decisions in ways appropriate to our unique settings, rather than relying on uniform prescriptions which ignore the particularity of teachers, learners, and language learning contexts. It is this recognition of diversity and the futility of prescriptions and supposed easy recipes that also informs the approach we take in this book. We hope that rather than prescribing how teachers should teach, this book will offer useful insights about psychology that enable them to make decisions appropriate to their own unique classroom lives.

Activity 1.3	**Analyzing classroom activities**

Let us now explore in more depth how some of our common classroom practices reflect different psychological perspectives on learning and teaching. Below are some typical examples of classroom activities carried out by different language teachers. Whether the teachers realize it or not, their different practices will be underpinned by their views of learning and of how best to help their students to learn.

As you read each example, make a note of the key features. Then try to identify which psychological perspective each activity reflects.

Imagine you are the teacher of the class carrying out the activities described. Which activities would you feel comfortable with? Are there any you would not feel comfortable using in a classroom? What factors would inform these feelings?

Classroom A

The teacher wants to teach the difference between 'since' and 'for'. She writes this sentence on the board:

'I've been here SINCE three o'clock.'

She asks the class to repeat the sentence. Next, she gives the class some more prompts. She says 'nine o'clock this morning' and the class completes the sentence 'I've been here since nine o'clock this morning'.

She then supplies the following prompts:

'2012', 'the day before yesterday', 'sunrise', 'my birthday', 'March'

The class duly completes the sentences.

Now she writes the following sentence:

'I've been here FOR three hours.'

She continues to give prompts until the class is repeating the structure correctly.

Classroom B

Teacher B wants to teach the order of adverbs in a sentence. He writes some sentences on the board:

'I went there yesterday.'

'Come here at once.'

'I worked in the garden at the weekend.'

'They played in the playground this morning.'

He asks the students to underline any adverbs of place (that show where) in red, and adverbs of time (that show when) in blue. He then asks them to examine the sentences to see if they can see any pattern or rule, before comparing what they find with a partner. Finally, he asks individual students to tell him what they discovered and explain their findings to the class.

Classroom C

Teacher C works in an area where there has been a recent earthquake. She draws two concentric circles on the board.

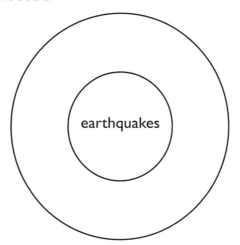

She asks the students to write anything they know about earthquakes in the big circle. They can include their feelings and experiences. She then asks the students to explain their 'circle maps' to their neighbours. After they have done this, she distributes four different recent newspaper articles—one to each student so they do not all have the same article—and asks the students to read them individually. Next, she asks a student with Article A to explain it to the class, and she does the same with the other three articles. Other students are invited to comment. Finally, students complete their own circle maps individually with other things they have learned. The teacher makes it clear that their circles are their own and might be different from those of other students. They then compare with others near them; if there are differences, they explain why they thought that piece of information was important.

Classroom D

Teacher D starts his lesson by asking the students to stand facing a partner. They imagine there is a mirror between them. While one student performs different movements, the other acts as a reflection and mirrors the movements. When the teacher feels the class has relaxed, the students are asked to explain how they felt while they were doing the activity, and the words and phrases are collected on the board.

You have probably recognized the psychological approaches underpinning these typical classroom activities that might be found in coursebooks. You have probably also noticed that complexity theories are not exemplified. Such approaches are new, and the challenge to coursebook writers and teachers is to try to incorporate them in their design of classroom tasks.

Summary

The central premise underlying this chapter is that any teacher's practice is informed by personal views of teaching, learning, and people, whether these are explicit or implicit. The activities teachers plan, their interactions with learners, and their expectations of those learners are all influenced by their fundamental understandings of learning and psychology. We have outlined some of the major theories of psychology that have affected the development of foreign and second language education. We hope these will help teachers to understand their own approaches to teaching and consider the implications for what they do in class. We have discussed the ways in which language education has been influenced by behaviourism, cognitive psychology, humanism, sociocultural theory, and, more recently, ecological and complexity perspectives. Throughout the chapter we have highlighted some important implications for teachers arising from these different approaches. We have stressed the importance of teachers understanding their own theories of teaching and learning, and how these influence their classroom practices. It is important to reiterate that rather than providing any prescriptions about how to teach, we would like to encourage teachers to evaluate their own theories of teaching and learning, and consider what is appropriate in their own settings. In the rest of the book, we shall refer back to this background chapter and explain how these psychological perspectives have influenced the different topics we discuss.

Questions for reflection

1 Think about your own ideas about teaching and learning a language. Do you think your ideas are influenced by or reflect—either consciously or unconsciously—any of the psychological perspectives discussed in this chapter?

2 Can you see any influences in your own workplace, or in an institution you are familiar with, of behaviourism, constructivism, or humanism? Do you find these influences positive or negative?

3 As a result of reading this chapter, are there any changes that you would ideally like to see in your classroom, your school, or your educational system?

Suggestions for further reading

Williams, M., & **Burden, R. L.** (1997). *Psychology for language teachers: A social constructivist approach*. Cambridge: Cambridge University Press.
This book provides an overview of developments in educational psychology at the time and considers their implications for language teaching, focusing in particular on a social constructivist approach to education. No previous knowledge of psychology is assumed and all concepts presented are carefully explained.

Buckler, S., & **Castle, P.** (2014). *Psychology for teachers*. London: Sage.
This book offers a clear, readable account of recent developments in educational psychology, exploring how psychological theory can support effective teaching and learning. It has a particular focus on the developing individual, and how to empower learners and meet their needs.

Lightbown, P. M., & **Spada, N.** (2013). *How languages are learned, fourth edition*. Oxford: Oxford University Press.
Written for teachers, this book provides clear explanations of key concepts in language acquisition research. It covers areas such as how first and second languages are learned, different psychological perspectives on second language learning, and areas of individual difference.

2

GROUPS

Introduction

Groups are a key component of almost all formal learning situations and while a well formed, functioning group can be a huge asset for learning, a dysfunctional group can represent a serious impediment. A simple way to regard groups would be as collections of individuals, but in this chapter, we hope to show that the group–individual relationship is not one-way. Instead, we shall demonstrate that it is not possible to understand individual learners without understanding the groups to which they belong, and that the influence of the group on the individual is as significant as the influence of the individual on the group. We will also consider the challenge we face as teachers of attending to the unique individuals in the class while taking into account the various group structures and dynamics that make up that class.

Any teacher knows that no two classes are the same and that each group of learners has its own unique group 'personality', which often makes it difficult to predict how an unfamiliar class will respond to activities. We regularly experience how a group of learners can change, not only over an extended period of time but even from lesson to lesson. In this chapter, we seek to answer some questions about the challenges of working with different types of groups and classes. How do groups form within a class and how does an entire class form a group identity? How can we harness group dynamics in ways which promote learning? What causes groups to change and in what ways? What role does the teacher play in the group and its dynamics? And how can we bring out the best in the classroom groups we work with?

The chapter will begin by exploring different meanings of the term 'group' and we will consider how belonging to particular types of groups can influence individuals and their approaches to learning and teaching. For the larger part of the chapter, we will focus on the classroom as a group and consider how individuals relate to and function as a class, as well as the ways in which all of us are fundamentally social beings. We will also reflect on how a class functions, the kinds of 'personalities' a group can develop, and what interactional strategies and power structures may exist within our classes.

Groups, culture, and communities

As humans, we participate in a number of different social contexts, all of which affect how we view the world, what we consider to be 'normal', and what we value and esteem. As outlined in Chapter 1, ecological and complexity perspectives on psychology have highlighted how, as individuals, we are embedded within a set of contextual systems (Bronfenbrenner, 1979; Davis & Sumara, 2006) which function at different levels, such as our national cultures, our local educational cultures, our classroom culture, and our family cultures. (See Figure 2.1 below.) In addition, some people move back and forth across national borders, some have friends and/or family in different countries, and all those relationships may change over time. Learners may also transfer from one school to another, or between classes within a school. Our membership of groups and communities is not static, and the many different contexts—past and present—to which we are connected have a considerable influence on us as individuals. People reflect on and interpret their experiences with different groups and cultures in unique ways to form their own 'personal cultures' (Holliday, 1994). In other words, although we may be members of the same group as others, we are likely to form our own unique connection to that group through the way we interpret ourselves in relation to it. This reminds us that we must be cautious with regard to generalizing about groups and individuals, given the very personal nature of an individual's connection to any particular group.

To consider the effects of these different layers of cultures and groups, we will start by working our way through the levels of **nested systems** in the diagram presented below:

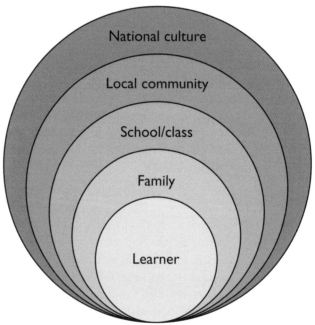

Figure 2.1 Nested systems (adapted from Davis & Sumara, 2006)

For many people, one of the macro-levels of cultural affiliation is related to national culture. Clearly, this is not true for everyone; for some, other broader cultural groups—such as ethnic or religious groups—may be more significant. However, for the purposes of illustration, we will look here at the example of national culture. Looking at national cultures reveals an important point about all cultures and groups: they are not monolithic entities. For example, each individual national culture varies in terms of social class, gender, ethnicity, and also often across regions and generations. A young, urban, working-class male will, for instance, be different culturally from an elderly, rural, upper-class female, even though they are members of the same national group. A further consideration is that many people have cultural affiliations with more than one national culture; a person may have parents from different countries and grow up with strong links to both of those countries. It is important to understand cultural and national ties, but not to oversimplify them, especially when we take increasing levels of population mobility into account.

A frequently cited distinction is made between cultures which are described as being **collectivist** (for example, many East Asian cultures such as Japan and China) and those termed **individualist** (for example, Western Europe and the USA), although naturally these positions are not absolute and individuals within these cultures can vary in their orientations (Triandis, Bontempo, Villareal, Asai, & Lucca, 1988). Generally, individualist cultures are believed to stress individual goals and independence, which promote a sense of competition and focus on the individual self. In contrast, collectivist cultures are thought to emphasize group goals and values, thereby promoting a culture of cooperation and putting the community above the individual. In the classroom context, such culturally based orientations can influence the way we teach, the way learners behave, and what the expected norms of behaviour might be for both teachers and learners.

As teachers, it is helpful to understand learners' cultural values to ensure a sensitive and empathetic approach to working within a certain cultural group and environment. Language teachers often come into contact with a range of cultural values; indeed, for many this is one of the great joys of the profession. However, it is also important for teachers to be able to recognize their own cultural lens through which they view their learners and language teaching. This lens affects the way we see teaching and what we expect of learners. It means we may be 'culturally biased', making judgements and assumptions based on our own cultural frames of reference and believing that our view is 'normal'. Instead, we need to be consciously sensitive to the values and cultural norms of the setting we are teaching in and the diverse individuals we are working with. Ideally, we would seek to work respectfully with this diversity in mind, cautious not to assume the primacy of our own cultural frameworks. A useful strategy to sensitize us to possible differences in understandings of learning and teaching can be to try to learn about the various cultural groups our students are from and seek to understand why they may approach learning in a certain way or hold certain beliefs. Within a group, we may also create the opportunity for dialogue between students about their own cultural perspectives in order to ensure group cohesiveness, a collective group identity, and an atmosphere of mutual respect, tolerance, and understanding.

Activity 2.1	**Considering different cultural backgrounds**

Imagine you are teaching a class of students from a range of cultural backgrounds. While teaching the class, you notice that there are frictions in the class which may stem from cultural differences. How would you deal with the following situations?

1 Some students in the class appear to resent one particular student who regularly interrupts you and asks a lot of questions.

2 One student in the class has a bad cold but does not blow his nose. His continued sniffling noises are annoying some other students in the class.

3 A group of students complain to you that they do not like participating in group-work or discussions with a particular student as they feel she is too quick to agree with everybody, thereby leaving no room for debate or language practice.

4 A student comes up to you after class to tell you that he finds the class a little intimidating because some of the students appear to be angry or quarrelling a lot of the time.

5 You are finding it very difficult to get males and females to work together. Single-sex groupings work well in the class, but there is strong resistance when you try to mix sexes for an activity.

All of the situations outlined in Activity 2.1 demand an awareness of and sensitivity to the cultural backgrounds and individuality of the learners in the class. However, sensitivity and awareness need to be reinforced by action, and teachers need to be aware of their role in establishing group norms within classes. At times, teachers play a dual role of both outsider and leader to the groups within their classes. The challenge is to manage these two roles. On the one hand, we must be able to step back and allow learners a sense of ownership of their own group norms. Yet on the other, we need to judge when the time is right to step in and demonstrate effective leadership, making those norms explicit and thus avoiding the risk of damaging misunderstandings potentially arising from cultural differences.

As can be seen in Figure 2.1, cultures function not only at the macro-level but also at a micro-level. Individual institutions or schools have their own 'culture' concerning norms of behaviour and patterns of interaction, and, again, these shape what we do, as well as the constraints—real or perceived—on how we approach our teaching. For example, in some secondary schools, pupils are expected to stand up when the teacher enters the room; not to do so would be considered impolite and could be interpreted by the teacher as an act of defiance or rudeness on the part of the pupil. Yet, in other settings, the same act of standing up when a teacher enters the room would be frowned upon, perhaps seen as a display of submissiveness in a perceived teacher–pupil hierarchy, which in a strongly defined egalitarian, open school setting would be viewed as inappropriate.

Also at a more micro-level, as teachers and learners, we are embedded in our own personal and family cultures, which, in turn, have their own values and norms. This means that all individuals have their unique, personal set of cultures that they bring with them to the classroom (see Holliday, 1994). The complexity of this web of interacting, multifaceted individual cultures for each individual student and teacher in any one situation illustrates the impossibility of generalizing about the cultural characteristics of settings and learners. Instead, teachers need to be flexible and responsive in making pedagogical decisions that are appropriate for their particular context.

All of the above suggests that it is important to develop good interpersonal and social skills as a teacher. Two skill areas are of particular relevance: social and emotional competence. (See Chapter 5.) These skills are concerned with the qualities of **empathy**, cooperation, social awareness, and relationships. They highlight the importance of having an open mind to diversity, seeking to understand others, and finding ways to cooperate with tolerance, respect, and sensitivity. Indeed, many of the qualities needed for working in multicultural environments can be supported with strong social skills and these are also skills worth promoting in our learners as multicultural communicators as well as in ourselves as teachers.

Activity 2.2	**Exploring the cultures of different groups**
	Make a list of some of the different groups or cultures that you belong to. Next to each, make a note of how you would describe yourself and your behaviour within that group.
	Are there differences in how you see yourself and how others see you in the different groups?
	Are there 'typical' patterns of behaviour and to what extent do they fit for you?

A final note to this section is a caution about not unduly emphasizing differences between individuals based on cultural backgrounds. It is true that we often find ourselves working in groups where each student brings a host of personal, social, and cultural influences to class and which result in a diverse mix of learners. However, it is important to remember that students are similar in many ways too, and that we can also focus on these similarities in our teaching and interactional approaches. We all wish to be respected, accepted, and given the chance to grow, develop, and learn. Indeed, these are core principles in positive group dynamics, and we will explore them further throughout this chapter.

The language classroom as a community and physical space

Nested within the other systems outlined above are the actual classrooms we work in, and these are the focus of the remainder of this chapter. Within a classroom collective, we may also create smaller groups and use pair- or group-work. Many of the issues relating to class-level group dynamics apply equally to different-sized groups within a class. (We discuss cooperative working structures, addressing this level of group, more explicitly later in the chapter.)

One way of thinking about a classroom is to consider it as a **community of practice**, a conceptual frame proposed by Jean Lave and Etienne Wenger (1991). They highlight the social nature of learning in classrooms, where learners and teachers work together, engaging in joint activities and sharing 'practice' through their relationships, with the ultimate common aim of learning together. Along the way, the community grows together, shares language, ideas, stories, and values, and becomes a culture of its own with particular shared ways of doing things and being together. Fundamentally, learning conceptualized from such a perspective is not about taking in knowledge but about taking part, engaging, and being able to participate in the life of the classroom and its related community. Conceiving of our classrooms as communities can be useful in transforming how we think of teaching—not as the imparting of knowledge in a top-down fashion, but rather as a social process which highlights the role of communication and interaction and the nature and quality of the relationships within the community. Thinking of our classrooms in this way challenges us as teachers to democratize our learning environments by enabling learners to become active participants. It also strengthens our understanding of learning as an active process of knowledge co-construction and of the importance of dialogue. (The concept of constructing knowledge is discussed in Chapter 1 in respect to social constructivist approaches to psychology.) Particularly in the language classroom, communication, dialogue, and interaction between learners play a vital role in helping those learners develop their linguistic, social, and cognitive skills.

The physical space in which we work can also be an important factor in promoting learning. People are known to respond to the stimulation provided by their environment emotionally as well as cognitively. We should not therefore underestimate the value of creating a positive emotional climate in our physical classroom spaces. In some teaching situations, teachers are able to do this through simple acts such as rearranging furniture, attending to light, temperature, and noise, or decorating the walls. Teachers may go further by empowering learners to take ownership of the space and encouraging them to bring in their own objects and ideas, although this will naturally depend on the institutional culture and its accepted practices and possible constraints. Nevertheless, as a general principle, we want to do as much as possible within our contexts to provide a facilitative physical learning environment—one that promotes well-being in the group, reduces stress, anxiety, and negative emotions, and allows learners 'space' to think, engage, and create. Ideally, the classroom should be a space which stimulates interaction, thinking, and engagement, but in view of the continuous high-speed stimulation in modern society, there is perhaps a need in classrooms for calm, quiet thinking space alongside interesting, interactive wall displays (see Dörnyei & Murphey, 2003).

The individual and the group

When discussing language learners, we often focus on individuals, discussing their profiles, styles, and personalities—sometimes as if they exist in isolation from others. Of course, considering the unique character of each learner is an important aspect of teaching; however, by switching our focus to the various groups to which the individual belongs, we can also appreciate how learners are fundamentally social and related to contexts and people. This implies that aspects of our psychology—such as our motivation, sense of self, beliefs, agency, or goals—are not solely our own but are co-constructed and mediated by our relationships with others and with the groups to which we belong.

To illustrate the social nature of learning, let us consider a topic that one might, at first sight, think of primarily or even solely in individualistic terms: **learner autonomy**. Autonomy could be seen as implying independence and the focus would thus be on individual learners, independent of others. However, people are socially situated and are engaged in all kinds of relationships with others which can facilitate or hinder their degrees of autonomy. Fundamentally, autonomy need not imply working alone, although in some instances it might. Instead, more recently, there have been developments which emphasize group goals, collaborative working structures, and the social and interdependent character of learner autonomy (for example, Murray, 2014). There has been research in a wide range of educational contexts which suggests that working cooperatively with others on a task can help learners to retain information more easily as well as promote motivation and positive group dynamics. Developments in technology also mean that we can be connected with others in a range of virtual environments, and our relationships in these contexts may also enhance autonomous learning behaviours. Indeed, the fundamentally social nature of foreign language learning implies an emphasis on social roles and relations with others for communication and use of the language. Two concepts proposed by Bandura (2000) refer to our beliefs that as a group or team we can successfully reach specific aims ('**collective efficacy**'), and feel empowered, willing, and able to work together to achieve joint goals ('**collective agency**'). These concepts help us to reconceptualize our learners, seeing them not as isolated individuals but as connected to other people and socially situated resources around them in their competences, achievements, beliefs, and potential.

Scholars such as David Little (1999) have highlighted how autonomy can be fostered through interaction and language use. Through talking, interaction, and reflection on our language learning beliefs and processes, we can gain **metacognitive knowledge**—knowledge about how we learn—and are thereby empowered to become more autonomous. Indeed, language is, at its core, a social, communicative undertaking which necessitates interaction; it is only through interaction that we use and learn the language. Language plays a crucial role in all learning, as it is through dialogue with others that we socially co-construct our understandings of the world. Autonomy is thus closely related to the kinds of relationships we form with others, and it can develop through the use of talk as a way to help us think, reflect, and gain awareness of ourselves, others, and language itself (see Littleton & Mercer, 2013).

As humans, we are fundamentally social beings and our general well-being is enhanced by being involved in healthy social relationships. (See also the section on positive emotions in Chapter 5.) We are known to benefit from friendships in which we both give and receive affection and support. This sense of security from our friendships in turn influences our ability to form other positive relationships. An important responsibility for teachers is to help learners in their need for **relatedness**. Relatedness refers to the fundamental psychological need to feel connected to other people, and we return to this concept once again in Chapter 6. Although human beings are said to have a basic need to belong with others (Baumeister & Leary, 1995), this does not mean that we cannot benefit from time alone. As inherently social beings, we need connection and supportive relationships with others, but while still feeling connected to others, we can profit from individual time. Indeed, in the classroom, it can also be beneficial to allow learners some thinking time, quiet periods, and the chance to work on their own occasionally. On the whole, we want to make learners feel included, welcomed, able to identify with the group, and related to others in it, thereby enabling a sense of belonging to the group. However, as teachers, we have no doubt witnessed how this is easier for some learners than others. In particular, highly anxious, shy, or introverted learners may be more reluctant to get deeply involved in a classroom community. While respecting some learners' possible needs for space and individuality, there are still ways for everyone to feel connected to the group and to maintain relationships to and within it.

As teachers, our relationships to the learners are perhaps the most central set of relationships, which strongly define the overall classroom dynamics, and we need to ensure an empathetic climate in which learners feel safe and esteemed as individuals. We can support our learners' relationships with us as teachers through many of the social skills outlined earlier, such as attentiveness in terms of smiling, genuinely listening, respecting their opinions, and integrating their input into decision-making processes. Such positive teacher–learner relationships impact not only on learners as individuals but also on us as teachers and, ultimately, on the class as a whole. We should also remember our needs for a supportive network of positive relationships as teachers. Nurturing our relationships with peers and colleagues, taking time, and making an effort to promote a positive set of working relationships based on respect, trust, and open communication are as important in staff rooms as they are in the classroom.

To conclude, there are many ways in which we can shift our attention from thinking of learners as isolated individuals to understanding them as social beings. In this book, we discuss different aspects of psychology, and while we often refer to individuals, we would like to see these different areas and individuals through a more social lens. It is for this reason that we have chosen to begin the book with this chapter on groups and thereby set the scene for all the remaining chapters. Consider, for example, learner motivation, which is the focus of Chapter 6. We can usefully think about the ways in which different levels of cultures can affect the development of a learner's motivation—by examining the motivational impact of interactions in various contexts, for example. However, we can also expand our understandings of motivation beyond the individual by recognizing collective and group motivation and the ways in which groups can enhance or restrict an individual's motivation. Further, we can reflect on how a class as a whole is motivated to learn a language and cooperate with each other. A defining factor in social and group motivation stems from the nature of group dynamics, which is what we will turn our attention to next.

Group dynamics

Group dynamics in the language classroom refer to the processes, relationships, and interactions between the learners as well as with the teacher. The importance of positive group dynamics is widely recognized by teachers, who know that the personality of the class and the classroom atmosphere are essential for successful teaching (see Dörnyei & Murphey, 2003). Students in EFL classes often work in groups or pairs, and fostering a positive atmosphere when working in such groups is essential. Activity 2.3 illustrates this further.

Activity 2.3

Fostering positive group dynamics

Remind your students that—given that communication is a key dimension of language learning—they often work in pairs or groups in their language classes. For homework, ask them to note down some short responses to the following questions anonymously.

1 What are the benefits of working with other people when you learn a language?
2 What things are you afraid of when you work in a group?
3 How should we work together when we are in a group?
4 How do you want other people to treat you when working in a group?

Collect these in at the start of the next session, mix them up, and redistribute them to the class. Ask students to reflect on the different responses they read. Put them in small groups and ask them to summarize the different responses to each question—including what they wrote themselves—and write them on a big sheet of paper. They can use mind maps, different colours, and add drawings if they wish. Each group's poster can be displayed in the classroom in order to help students reflect on group behaviours the next time they work together.

Read the papers yourself and reflect on your learners' views about working with others. What have you learned after listening to their views? Were there any surprises? How can you incorporate explicit discussion of group dynamics and the benefits of group-work into your teaching? (Based on an idea in Murphey, Falout, Fukuda, & Fukada, 2014, in which they discuss learners' perceptions about ideal classmates to work with.)

Within a classroom group, each member has a role in defining and making up the group; at the same time, everybody is influenced by being part of the group. It means that everyone in the class is interdependent and we cannot understand the personality of the whole group by just looking at its individuals. The implication of this is that we need to attend to the quality of the relationships between everyone in the class—teachers and learners. Ideally, we want to attain a sense of community, harmony, and a positive set of relationships amongst the learners, in which they respect and accept each other. Essentially, group dynamics depend on individual learners, their relationships and forms of interaction, the social structure of the group, and many other contextual factors as well as, crucially, the role of the teacher. We will now consider group dynamics from all of these perspectives by reflecting on how groups form and become cohesive, how we can ensure positive group dynamics, and what we know about roles of leadership and power in the language classroom. Empathy—the ability to understand the world from the perspective of others and put yourself in their shoes—is an essential skill for building the positive relationships that contribute to positive group dynamics. In communicative foreign language classrooms, there are many opportunities to enhance and promote empathy, while simultaneously practising students' language skills. (See Hadfield, 1992, for practical classroom activities.) As teachers, it is vital that we empathize with our students, remembering what it was like to be learning a foreign language and, in some contexts, what it means to be a teenager. One very helpful strategy can be to begin learning a new foreign language again to remind ourselves of how it feels to be limited in linguistic expression and self-presentation.

Activity 2.4	**Developing empathy**

For this reflective task, find a colleague with whom to meet and share experiences of being a learner. Try to empathize as much as possible both with your former self and with your partner's stories and experiences. Remember that an essential element of empathy is actively listening to the other person. This means listening carefully and consciously to the meaning and message of what your partner is saying. These exercises can help sensitize us to what foreign language learners are going through and also to what it means to be empathetic as a teacher. Tell your partner about:

- a time when you learned something completely new, with no previous knowledge or skills in that area. It could be a foreign language or some other skill. What happened? How did you feel? How did you behave and why? How did others react towards you and how did you respond to this?

- an experience from your time at school as a pupil when something positive happened to make you feel proud, happy, or loved. What happened? How were you treated by others, and what were your expectations, feelings, and thoughts? Why do you feel you have remembered this incident and what was important about it for you as a learner at that time?

- a teacher, colleague, or friend whom you admire and consider as being or having been particularly empathetic. How does/did this person show empathy? How does/did talking with the person make you feel? What specific empathetic skills and behaviours could you emulate? How do you think that individual was feeling during particular incidents?

Group formation processes

As teachers, we recognize how our classes develop and change over time. While this is due in part to changes in the individuals themselves, it is also, to a large extent, due to the maturing of the group as a whole and the establishing of a group identity and culture. Groups never stop evolving and adapting to contextual factors and developments. Traditionally, groups are thought to go through five recognizable stages of development. Tuckman (1965) named these 'forming', 'storming', 'norming', 'performing', and 'adjourning', which are all believed to be normal parts of group formation processes necessary for the group to function effectively. Dörnyei and Murphey (2003) explain that, for teachers, it can be quite comforting to know and recognize these stages within a group, firstly, in order to enhance the group development processes and allow the group to form as it needs to, and secondly, to anticipate future developments. Not all groups go through all stages to the same extent or for the same length of time, and some may return to earlier stages. Our discussion here is useful for understanding the nature of group development, but this should not be interpreted as a rigid, fixed sequence of events; issues in a group concerning relationships and trust, as well as modes and forms of communication, are constantly in flux. However, these sequential patterns of group formation are sufficiently recognized that they help us to understand some of the issues and processes at play as our classes form into effective, positive classroom communities.

Activity 2.5 | **Fostering positive group dynamics**

Which of the following activities would you choose to use with a new group of students that you will be working with for a length of time in order to foster positive group dynamics? What would be your reasoning for and against any of these activities?

1 giving a test to establish any gaps in knowledge at the outset
2 asking students to work in pairs to interview each other and then introduce their partner to the whole class
3 working together on a learning contract consisting of rules for the whole class
4 singing a song about friendship
5 using the activity 'find someone who …' with questions such as 'Find someone who was born in Brazil', in which students have to mingle and complete questionnaires
6 asking students to work on a 'spot the difference' picture description activity in pairs.

What activities have you used successfully with a new class? What was the rationale in terms of group dynamics of using or not using various activities?

The first stage, 'forming', takes place when a group forms and begins to become a recognizable group. Most teachers are aware of how anxiety-inducing it can be for learners in a new class and how important it is to start by creating group bonds, positive interpersonal relationships, and alleviating learner fears. To this end, first sessions with learners are important in establishing a positive atmosphere, showing them there is nothing to be afraid of, establishing ground rules, and generally setting the tone for the coming months of working and learning together.

For these reasons, many teachers begin courses with various forms of icebreaker activities designed to promote positive group dynamics and familiarity amongst members. As the group is forming, it is usual to avoid controversial issues, conflict, and situations that might feel threatening for any of the group members. This means teachers have a vital role to play at the outset in directing and guiding group processes and establishing a positive group climate. Given the importance of establishing positive group dynamics, it is well worth teachers investing time and energy at the beginning in tasks designed to promote constructive, open communication and allow a climate of interpersonal trust to develop.

Gradually, however, the relative harmony established at the outset will naturally give way to the 'storming' stage, in which people feel more familiar and confident to start disagreeing more openly, and in which competition amongst members for their position within the group takes place. It is also normal for the group to establish some independence from the teacher and, indeed, possibly challenge the teacher's authority. Teachers can view such developments as a sign of progress and accept them as a stage in a process that the group will ultimately be stronger for having gone through (Dörnyei & Murphey, 2003).

The 'norming' stage occurs when things settle and a degree of cohesion in the group emerges based on shared goals and norms. There is a sense of openness in the way the members of the group react towards each other, but this goes with an established set of norms and interactional patterns. Many groups may continue to function at this level; however, others may reach the 'performing' stage, in which the group is highly motivated, cohesive, and interdependent, and in which the teacher is able to step back and take more of a facilitatory role. The final stage of 'adjourning' concerns the stage when a group comes to an end and separates. Researchers in the area of group dynamics explain how the dissolution of a group can be linked to anxiety for some and that it is important for people to have the chance for closure in order to proceed to the next stage of their lives. People need to leave groups with a favourable memory of that group, yet ready to let go, move on, and positively interpret their time and achievements in and with the group (Dörnyei & Murphey, 2003).

Leadership and group roles

As we touched upon earlier in the chapter, teachers have to adopt a variety of roles in their interactions with learners, and these roles depend very much on the task at hand and the current stage of group development. Sometimes we need to be in the role of the controller or director and at other times we need to become a facilitator or participant. However, a role we never relinquish is that of group leader, and one of our principal responsibilities remains to manage and develop the groups of learners we work with (Harmer, 2011). As teachers, we will typically be the central focus in our classrooms and the one most likely to affect the classroom atmosphere and group dynamics. We do this both directly and indirectly, through our behaviour and our attitudes to the group, to individuals, to the subject, and to tasks themselves. Thus, there is a widely recognized acceptance that teachers are the leaders in the classroom and, indeed, in many cultures and settings there is an expectation that they will behave accordingly. Our leadership role in the classroom means we have certain functions to fulfil, such as promoting positive group dynamics, establishing an atmosphere of trust and mutual respect, ensuring the group functions and achieves its goals, and keeping the group productive and on task.

There are three principal styles of leadership that were identified by Kurt Lewin and his colleagues and which are still referred to in many leadership studies today (Lewin, Lippitt, & White, 1939). These are autocratic, democratic and *laissez-faire* **leadership styles**. Autocratic or authoritarian leaders make the majority of the decisions, dictating rules and group norms with little or no discussion or input from members of the group. An exaggerated form of this would be a dictatorial and controlling style, removing freedom and choice from other group members. In contrast, democratic leaders encourage the group to take responsibility and contribute to group decisions and goal setting collectively. The third style is that of *laissez-faire* leaders, who typically do not exercise their authority and offer no guidance or support at all to the group, its development, or its decision-making processes. Unlike the *laissez-faire* leader, a democratic leader does exert some degree of authority, but this is done through democratic processes in a way which balances the need for structures and the need for other people's freedom and agency.

Perhaps unsurprisingly, the teacher leadership style generally believed to be the most effective is the democratic style, which ensures that the class has direction and structure but that learners feel empowered, respected, and involved in the development of the class and its contents. An excessively *laissez-faire* style can be problematic in the classroom as learners may lack sufficient support, structure, and direction to guide their learning processes and in-class behaviours. In contrast, an overly autocratic style cripples learner engagement, creativity, and investment, and tends to foster an unproductive, aggressive, competitive working climate. More democratic teachers are able to embrace their responsibility as a teacher and adopt the role of facilitator in order to promote learner autonomy and enhance the cooperative learning potential of their classrooms. This delegating and democratizing of power to the group is not without its challenges for the teacher, who has to remain attentive to needs and changes in the group which may necessitate a switch in role and more directed leadership at certain points. Essentially, democratic teachers never completely renounce their power in the classroom, but use it judiciously for the benefit of the entire group. The extent to which a democratic leadership style may or may not be expected from a teacher can depend on the local contexts and cultures; while teachers may strive for such a democratized power structure in their classrooms, developments in that direction may need to be introduced more gently, as a step-by-step process, depending on the specific expectations and constraints of particular contexts (see Dörnyei & Murphey, 2003).

In addition, teachers may have an overall leadership style tendency, but they will also need to be flexible in responding to group needs. In relation to the group formation processes outlined earlier in this chapter, researchers have found that certain leadership styles are conducive to group development at certain stages. For example, at the outset with a group, the teacher will need to be the one who sets the tone, boundaries, and some of the rules, and during the 'storming' stages, the teacher will need to retain some degree of control, while, at the same time, allowing the group to find its own identity, structure, and boundaries. Generally, as the group develops, the leader should be able to take on a less prominent role in managing the group. This does not mean withdrawing and taking on a *laissez-faire* approach; rather, it means that the teacher, as leader, needs to continue to monitor and promote positive group dynamics and cohesion, but allow the group to grow and gain independence (see Dörnyei & Murphey, 2003).

Finally, not only teachers take on leadership roles; learners can also adopt these and other roles within the group. Roles are usually thought of either as emerging naturally from the interactional patterns in the group—informal roles—or as being assigned by the teacher or through a vote—formal roles. Learners need to be encouraged to explore different roles, but a successfully functioning group benefits from everyone having a role—formal or informal—within the group structure. Leaders within the student body will either emerge spontaneously or be assigned that position by others. Care must be taken that learners do not informally take on undesired roles within the group, such as the role of scapegoat or outsider (Dörnyei & Murphey, 2003). A particular challenge for language teachers is that there may be certain learners in a class who, by virtue of their language proficiency, are assigned leadership roles but who, in other domains where foreign language proficiency is not an obvious asset, may be unfamiliar with the role of leader. In such cases, there may be reluctance on the part of the student to accept the leadership role, or on the part of others to acknowledge this individual in an unfamiliar social role. Language learners bring other aspects of their social identities into the language classroom and, as language teachers, we need to recognize these multiple identities and how they may affect group positioning. We need to be sensitive to the roles being adopted and enacted in the group, and decide how to engage with them in ways that are constructive both for the individuals and for the group as a whole.

A particularly important type of role in the language classroom is that of role model. We especially want learners to be confronted with positive role models in terms of language learners—not necessarily those who appear to have a natural 'gift' for languages and succeed apparently effortlessly (see the section on mindsets in Chapter 4), but rather those who have had to work purposefully to achieve their language learning goals. A powerful form of modelling suggested by Murphey and colleagues (for example, Murphey & Arao, 2001) is the use of **near-peer role models**. These are peers who are close socially, in age, and/or in proficiency to the learners and whom they can admire and respect but also see as representing realistic, attainable goals. Encouraging learners to form an imagined relationship with such a role model can be valuable for their motivation, agency, and sense of efficacy.

Power in the classroom

An additional related issue in the classroom connected to leadership styles and working structures concerns the distribution of power in the classroom. In this respect, teachers may differ in their teaching styles, with some being more in need of control and others tending to be more democratic in style. As Ehrman and Dörnyei (1998) emphasize, power is not inherently a 'dirty word'. They explain that teachers are mandated by their jobs and institutions to exert 'legitimate power' in the language classroom. However, as with any other tool, it can be used positively or negatively by teachers. This means that there will be times when leadership is expected of the teacher—in which case they exert their authority—but it should never be driven by their own ego needs.

Bonny Norton (2000, 2013) makes the point that a person's position within any group or set of relationships implies some form of power structure, which may be explicit or implicit. Returning to the idea outlined at the beginning of this chapter of understanding classrooms as communities of practice, Norton's work draws our attention to opportunities for learners to take part in classrooms and their rights to have their contributions recognized and valued. Any community is imbued with power structures; as teachers, we need to be aware of what these are and consider how we can empower all of our learners to have equal opportunities to participate in our learning community. A particularly problematic issue connected with power and group dynamics concerns bullying in the classroom (see Forsyth, 2014). Bullying is when one person or group uses force, threat, or coercion over another person or group of people perceived as being somehow less powerful than themselves. Bullying is a complex problem, far beyond the scope of this book and chapter. Nevertheless, it is an important element of classroom power structures and learners' networked lives beyond the immediate classroom that teachers need to be aware of and sensitive to. It is hoped that a cohesive group environment—with positive inter-group relations, mutual respect, trust, and an open culture of communication—might reduce the threat of bullying. However, rules of behaviour, taking reports of bullying seriously, and mediation programmes can serve as important measures to diminish the threat of bullying (Forsyth, 2014).

Competitions, collaborations, and cooperation

A particular form of interaction that may promote aggressive relationships and be highly problematic in terms of power struggles emerges from competitive group structures. Many of us will have used competitions in class to add an element of fun or drama, to spice up games, and to energize short-term motivation. We may also have specific pedagogical purposes depending on how we choose to define the winner. It should not necessarily be in terms of achievement; we may seek to highlight creativity or reward group cooperation on a task. Generally, however, competition needs to be employed with great caution, given the risks it poses to group cohesion, the high anxiety it can cause for some learners, and the potential for exclusion of certain members of the class. Essentially, a competitive climate

A cooperative environment

means that we are deliberately pitting the students against each other and there can be only one winner—meaning that all the others must in some way be losers. Competitions also tend to stress the outcomes of learning, rather than the process of development. The potentially damaging implications of these side effects of competition for learners' self-esteem, self-efficacy, and beliefs about the goals of learning are apparent. (See Chapter 3 on the self.) Additionally, such competitive climates and activities can be detrimental to long-term motivation as they can reduce learners' intrinsic motivation by focusing their attention and goals on an external reward. (See Chapter 6 on motivation.)

Given the rise of communicative language teaching, it is unsurprising that many classroom tasks require cooperation and working together with others. We are aware how beneficial this can be for the learners in terms of extending their thinking, using the language for communicative purposes, and contributing further to positive group dynamics. Yet working in groups might not always be successful and it is important to consider some prerequisites for effective collaboration. Collaboration is based on the fundamental premise that we learn through social structures and effective working with others, and that this can be achieved through structured cooperative activities. However, group-work does not, in itself, necessarily mean cooperative group-work. Working on a cooperative task means learners need to share ideas and resources, help each other, and provide constructive feedback. Cooperation takes place when learners have a need to work together in order to carry out the activity successfully. Learners need to know how to collaborate effectively with others; they need to feel a shared sense of responsibility, recognize a common goal, and feel willing to work together in a climate of mutual respect and support. Often the general group atmosphere and dynamics can contribute positively to ensuring that pair- or group-work within the larger class also functions effectively. However, the teacher may wish to assign roles and specific functions within a small group and even break down global tasks into smaller ones in order to facilitate the smooth functioning of a cooperative group. Teachers may also choose to deliberately highlight, discuss, and teach strategies for working cooperatively. These may include strategies for asking for people's opinions or help, listening actively and respectfully to each other, reflecting on somebody else's input, giving constructive feedback, negotiating, helping each other, and coordinating the efforts of all group members towards the common learning goal (Ehrman & Dörnyei, 1998).

Group cohesion

To end this chapter on a positive note, we want to return to considering the characteristics of groups that function well and have an atmosphere conducive to learning. Among the most widely cited features of such a group are strong group cohesion and shared group identities. A cohesive group is one in which all the members of the group are accepted and cooperate, working together towards and committed to common goals, and when subgroups are also integrated into the class as a whole, ensuring a group identity. Generally, in such a positive group climate, learners are more inclined to be engaged and focused on the goal of learning. However, group cohesion is also complex. It is dynamic, changing over time, and a group could potentially be cohesive but still refuse to work towards a common goal.

What brings about group cohesion? Usually it develops gradually, and many of the stages of group formation outlined above will contribute to it. Group cohesion is aided when the people in the group like each other, trust one another, and generally have positive inter-group relationships, including the relationships with the teacher. Cohesive groups can be thought of as being unified and focused on common goals. Attending to many of the issues addressed throughout this chapter will hopefully support the formation of a cohesive group. An additional way to promote positive group dynamics, especially during the early stage of group formation, concerns the establishment of group rules. Each group has its own social structure and accepted 'norms' of behaviour. Sometimes teachers may formalize these through the use of 'learning contracts', in which students and teacher collaboratively codify a set of 'rules' for successful and effective group

Group cohesion

functioning. These documents outline the rules of the group and expectations of its members, including learners' expectations of the teacher. Indeed, the process of working on learning contracts as a group can, in itself, be extremely productive, allowing issues to be discussed and agreement to be reached as a collective. On other occasions, these rules of behaviour might not be formally written down but everyone in the classroom culture knows what is expected and what can or cannot be done.

Collaboration and cooperation are key features of any successful working community of learning. However, a word of caution is needed. In groups where the desire or need for harmony or conformity is too great, then there is a danger of what is known as 'groupthink' (Dörnyei & Murphey, 2003). In overly cohesive groups with a strong sense of group loyalty, learners may feel pressure to conform and not express conflicting opinions, with the result that creative and critical thinking within the class is smothered. Groups may also develop a 'norm of mediocrity' (Dörnyei, 2005), which discourages group members from challenging themselves or realizing their full potential out of the wish not to disrupt the group cohesion or norms. Therefore, while we want to promote positive group cohesion, this must not come at the cost of individuality and critical thinking. As teachers, we must constantly seek to challenge our students' thinking and opinions in order to stimulate a healthy range of differentiated perspectives within the group.

As a final point, we ought to stress that social groups are not static; they are constantly developing, often taking on new members while losing old ones. Individuals' feelings of group membership, or belonging to a group, inevitably change over time. People rarely feel an instant sense of belonging to any group, as these feelings take time to develop. Membership of a group often begins through what is known as **peripheral participation** (Lave & Wenger, 1991)—that is to say, new or prospective members often spend time either observing from the edges of the group or participating in minor roles. Over time, this peripheral participation facilitates recognition from other group members, which, in turn, encourages a fuller sense of belonging to the group and more active participation in its events. Individual members of a group rarely feel the same levels of belonging or commitment to a group and its norms at the same time.

Activity 2.6	**Membership of social groups**

Think about some of the different social groups to which you have felt a strong sense of belonging. These can be groups from any walk of life, in either educational or non-educational contexts. Think about some of the ways in which your feelings towards the group changed over time. Do you remember how you felt as an outsider or peripheral member of the group? Do you remember any key signs or events that indicated you were recognized as a legitimate member of the group? Do you remember any particular thoughts or feelings you had that suggested you were drifting away from the group?

From a practical perspective, the ability to recognize and understand the signs of group membership and belonging is a valuable skill for all teachers. For language teachers especially, the nature of the subject being taught places an increased value on this skill. Social groupings of all kinds, from pairs to the whole class, and communication between the members of those groups are essential features of formal language instruction. Effectively managing and nurturing those groups, recognizing when individuals identify with group norms, and encouraging this sense of identification, are core tasks for language teachers.

Summary

Successful classroom management depends on many of the issues outlined in this chapter and it is clear how complex and challenging it can be to effectively manage our groups of learners while also attending to the unique individuals within the class. If we concentrate on promoting positive group dynamics, we can simultaneously address many of the needs of individual learners, such as their need for belonging, positive affective climates, supportive relationships, respect, trust, acceptance, and a purpose within safe, non-threatening learning environments. Positive group dynamics mean positive social relations for individual learners in the group too. We cannot take the learner out of the group, nor the group out of the learner: attending to one means implicitly attending to the other. On the whole, we would agree with Dörnyei and Murphey (2003, p. 170), who conclude their book on group dynamics by saying that this topic is 'one of the—if not the—most useful academic subdiscipline for classroom practitioners.' All our language classrooms need to begin with us helping to develop a positive set of interpersonal relationships in the group, which will, in turn, generate the positive classroom atmosphere we know is conducive to and necessary for successful language learning and use.

In the next chapter, we will turn our attention to the individual, but we must remember that the individual is always situated within a range of groups, cultures, and broader contexts, which simultaneously shape and are influenced by that individual. As John Donne said, 'no man is an island', and while for practical purposes in this book, we may focus on individuals and their psychology, these can never be truly understood as separate from the groups and cultures within which they are situated.

Questions for reflection

1 Looking at the coursebooks or materials that you currently use in your classes, which exercises encourage cooperation among students? Which can be completed individually?

2 Think of the various classes you have been in as either a learner or a teacher. What are the most positive elements of these groups and settings that you would like to bring together in the classes you work in? Think in terms of the physical dimensions of the space as well as the social and emotional components.

3 Think about the classes that you work with. How often do you consider the 'personality' and needs of the groups as a whole compared with those of individuals? Which groups might need some help in developing more positive group dynamics and how might you want to go about this?

Suggestions for further reading

Dörnyei, Z., & **Murphey, T.** (2003). *Group dynamics in the language classroom.* Cambridge: Cambridge University Press.
This is the only widely available book dedicated to the topic of group dynamics and language learning, and it offers an excellent accessible overview of issues such as group development, group norms, student roles, leadership functions, and conflict management. The book also has a pleasingly practical orientation, having been written for teachers by teachers and with practical considerations playing a strong role.

Schmuck, R. A., & **Schmuck, P. A.** (2001). *Group processes in the classroom.* Boston, MA: McGraw-Hill.
A rich, comprehensive book which takes a social psychological perspective on classrooms and their group dynamics and considers additional vital issues such as peer pressure, diversity, inclusion, cooperative learning, and school structures. It also includes many excellent classroom practice activities and ideas.

Hadfield, J. (1992). *Classroom dynamics.* Oxford: Oxford University Press.
An incredibly useful resource book for teachers with activities and tasks designed to help teachers establish good working relationships with students in the foreign language classroom and accompanied by a succinct summary of key themes and issues.

3

THE SELF

Introduction

Imagine being asked to describe yourself as a teacher; what things would you mention? Perhaps you would talk about your perceived strengths, weaknesses, preferences, dislikes, pet hates, fears, ambitions, motivations, personality characteristics, etc. You might refer to key experiences in your past as well as people who have been influential for you along your life journey. You would perhaps also talk about your hopes and ambitions for the future and how you imagine your future to be. All of these (and more besides) represent your sense of self as a teacher. Even the apparently simple task of thinking about yourself as a teacher is a complex undertaking. Now imagine how messy things become when you start to think about other areas of your life and expand your sense of self to incorporate how you see yourself in other roles, for example, as a parent, partner, carer, or learner. Bringing all these different aspects of your perception of your 'self' together reveals just how vast and complex any individual's sense of self is, and how it stretches across time to incorporate experiences in our past and our hopes for the future.

The immense scope of the self makes it a fascinating topic for researchers to investigate; however, it also explains why research in this area has been so fragmented and why a multitude of self-related terms has proliferated to try to capture and describe the self. In order to make researching the self manageable, researchers have had to set boundaries. In doing so, they have chosen to break the self down into different components or explore specific facets, each with its own separate term. Typically, these different aspects of the self reflect distinctions that people are able to recognize, such as our sense of self in respect to specific areas of our lives, or our sense of self in terms of particular types of thoughts or emotions—such as our beliefs about our competence to perform certain tasks or actions.

In this chapter, we will look at what we know about some of these facets of the self in respect to language learning and teaching. However, we feel it is important to remember that these are all parts of your overall sense of self. It is the ways in which all these different facets of the self interact that give us our overall sense of who we believe ourselves to be. Thus, although we often refer to people as having multiple selves, the way we experience our sense of self in our daily lives usually feels much more coherent than this. Without this sense of coherence, we would find ourselves confused, disoriented, and open to all kinds of mental stress.

Activity 3.1   **My sense of self as a teacher**

1   Think about yourself as a teacher. Write down six things that describe you as a teacher, for example, your strengths, weaknesses, characteristics, or teaching style. Write them in the first column. If possible, compare your list with someone else's.

2   In the second column, write down how you feel that aspect of your self affects your behaviour in the language classroom. For example: 'I feel that I am very social and this perhaps means that I pay a lot of attention to social relationships in class and use more group-based collaborative activities.'

	Who I am as a teacher	**My behaviour / what I do in class**
1		
2		
3		
4		
5		
6		

Photocopiable © Oxford University Press

These are all aspects of your **self-concept** as a teacher. This might not be the same as your sense of self as a parent, as a sportsperson, as a musician, or in any other role you play. Together, however, these aspects make up part of who you are and guide how you behave in the classroom. In this chapter, we will begin by explaining why the self is so important in educational settings for both teachers and learners. We will then consider how the self can be defined and what insights for language teaching these different perspectives have generated. Given our interest in helping learners develop a healthy sense of self in relation to language learning, we will then consider how individuals form their sense of self over time, as well as particular challenges for a learner's sense of self in everyday classroom life. The chapter concludes by reflecting on what we can do as teachers to promote a healthy sense of self in both our learners and ourselves.

Why is it so important for teachers to understand the self?

Perhaps not surprisingly, our beliefs and feelings about ourselves strongly affect the ways we behave, how we engage with others, the goals we set ourselves, the challenges we take on, and our willingness to persevere in the face of difficulties. The self connects all the other chapters in this book, linking our motivations, emotions, levels of anxiety, use of strategies, willingness to communicate, sense of agency, and position within a group. So, in Activity 3.1, you might see yourself as a patient teacher, which might lead you to spend time explaining things to individuals. Alternatively, you might see yourself as an active person, which might lead you to select activities involving movement. Our sense of self plays a key role in how we navigate all our encounters in our daily lives, including every educational and language-related encounter, whether as a teacher or learner.

Our perception of who we believe or feel we are also lies at the core of our ability to **self-regulate** (see Chapter 7), which includes how we monitor and evaluate our own behaviour and select appropriate strategies to help us to learn and use language. A key component in self-regulation is our ability to judge our own competences in order to know when and how we need to use such strategies. Further, our willingness to use strategies and to plan and monitor our own progress is also related to our confidence to do so. This awareness about ourselves is crucial to how we learn and is linked to our unique capacities as humans to be able to reflect on our selves and our experiences and then to use this knowledge to guide our subsequent behaviour and future goals. Believing we are capable of doing something or achieving a certain objective is a vital element of being willing and able to take control of and responsibility for our actions— also called **agency**, a topic that we address in Chapter 7. It is a desirable goal for teachers to promote this feeling of competence and empowerment in learners.

However, two things are important to note at this point and to bear in mind throughout the chapter. Firstly, our sense of self may not necessarily be an accurate reflection of our actual abilities or performance, but rather it consists of what we believe to be true of ourselves. Whether we are right or wrong is, in some ways, less important than our self-beliefs and how these beliefs guide our behaviour. Secondly, learners need to hold a positive but, importantly, realistic sense of self. There is no point in learners developing an overinflated or unrealistic sense of self, as this can lead not only to problems in self-regulation but also potentially to undesirable behaviours such as bullying and cheating.

Fundamentally, if we wish to take a learner-centred approach to our teaching, then we must begin by understanding the individuals we work with and how they see themselves. An appreciation of our learners' sense of self can be vital in helping us to empathize and form meaningful social relationships with them, in anticipating their concerns, and in interpreting their behaviours and responses to classroom tasks and feedback. Seeing the language learning experience through learners' eyes and appreciating their perception of how well they feel they are positioned to cope is an invaluable insight to have in our pedagogical toolkit.

Activity 3.2   **Knowing your learners' sense of self**

Think of a class you teach currently and consider the following questions in relation to the individual learners.

1 Are you aware of how your learners view themselves in respect to language learning?
2 Do you know how they would describe themselves in terms of their strengths, weaknesses, characteristics, or learning style?
3 How might you elicit this information from the learners?
4 How comfortable do you think your learners would feel about describing their views of themselves as language learners?

Multiple ways of understanding the self

It is hard to know where to begin and which of the terms concerned with the self to discuss, but we have chosen to concentrate on those aspects of the self which have been the focus of research both within foreign language learning and beyond it, in educational psychology. We have also opted to present our understandings of them in ways we think especially useful for practice. However, before we look at individual constructs and what we know about them, it is worth reiterating some key points that affect any discussion of the self. As explained in Chapter 2, who we feel and believe we are strongly reflects how we interact with and interpret the environments and contexts in which we live and learn. Nobody becomes who they are in a vacuum, separate and distinct from cultural and contextual influences. During our lifetime, we learn to interpret feedback from others, especially those whose opinions we value, as well as developing our understanding of our sense of self from various environmental clues. The societies and communities in which we live also esteem certain values and we use these as benchmarks to evaluate ourselves. Therefore, it is impossible to conceive of the self without understanding how it relates to contexts and social encounters. However, in our discussion of self constructs, it will become apparent that some definitions of self stress the interaction of a particular aspect of the self with the environment more than others.

Self-efficacy and second language linguistic self-confidence

The first term we will look at is **self-efficacy** (Mills, Pajares, & Herron, 2007). This is a cognitive self construct in which the focus is on one's evaluation of one's ability to do something successfully in a specific situation, such as a specific language task—for example: 'I believe I could successfully do a listening exercise of multiple-choice questions based on an authentic Polish radio broadcast.' There has been a considerable amount of work in this area in second language acquisition (SLA) and self-efficacy has been shown to be tightly connected to learners' levels of achievement, use of strategies, levels of anxiety, and ability to self-regulate and manage their learning.

A related construct in SLA is **L2 linguistic self-confidence**, which refers more specifically to learners' confidence in their ability to communicate in a second language

(L2). Much of the work in this area has been conducted in the bilingual setting of Canada (for example, Clément, 1980), in which the Francophone and Anglophone communities coexist side by side. The research in that context has shown that a high level of L2 linguistic self-confidence is connected to positive attitudes towards the second-language culture, a willingness to seek opportunities to use the language, and lower levels of anxiety in using the language. Clearly, these are all characteristics that all teachers would seek to engender in their learners whatever the setting.

Both of these facets of the self centre on whether we believe we have the capacity to do something specific in respect to learning or using the language. They are often referred to as **expectancy beliefs** (see Chapter 6 on expectancy–value theory) and they link to whether we expect to be able to achieve something or carry out a certain task. Both of these self terms generally refer to a very specific context, and are considered to be primarily cognitive terms, reflecting people's beliefs about their competence in respect to a particular task rather than to a specific setting. For teachers, it is important to understand these beliefs, as they can form the 'building blocks' of other aspects of the self, such as the generally more broadly defined self-concept (Bong & Skaalvik, 2003).

Self-concept

Self-concept tends to be a more globally defined term that can refer to people's cognitive beliefs about their abilities as well as to their affective evaluation of their competence in a specific domain. However, what we mean by the term 'specific domain' needs some clarification. For example, at one level we might refer to the domain of academic learning in general, but we may also identify a more specific domain relating to foreign language learning. Even within the domain of foreign language learning, we can consider additional domains connected to the learning of particular foreign languages, or learning at specific skill levels such as speaking, writing, reading, or listening. Thus, we can talk about writing self-concept and reading self-concept. While we can talk about our learners' language learning self-concept, as it does have a unique and recognizable character and content, it is important to note that it may share elements from other domains, such as the learners' experiences of learning other subjects. This implies that when talking to learners about their language learning self-concept, we need to recognize that it cannot be isolated from other aspects of their academic self-concept, as the various domains can influence each other and the way learners come to see themselves. The practical implication is that in order to more fully understand learners and help them with their learning, teachers may wish to take an interest in their self-concept. Some teachers find that asking students to describe themselves as language learners—in writing, speaking, or in some form of self-representation such as a collage or blog—can provide invaluable information about the basic picture they have of themselves as learners of language and, indeed, of other things.

An important concern for all self-beliefs is the extent to which a learner may generalize a particular belief. Consider, for example, a learner who claims, 'I can never do any listening exercises.' The use of 'never' and 'any' implies that the learner has extended a specific belief from an experience with a particular task—such as 'I find it difficult to do listening exercises from live radio broadcasts with lots of background noise'—to a more general belief that they cannot do any listening-related tasks in the language. Of course, people often make these kinds of generalizations; this is perfectly normal and unavoidable. However, teachers need to remain aware of some of the risks associated with learners generalizing beliefs to all settings, especially since a generalized self-belief is much more difficult to challenge and change than a more specific one. While we can think of the self as a set of patterns that we recognize about ourselves, it is important that we remain open to the idea of the potential for change. Activity 3.3 illustrates this point.

Activity 3.3   **Responding to a learner's self-concept**

The following are statements from a female native speaker of German called Joana (a pseudonym) studying at a university in Austria, as reported in a study by Mercer (2011). Some of the statements relate to Joana's academic self-concept and some to her language self-concept. Decide what each statement tells you about her self-concept. When you have done this, decide how you would work with her if you were her teacher.

1 '… I can't study by heart, I can't even study a few pages by heart, I can't do it, I can't do it, I just can't memorize it that well and I can't memorize word by word …'
2 'I need that personal link by people I like … I am not that type of student that reads books … studies at home, you know, in their room and just doesn't need any other feedback … I couldn't study without having personal links …'
3 'I used to be good at school and I'm just used to being good which is something like a habit. I know I would be a lot better in writing if I had read more. I'm just not a reader but I think I can improve on writing a lot and it has to do a lot of practice … the more often you write … the easier it gets …'
4 'I can't pronounce my *th* anymore and that's like when I'm tired or something like that and then I start like pronouncing things weirdly …'

Some of the statements above relate to more general beliefs and some to her abilities in very specific terms in a particular skill area. The main point is that if teachers understand how their learners see themselves, we can work with individual learners to help them to tackle perceived problems, set individual goals, and find appropriate working strategies and styles.

Self-esteem

Self-esteem can be understood as our overall affective evaluation of ourselves—what we feel about ourselves generally—and the term **self-worth**, with which it is frequently used interchangeably, also captures this more emotional, holistic sense of self. Although these terms are understood as referring principally to an affective construct, it is unlikely that we can meaningfully separate cognition and affect. (See Chapter 5 for a more detailed discussion of this point.) If we think of self-esteem as including a cognitive dimension, it becomes very similar as a construct to more holistic definitions of self-concept. For us, it is important to note that what individuals feel about themselves and what they believe about themselves are closely intertwined.

Our global self-esteem emerges from the interaction of all the many other beliefs and feelings we hold about ourselves, such as our domain-specific self-concepts and our self-efficacy beliefs. How influential these various beliefs are for our overall self-esteem depends on the relative importance in our lives of the areas they represent. So if, for example, a learner holds negative self-beliefs in respect to music but this domain is not important or valued by the learner, then the effect on his overall self-esteem will be limited. However, should that learner come from a family of athletes and be a keen athlete himself, then holding negative self-beliefs about himself in respect to an area of sport is more likely to have a bigger impact on his overall self-esteem.

Generally, understanding the composite nature of the self and the multiple domains from which it is composed can help us in our interactions with our learners. If we encounter learners who seem to be focusing on negative aspects of the self and developing a negative sense of self, we can help by encouraging them to focus on the other aspects in which they may have more positive feelings. In doing so, we can shift their attention to also include positive dimensions of their self-concept and perhaps find ways of connecting these areas with language learning. It is important for everyone to appreciate that we all have aspects of our selves that we feel positive and negative about and we need to try to keep these in balance in our overall self-perception.

Identity

Identity is another term that has been variously defined and is often used interchangeably with the term 'self'. For our purposes, we are going to consider identity as the way we view ourselves in respect to specific contexts and groups—real or imagined. Thus, we talk about learner identities as being individuals' sense of self in relation to specific learning settings and roles. In the case of language learners, we are interested in this sense of self in relation to settings and roles concerned with language learning and use. As with all self constructs, each learner has multiple identities reflecting the multiple roles, social groups, and settings with which that individual is connected. These roles may also potentially be in conflict within a single individual; for example, a person may feel a strong, positive identity in one setting—for example, a learner of English using the language competently in an online gaming world—that is challenged or even contradicted in another—such as the same learner struggling to use English effectively in an academic writing course.

Adolescents are in a particularly difficult position that requires sensitivity and understanding, as they may need to balance conflicting roles. For instance, learners may be keen to display to a teacher and parents their hard-working and committed student identity. Yet, at the same time, they may feel the need to go to great lengths to conceal such an identity from their peers in class, to whom they may wish to display a very different identity by enacting the role of 'cool classmate' (see Taylor, 2013). In addition, we must remember that our learners hold a host of other identities and roles beyond the bounds of the language learning classroom, for example, as a footballer, collector, gamer, or musician. It can be beneficial for teachers to allow learners to express those identities and integrate them into their in-class identities through activities such as writing, discussion, and presentations in the foreign language connecting with other domains and roles in their lives.

Activity 3.4	**Multiple identities**

Make a list of some different activities you commonly find yourself doing, for example, cooking a meal at home, preparing lessons in the staffroom, driving a car in a city, or playing football. Next to each activity, make a note of how you view yourself in respect to that activity. For instance, when preparing lessons, one might view oneself as an experienced professional commanding respect, while cooking in the kitchen at home, one may see oneself as rather inept.

One way of discussing identity in the research literature has been to talk about a learner's sense of self in relation to '**communities of practice**' (Lave & Wenger, 1991; see Chapter 2). These refer to communities which share certain characteristics and of which individuals seek to become 'legitimate members', such as a school staff room or an online social networking space. They can be actual spaces and discourse communities or imagined communities of practice. So, for example, we can think of learners as seeking to become members of classroom or institutional communities of practice in which they work at learning the behaviours and language needed to be successful in that community. We can also think of language learners as seeking to become members of communities of practice in terms of target-language cultures or contexts of use. More recently, work has focused on the role of imagination (Pavlenko & Norton, 2007)—how learners may form identities in their imagination with imagined groups of users and how motivating such images and imagined identities can be. As teachers, we can help learners create an identity with an imagined L2 community and support them in sustaining a positive, motivating relationship with that setting. This could be achieved through projects about the setting, and imaginative tasks which might involve them envisaging themselves in roles and situations in that context. (See Hadfield & Dörnyei, 2014, for specific task ideas.)

Finally, research into identity has also revealed some interesting findings concerning the role of power in classrooms and the identities learners feel they can display and make their own (Norton, 2014). For example, a learner may feel competent in using the language in certain social settings but feel limited in opportunities to speak in class, which may be inhibited through perceived teacher behaviour or peer hierarchies. As teachers, we need to ensure that classroom structures for engagement and participation are enabling for all learners and provide a safe setting for them to have the confidence to express and enact their multiple identities. (See Chapter 2.)

In addition, work with bi- and multilinguals (Hemmi, 2014) has revealed interesting insights about the extent to which having bilingual identities can be perceived by individuals either as positive and beneficial for their lives or as negative, leading to conflicting, insecure identities in which individuals may feel quite literally divided. In today's increasingly globalized multicultural and multilingual societies, there is perhaps an assumption that bi- and multilingualism is to be positively embraced; but in the context of education, it is worth retaining a degree of caution about potential problems and conflicts that may accompany multiple identities for some individuals. Especially with increasing migration and a growing interest in many parts of the world in Content and Language Integrated Learning (CLIL) and other bilingual teaching approaches, it is important to understand the challenges of a multiplicity of identities. Such challenges may be faced not only by the learners themselves but also by their teachers, who have to deal with multiple roles and potentially divided identities in their professional contexts.

Activity 3.5

Me as a language learner

1 Ask your students to think about how they see themselves as language learners, for example, their strengths, their fears, and how they like to learn. Give students the figure below or tell them to copy it from the board. Ask them to write in it any words or add any pictures that they feel describe how they see themselves as language learners. Depending on how advanced the learners are, they can think about metaphors or the use of colour to convey their ideas. Ask the students to complete the figure at home and bring it to class ready to discuss with a partner they feel comfortable working with.

2 In class, ask students to describe themselves to their partners. Then give them another blank figure each and ask them to fill this in with how they would like to see themselves as a language learner one or five years from now. Each pair should compare their past and future figures and discuss what steps they will need to take to become the language learners they would like to be. You can collect the figures of their current and future selves from them and, as feedback, offer suggestions as to steps they could take to meet their aims.

How does an individual form a sense of self?

A person's sense of self is formed in a myriad of complex ways and the most influential factors can differ for individuals and across age groups. Young children go through different processes and conceptualize their self in different ways as they mature into adults (Harter, 1999). For example, young children tend to see themselves in more descriptive terms, rather than being able to evaluate these self-descriptions. They also tend to describe themselves in very concrete, episodic ways, as they are not yet able to see connections with others and make abstractions. Given that the majority of foreign language learning takes place amongst secondary-school-aged learners and adults, we will focus our discussion on these age groups.

Naturally, as we get older, we form more coherent self-concepts; for language learners, this is most notably based on how they interpret past experiences of learning generally, and language learning in particular. This means that as teachers, we need to appreciate what kinds of language learning and use experiences learners may previously have had and how they have interpreted these. In order to gain this kind of insight about each learner's sense of self, it can be useful to ask the class to write their language learning history. This can be done in writing, orally, through multimedia such as photo collages, or by bringing items of meaning to class. Such activities can open pathways of communication to challenge any inhibitive beliefs and help learners reconsider their evaluations of and relationships to any perceived negative past experiences.

Cultural factors

We also use social and environmental clues to make sense of who we feel we are. These can be macro-level clues, such as the characteristics that a certain culture or educational setting values and whether we feel we have these or not. It is important for language teachers to appreciate that different cultures may esteem different personality traits and values, and this can affect the learner's sense of self. One distinction featured prominently in the research (Markus & Kitayama, 1991) is between the values esteemed by collectivist cultures and how they may differ from those appreciated in more individualist cultures. (See also Chapter 2.) A pattern that appears to reoccur in research conducted in different cultural settings concerns differences in learners' self-concepts according to academic subjects and gender. Boys have typically been found to have higher self-concepts in maths, sciences, and related subjects, whereas girls tend to have more positive self-concepts in other areas, one of these being language-related domains. These widespread differences have been attributed to socialization patterns in which the general discourse in a culture tends to 'label' and position a subject as a girls' or a boys' subject. The implication for language teaching is a need to be especially attentive to the self-related needs of boys, given that they may commence their language learning careers from a deficit position.

Experiences of success and failure

Naturally, a person's sense of self can also be influenced by experiences of success or failure in a particular setting. However, it is important to note that success need not necessarily be defined in standardized terms: it is the learners' own interpretations of experiences as being successes or failures that influence their sense of self. For some learners, receiving a B on a test may be a great success, while for others, it could be perceived as a failure. Therefore, it is how individuals process particular events that affects their sense of self, and not just an external standard. In language learning, it is especially important to note the potential influence of perceived successful or failed attempts at using the language in the world outside the classroom and the role these experiences play in learners' sense of self in respect to the language. (See Chapter 4 for a more detailed discussion of learner perceptions of success and failure.)

Internal comparisons

Another related self-formation process stems from comparisons learners make internally about their abilities across domains (Marsh, 1986). This is when learners compare themselves across subjects and draw conclusions about their abilities in one domain through comparison with their experiences in another. In respect to language learning, it is highly likely that if learners are learning more than one foreign language, they will compare their experiences across languages. An interesting effect of this internal comparison is that the self-concept in one language is often enhanced and the other weakened as a consequence of this cross-domain comparison, even if their proficiency and test scores are the same. Similarly, this same internal comparison can take place across skill areas within a language, thus potentially leading learners to strengthen their sense of self in respect to one skill, such as speaking, while simultaneously weakening it in respect to, say, writing (Mercer, 2011). Once again, it can be useful to ask learners how they see themselves in different skill areas and encourage them to reflect on how and on what basis they form their respective evaluations.

Feedback

Another major source of information in forming our sense of self stems from how we judge the feedback—both explicit and implicit—that we get from others. Obviously, feedback can have a considerable impact on a learner's sense of self and this means that teachers need to take great care with the feedback that they offer. For one thing, learners tend to be highly astute at evaluating the 'authenticity' of feedback; they can discern whether praise from teachers is 'genuine' or not and they tend to ignore or devalue what they perceive as being 'empty' praise (Hyland & Hyland, 2006). Therefore, teachers need to ensure that all feedback and praise is credible. Learners also need to respect and value the person from whom they receive feedback. Interestingly, parents can be very influential as feedback-givers while children are growing up, but as they get older, children start to depend on feedback from those they feel more qualified to judge—in academic fields, usually teachers. In the field of foreign languages, encounters with native speakers can also have a considerable impact on a learner's sense of self, in some cases overriding or undermining feedback from teachers (Mercer, 2011).

A source of indirect feedback is what are known as 'reflected appraisals' (Mead, 1934; Cooley, 1902). These refer to how learners interpret clues from other people and their environment about what they believe others think of them. This indirect form of feedback can be a challenge for educators. How learners interpret our behaviour as teachers may not reflect our intentions, which, indeed, may be quite the opposite. While it is difficult to fully anticipate what meaning learners may assign to our behaviours and the subsequent implications for their sense of self, an awareness of these processes cautions us to be more conscious of the implicit messages that we may convey to learners through our in-class behaviour. For example, praising one particular learner may lead others in the same class to feel less competent when they notice that they did not receive any praise.

Our use of language can also indirectly convey important messages about ability. Consider the different messages if you say to a learner, 'Anna, you are really good at learning vocabulary' compared with 'Anna, you did a great job on this vocabulary test'. The first conveys the impression of an overall general competence, whereas the second concentrates on the learner's performance on a specific task. While the first may seem like effective feedback at first sight, in the long run, it can have detrimental effects. Imagine that Anna encounters difficulties with her next vocabulary test; she may then start to question her ability, believing that it is something she either has or does not have, rather than something that can be worked on and improved (see Dweck, 2006). The area of implicit messages conveyed by teachers though their behaviours and use of language is also related to possible **self-fulfilling prophecies** (Weinstein, 2002). This theory suggests that when we, as educators, believe something about a learner—such as a belief about a learner's ability or temperament—we are likely to start treating and interacting with that individual in a way that directly or indirectly conveys that evaluation. This may, in turn, influence that individual's self-beliefs, approaches to learning, and, eventually, actual learning outcomes. In some cases, this can lead to very positive outcomes—the so-called **Pygmalion effect**—where a teacher's strong belief in the potential of a learner encourages that individual towards high achievement (Babad, Inbar, & Rosenthal, 1982). However, this is not always the case and teachers' negative evaluations and the ways in which they implicitly communicate these evaluations to learners can function as strong impediments to learning in the opposite process known as the **Golem effect** (Babad et al., 1982). Of course, it is unrealistic to expect all learners to be successful all the time, but we would suggest that a wise strategy for teachers may be to believe that the best is possible from all students. This hope may not be realized in all cases, but it reduces the risk of teachers hindering learners through their own negative assessments of certain individuals. Furthermore, such an approach is likely to create a much more positive and encouraging environment for learning to take place.

Social comparisons

Another key influence in forming our sense of self stems from **social comparison processes** (Festinger, 1954). These comparisons are external and involve individuals comparing themselves to others in order to gain a sense of their competence and abilities—effectively, measuring themselves against the people around them. Sometimes these comparisons may be imposed by the learning environment, such as in competitive classrooms where the standing or rating of the individual learners is made visible. Naturally, for those doing less well, this can be extremely dispiriting and detrimental to their sense of self. However, social comparisons can also be driven by the learners themselves in two possible directions, in what are known as either **upward** or **downward social comparisons**. Upward social comparisons are when learners consciously or unconsciously compare themselves to those they perceive as being more competent than themselves. Depending on whether they believe they can attain that same level (see Chapter 4 on beliefs), such a comparison can be motivating and positively reinforcing for their sense of self. However, if the other person seems to represent an unattainable goal, then the effect can be negative for their self-concept and ultimately demotivating. Downward social comparisons are when learners compare themselves to those they perceive as being less competent than themselves. Learners can be driven to engage in downward social comparisons in order to make themselves feel better and enhance their sense of self by feeling more competent than others. In both cases, we need to exercise caution as we want all our learners to continually strive to improve and yet maintain a realistic but positive sense of self. This suggests the importance of encouraging learners to focus on their own sense of progress, rather than on outward social comparisons.

An interesting related effect of social comparison processes that has particular implications for education is what is referred to as the '**big-fish-little-pond' effect** (Marsh & Craven, 2002). Learners in streamed or ability-grouped classes, or even in selective schools, may develop a lower or higher self-concept respectively than those in more heterogeneous groups, given that the peers to compare themselves with are naturally a selected population. In other words, a child in a high-ability group may develop a lower self-concept than another with similar abilities in a mixed-ability group due to the high level of all the child's peers. Similarly, a child in a low-ability group may develop a relatively high self-concept surrounded by peers of similar ability. However, to complicate matters, there is also an effect known as 'basking in reflected glory', by which individuals may enhance their own sense of self by associating with the success of other individuals, educational groups, or institutions (Cialdini et al., 1976). Although the area is clearly complex, it has important implications worth considering for selective or streamed language classes.

Activity 3.6	**Comparing your sense of self to others**

Imagine that in your free time you were a keen tennis player. Do you think you would prefer to play tennis mostly against weaker opponents so you could show how good you were? Or would you prefer the challenge of facing stronger opponents, even though regular defeat would be the most likely outcome? In which environment do you think you would improve as a tennis player? How about in other areas of your life? Do you think you tend to prefer being a 'big fish' or a 'little fish', and how consistent is this tendency across areas of your life? How would you feel as a language learner? Would you prefer to be in a class with people mainly of a higher or lower proficiency than you?

Finally, to understand how learners view themselves in relation to language learning, we also need to appreciate what other beliefs those individuals may hold about the nature and processes of language learning. These can impact strongly on how they interpret their sense of self and whether they feel they have the potential to change and improve. For example, the area of mindsets is closely related to self. (See Chapter 4 for a discussion of beliefs and mindsets.) Clearly, if learners have a negative sense of self as language learners but feel that their abilities can fundamentally be changed, then they are more likely to be open to interpreting new experiences of success positively and seeking chances to improve. However, those who hold a negative sense of self as language learners and do not believe that their abilities are something that can be changed are likely to show a helpless response and be difficult to help improve.

Self-driven behavioural styles

Forming our sense of self is an ongoing, lifelong process. Essentially, we never have a completed sense of self but, throughout our lifetime, remain a 'work in progress' (van Lier, 2004). An interesting dimension to understand in self-formation—introduced above in the section on social comparisons—is the idea that how we evaluate ourselves can be driven by different forms of self-related motives (Mruk, 2006). Firstly, we can act in order to get an accurate sense of self, referred to as self-evaluation. We can also seek simply to maintain a view we hold of ourselves—self-protection. This may reinforce either a negative or positive set of self-beliefs—in other words, we simply wish to confirm that we are as we thought we were. Alternatively, we can be driven to act in ways that improve our sense of self and make us feel better about ourselves—self-enhancement. Appreciating the drives underlying learner behaviours can help us to view more critically behaviours that at first sight may not be easy to comprehend.

Consider, for example, the learner who, despite having poor grades, refuses to do homework and consistently forgets worksheets, etc. This learner may have a host of reasons for this behaviour, but one may be a form of self-protection. If learners believe that they are not good at languages and this is not something they can change, they may deliberately set up hindrances to their success, as it would be easier and more comfortable to blame these for their anticipated failings than to blame themselves. Such actions are called **self-handicapping behaviours** (Rhodewalt & Vohs, 2005). These refer to obstacles that people may deliberately put in their own way so that they can blame any perceived and usually expected failure on those obstacles, rather than risk any further threat to their sense of self.

Promoting a healthy sense of self in learners

To conclude this chapter, we would like to consider what we can do as teachers to promote a healthy sense of self amongst all our learners in respect to language learning. At this point in the chapter, we are deliberately using the term 'healthy' as opposed to 'high' or 'low', or 'positive' or 'negative', in order to stress the importance of a learner's sense of self being realistic—and therefore healthy for optimum learning (Branch & Wilson, 2009). Obviously, the first caveat that needs to be raised is that, as this chapter has shown, the self is so complex that it would be naive to think that we can easily influence or change how learners view themselves. Yet there are things we can do that are known to promote, or at least facilitate, the development of a healthy sense of self in learners.

Firstly, it is important to revisit our understandings of different facets of the self. Research suggests that some facets are more open to change, and to different degrees of change, than others. Generally, the more global sense of self, that which is developed over the course of a lifespan, is the most resistant to change. In contrast, the more specific, less holistic components of the self can change more readily and these, in turn, can potentially affect the more global aspects of the self over time. Another useful distinction is between core beliefs about the self and more peripheral beliefs (Markus & Wurf, 1987). Self-beliefs which are central to how learners view themselves—possibly across different domains—are typically less open to change, whereas beliefs that are less fundamental to the self-belief system and may be specific to one context are potentially more dynamic. Therefore, in order to effectively help learners to develop a healthy sense of self in respect to language learning, we are advised not to seek to change a learner's global sense of self-worth. Instead, it is likely to be more effective to work on specific facets of the self and seek to enhance these smaller segments, which ultimately can lead to bigger changes in the overall self. This means helping learners to develop positive self-efficacy by empowering them with a sense of control, for example, through strategy training (see Chapter 7) and also through fostering positive mindsets and attributions for success and failure (see Chapter 4). In doing so, we may promote a positive sense of expectation and agency in relation to specific tasks and aspects of language learning.

Another important way of engendering a positive sense of expectation in respect to a set of skills or tasks is through experiences of success. However, these need to represent genuine, believable experiences of success in order to be positive for the learners' sense of self. Scaffolding activities (see Chapter 1)—by providing differing degrees of support, offering multiple grades of difficulty for tasks and activities, and allowing for different paces of working—can be vital in enabling all of our learners to experience success. A recent development linked to the autonomy movement has been the use of 'can do' statements, which are particularly helpful in making salient a sense of progress and helping learners to focus on what they can do, rather than on what they cannot do.

A further element of our teaching that we can attend to is creating a positive class atmosphere to reduce anxiety; we can pay attention to how we deal with mistakes, the kinds of praise and feedback we offer, and the way we generally interact with learners and show them respect and support. Such a climate is crucial if we are to enable learners to experience success, take risks and push themselves to greater achievements and higher levels, feel valued and respected for who they are, and ultimately, gain confidence.

Summary

Although the focus in this discussion has so far been on learners, it is important to remember that our own sense of self as teachers is equally powerful in influencing how we choose to teach and present ourselves in the language classroom; how we manage our daily encounters in the school setting with both colleagues and learners; and how we cope with challenges to our familiar routines and modes of teaching. To be effective and progressive teachers, we need to feel competent but also willing and able to take new steps in our approaches to language teaching and for this, we need a healthy but realistic sense of self as language teachers. The various ways in which we deal with our own mistakes and challenges can serve as a positive role model for our learners. We can show them how to be open to new ways of learning; how mistakes are opportunities for learning; and how we should challenge ourselves to pursue higher goals. Similarly, in our interactions with our learners we can demonstrate our openness to, respect for, and acceptance of learner diversity. Essentially, in this chapter, we hope to have shown how complex our sense of self is, as well as how central it is to all that we think, feel, and do. Its role in our motivation is examined in more detail in the next chapter.

Questions for reflection	1 What differences—and consistencies—have you observed in yourself across academic domains? How about in respect to any foreign languages you have learned? Do you feel differently about yourself when, say, speaking and when writing in the language? Do you feel more confident in respect to certain writing tasks than you do to others?
	2 Imagine a learner in your class who seems to be working very hard but not really making much progress and is consequently starting to doubt his abilities. What kind of feedback would you give this learner? What kind of factors would influence your choice of words and actions?
	3 Think about your own life. Have you ever acted in a self-handicapping way? What kinds of things did you do and why? Have you ever witnessed any learner behaviours that you feel could perhaps be interpreted as a form of self-handicapping? What steps could you take to intervene and help such learners?

Suggestions for further reading

Mercer, S. (2011). *Towards an understanding of language learner self-concept.*
Dordrecht: Springer.
This book presents qualitative research conducted with tertiary-level EFL learners.
It describes general understandings of self-concept amongst foreign language
learners at all levels, covering many of the points made in this chapter, and is useful
for gaining a greater understanding of learners' self-concepts and their formation.

Mercer, S., & **Williams, M.** (Eds.). (2014). *Multiple perspectives on the self in SLA.*
Bristol: Multilingual Matters.
This collection of papers presents a variety of ways of looking at the self in SLA.
Each chapter outlines the particular perspective taken and also considers the
implications for practice, although the book is primarily aimed at academics with
an interest in the self.

Taylor, F. (2013). *Self and identity in adolescent foreign language learning.* Bristol:
Multilingual Matters.
This is a highly interesting book looking at how learners balance their private
and public selves in the context of learning a foreign language. It links together
various aspects of psychology and relates these to issues of the self. It is especially
useful for teachers working with teenagers who want to develop an empathetic
understanding of their learners' sense of self.

4

BELIEFS

Introduction

This chapter examines the nature of beliefs, illustrating ways in which our beliefs influence our actions, and, more specifically, our approach to learning and teaching. We will see that some beliefs are helpful to learning, while others can be unhelpful; thus, teachers can play an important role in fostering beliefs that facilitate learning. Our beliefs can change; they evolve over time and are influenced by context and culture, including the culture of the classroom. We begin the chapter by thinking a little more carefully about what we mean when we use the term 'beliefs' in connection to learning. We then move on to focus on three different types of beliefs that are important in classroom settings and that teachers need to understand and work on in order to facilitate learning:

1 the beliefs individuals hold regarding the nature of knowledge and learning

2 various powerful beliefs that people hold but may not be aware of or able to articulate

3 the beliefs learners develop in order to explain their own personal successes and failures.

In the final part of the chapter, we turn our attention to specific manifestations of beliefs in language classrooms, and here we look at not only learner beliefs but also those of teachers. We hope to encourage teachers firstly to develop a greater awareness of their own beliefs about language learning and language learners, and ultimately to understand their own role in influencing the beliefs of the learners with whom they regularly interact.

What are beliefs?

All of us have beliefs about who we are, the world we live in, and how we should act within that world. Some of these beliefs are deeply held and central to how we regard ourselves, while others may be altogether more peripheral. Similarly, those of us involved in language learning have beliefs about the nature of and processes involved in teaching and learning a foreign language, as well as about our own capabilities. These beliefs affect how we approach learning or teaching, and it is the

nature of these beliefs—and the ways in which they can influence our actions—
that we explore in this chapter. Before going further, let us look at some beliefs that
teachers hold and consider how these might influence their actions.

Activity 4.1	**Exploring teachers' beliefs**

Here are statements collected from teachers in schools in Thailand (Maiklad, 2001). What
do you infer about the beliefs of each teacher from the statements? In each case, how
would you expect that teacher to act in the classroom?

Statement	Belief
'Learning … is … receiving knowledge and understanding it.'	
'If you ask me which one students should master first, it must be correct grammar. Then they will have confidence. With this confidence, their fluency will occur soon after.'	
'They can learn well if they have a chance to touch or to see.'	
'I think the best and most efficient [method] is to teach them to speak … to teach them to listen and to speak … I think that I should let them try out the language.'	
'Children are like white clothes. Nothing is painted on them. Language is a new thing in their life. So in the beginning, they just try and test things. They may speak correctly or incorrectly.'	
'[W]hen students speak, I stop them immediately after they make mistakes. And I correct them by saying the right thing and tell them that the right one should be like this.'	
'In the classroom I expect [the children] just to understand the knowledge I transmit to them and to use it.'	

Photocopiable © Oxford University Press

We can see from this activity how teachers' beliefs can have a profound influence on
their classroom actions. If, for example, teachers believe that knowledge is transmitted
from teacher to students, they are likely to teach by presenting and practising language
forms. If, on the other hand, they believe that learning involves actively constructing
knowledge, they are likely to put learners in situations that involve using the language.

A common-sense definition of a belief is that it represents an acceptance or conviction that something is true. Nevertheless, if we unpack this definition a little, we can see that it is somewhat unsatisfactory since it suggests that beliefs are binary: we either believe something or we do not. Of course, this is not the case, as we believe some things more strongly than others. It is more accurate to think of beliefs as existing on a continuum from 'slight hunch' to 'firm conviction'.

Believing or knowing?

Since researchers began taking a serious interest in the role of beliefs in language education in the mid-1990s, numerous terms have been used to discuss and examine beliefs in SLA. The literature contains terms such as **(meta)cognitions**, personal theories, philosophies, and perceptions (Kalaja & Barcelos, 2003). In their influential book investigating beliefs within the field of language learning, Paula Kalaja and Ana Maria Barcelos describe beliefs as being the opinions and ideas that teachers and learners have about the process of learning a foreign language.

If we think a little about this description of beliefs—about the opinions and ideas that teachers and learners hold—then one key distinction that needs to be made is that between belief and knowledge; we may know that the Earth orbits the sun, but some people may also believe that some form of intelligent life exists elsewhere in the universe. This is a relatively clear-cut example. However, there are cases when the borders between belief and knowledge are not so clearly demarcated. There may be certain beliefs that we hold so strongly that we cease to recognize them as being beliefs, regarding them as incontrovertible facts. When individuals fail to identify their beliefs as such, they are less likely to reconsider them or to be receptive to challenges to those beliefs (Woods, 2003).

In respect to language learning, individuals are likely to be more certain about some beliefs than others. For example, consider an adult learner who believes strongly that adults are unable to improve their pronunciation skills no matter how hard they try. How might this belief affect his attitude to improving pronunciation? How willing might he be to engage in conscious strategic efforts to improve his pronunciation and how open to techniques suggested by the teacher? In contrast, another learner may hold a similar belief about the inability of adults to improve their pronunciation in a foreign language but without the same degree of certainty. Such a learner may be more open to suggestions from the teacher about working on her pronunciation skills and more willing to try alternative approaches. Those beliefs that are deeply entrenched and that we feel most certain about are less susceptible to change than beliefs which we hold with less conviction. More often than not, these strongly held beliefs are those which are central to our self-concept or to which we feel some form of emotional attachment. (See Chapters 3 and 5.) It is clear that when individuals hold very firm beliefs about language learning, it can be hard for teachers to encourage those students to reconsider them.

In addition to the strength of a belief, we should also address the issue of how helpful, or otherwise, different beliefs can be; some beliefs are conducive to successful learning—**facilitative beliefs**—while others hinder learning—**debilitative beliefs**. However, deciding what constitutes a facilitative or a debilitative belief can be problematic. It is difficult to make generalizations as there is considerable variation across individuals, and even within an individual: what is facilitative for one person may not be for another and what is facilitative for somebody in one context or at a certain time may not be in another. Nevertheless, for us as teachers, it can be helpful to consider what beliefs our learners hold and how these beliefs may be affecting their learning in positive or negative ways. Activity 4.2 illustrates this point.

Activity 4.2   **Analyzing facilitative and debilitative beliefs**

Consider the following statements made by learners of English in Malaysia (Choy, 2003). What underlying beliefs do they reflect and do you believe that these are likely to be facilitative (F) or debilitative (D) beliefs for the learners you typically work with?

Statement	Belief	F/D
'When I learn English I usually wait for my teachers, who are expert and authority in English, to teach me and help me learn the language.'		
'I depend on my teachers to give me model essays to memorize so that I can use these to help me write my own essays.'		
'I have difficulty understanding English in school. I do not understand my lessons and I do not like the language because it is very difficult to become good in it.'		
'I like to learn English because it is an international language and I can use it to communicate with people from other countries.'		
'I am afraid of using the wrong words when speaking English … I am afraid of making mistakes. I often repeat to myself or write down on a piece of paper what I want to say to avoid mistakes.'		
'I look up to people who speak English well and I think others will look up to me if I spoke the language well also. Therefore I want to learn the language well.'		
'I am willing to practise until I am better in the language. I usually try to watch more English videos to help me understand and speak better.'		

Photocopiable © Oxford University Press

As a teacher, how would you respond to learners in your class holding beliefs that appear to be hindering their learning?

As teachers, we are constantly evaluating the actions of learners and, by extension, the beliefs that underpin those actions. This is an integral part of the teaching process. Nevertheless, these evaluations are, to a great extent, shaped by our own beliefs about language learning. This suggests that we need not only to pay attention to the beliefs of learners in our classrooms but also to develop a greater awareness of our own beliefs and how they are affecting the decisions we make. Of course, it makes sense to intervene and help in cases where we feel that a specific belief is having a debilitating effect on an individual's learning. However, we need to take care that we do not simply impose our own beliefs on all our learners; there may be specific beliefs that work for certain learners in certain situations but not for others.

Beliefs in context

In the past, beliefs were often characterized as residing in the mind of the individual. Within this framework, beliefs were regarded as static, discrete cognitive entities. However, since the mid-1990s (see Benson & Lor, 1999; Kalaja, 1995; Kalaja, Menezes, & Barcelos, 2008), there has been a shift towards more contextualized understandings of beliefs. This means that different aspects of the context or situation are acknowledged as playing a role in how individuals form their beliefs.

Contextual factors affect our beliefs in different ways. It can be useful to think of these contextual influences as occurring at a number of levels. As we discussed in Chapter 2, it is possible to distinguish between different levels of context. In the current discussion, we will focus on three basic levels: macro, micro, and interactional. At the macro-level, we would include national or educational cultures that affect individuals' beliefs. At the micro-level are aspects of the immediate situation, such as the lesson, teacher, and peers. At the interactional level, there are particular experiences or interactions with specific individuals. Of course, in real life, things are likely to be considerably more complex, with overlap between levels of beliefs. Nevertheless, this basic three-level distinction may serve as a useful guide for teachers trying to understand the various factors influencing the formation and development of beliefs inside their classrooms.

Beliefs and cultural background

As members of any society, we all learn tacitly through our continual, lifelong interactions which particular beliefs are valued within that society—a process known as **socialization**. Since we are exposed to such beliefs from an early age and they are being constantly reinforced throughout the lifespan, they tend to be the most stable and resistant to change. Of course, some people move between different societies and cultural settings and in such cases beliefs may be challenged and evolve in response to these challenges. The implication for language teaching is a need to recognize and accommodate the various beliefs about language learning that may be 'typical' for a given culture. In particular, in cases where teachers and learners do not share the same cultural background, some degree of mutual understanding and respect is required, and attempts by teachers to 'impose' their culturally based beliefs on learners holding other beliefs are likely to encounter resistance. This conflict between different cultural beliefs about education can also manifest itself when teachers in one socio-educational context attempt to use educational materials developed in, and perhaps for, another.

Situational and interactional factors

As we discussed in Chapter 2, it is important not to oversimplify the impact of cultural factors. Individuals within a particular culture do not all hold identical beliefs. We are also influenced by factors in our family settings and in our various social relationships, as well as by specific situations or interactions. A situational view of beliefs implies that schools and classrooms play a significant role in influencing the beliefs of the individuals within them, and that a key role for teachers is to work towards creating a classroom culture that generates a facilitative set of beliefs about language learning among learners. Let us consider a teacher dealing with a group of young learners taking their first steps in foreign language learning. As with any group, some individuals are likely to be more successful than others. How does the teacher choose to respond to that success? Some teachers may highlight the successful outcome and the speed with which those successful learners 'picked up' the language, implying that these learners have some form of natural aptitude or talent. In such an environment, learners may come to believe in a strong link between innate talent and successful outcomes. On the other hand, in cases where the teacher chooses to focus on the process rather than the outcome, or on efforts as opposed to notions of talent, learners are more likely to develop a belief that their own efforts can lead to success.

The individual choices teachers make are subjective judgements based on their own beliefs and understandings of language and learning. As such, teacher beliefs are a major contributory factor to the culture of any classroom and, by extension, to the beliefs of learners within it. This presents teachers with three crucial challenges: firstly, to be aware of their own beliefs; secondly, to understand how these beliefs impact upon their teaching and students' learning; and thirdly, to consider ways to promote the beliefs they consider most helpful to learners.

At another level, learners' belief systems are also affected by their own unique experiences and their interactions with other people around them. Let us imagine a learner with a family member, say a sister, who has married someone from a different linguistic background and has successfully made efforts to learn that language. Conversations and interaction with this sister may prove to be a significant influence on this particular learner's beliefs about language learning. In this case, these beliefs would be unique to this individual, not shared by the whole class.

Emotional factors

A further important aspect of beliefs is their emotional nature (Frijda & Mesquita, 2000). Individuals can feel strong emotional attachments to their beliefs and this has powerful practical implications. (The connections between beliefs, emotions, and behaviour is a topic we return to in Chapter 5.) The essential underlying theme of this chapter is that learners' beliefs about the nature of language learning influence their approaches to learning; therefore, teachers need to be both aware of these beliefs and equipped to help learners re-evaluate any beliefs that may be impeding learning. In order to achieve this, teachers need to understand the emotional significance of some beliefs.

From a practical point of view, teachers ought to be aware that learners can be more emotionally attached to some beliefs than to others; this connects back to the distinction between core and peripheral beliefs that we made at the beginning of the chapter. A strong emotional attachment to a particular belief can be problematic when the teacher judges that belief to be harmful to learning. For example, let us think of an adult learner who has always done things in a certain way and strongly believes that this is the best—even the only—way. However, you, as the teacher, disagree; you have been watching patiently as this learner makes no progress at all, offering gentle suggestions, all of which seem to be ignored. What can you do in such a situation? You cannot simply ignore the belief and its damaging effects. It may well be the case that the more the learner persists with this belief—and the less successful the learning efforts—the greater the emotional investment. This may be highly irrational and, in such cases, a purely rational approach from the teacher encouraging the learner to reappraise these beliefs may, in fact, be counterproductive if not handled skilfully. Simply pointing out the flaws in the current approach and suggesting an alternative may cause the learner to resist and become even more invested in the belief. In order to help learners reappraise their beliefs, teachers need not only to be aware of the specific beliefs that learners hold but also to understand something of the emotional significance those beliefs have for learners, and to develop non-threatening strategies that encourage learners to re-examine them.

Beliefs across time

In the previous section, we discussed how beliefs are liable to change across different contexts. Beliefs may also evolve over time. At one level, changes in beliefs reflect various changes in cognitions that occur across the lifespan; these tend to be predictable and are common to most people. At the same time, changes in beliefs are also shaped by our own particular experiences and social interactions that occur over time; these changes are unique and individual. Beliefs are not static, but neither do we suddenly come to believe or disbelieve something. There is likely to be a questioning process, with doubts gradually creeping in as to the veracity of certain beliefs, or a gradual strengthening of other beliefs occurring as a result of confirmatory experiences or interactions with others. In fact, it is possible to argue that all our beliefs are, to some extent, in a state of flux and that the major difference is one of degree, with beliefs at the 'strongly held' end of the continuum being more stable.

The recognition that beliefs are situated and dynamic represents positive news for teachers, as it suggests that learner beliefs can change and are influenced by the learning environment. As teachers, we have a role to play in the development of positive learner beliefs. We are in a position to monitor and assess the various beliefs that our learners hold in our teaching situations and use these assessments to encourage both the questioning of what we regard as unhelpful beliefs and the strengthening of facilitative beliefs.

Types of beliefs

We can hold beliefs about any aspect of learning and teaching processes, the language itself, how it is best learned, and ourselves in relation to these processes. However, certain beliefs appear to be more influential than others in enhancing or hindering learning. We have chosen here to focus on three central sets of beliefs: **epistemological beliefs**, **mindsets**, and **attributions**.

Epistemological beliefs

We all have beliefs about the nature of knowledge and learning: what knowledge is and how it is acquired. These are known as epistemological beliefs. To a certain extent, these beliefs are a reflection of the particular time and place in which we live. In different periods of history and in different cultural settings, various theories of knowledge have tended to dominate. The issues of what constitutes knowledge and how knowledge is transmitted are complex. For the purposes of our current discussion, it is helpful to provide an outline of some of the main principles regarding epistemology.

The fundamental epistemological question underpinning language education concerns what it means to learn or to know a language. One key distinction that has been made is between learning how and learning about. When we learn or know <u>how</u> to do something, this means that we develop an ability to perform a certain skill. For example, we learn how to drive a car without necessarily knowing the detailed workings of a four-stroke engine. On the other hand, when we learn or know <u>about</u>, we develop an understanding of how something operates or how a skill is performed, without necessarily being able to perform it. So, staying with the driving illustration, it is possible for somebody to understand when and how to change gears on a manual car but not actually to be able to perform the task in real time. In the case of language learning and teaching, if we believe that knowing a language means understanding its formal properties, then we may favour an approach to teaching that stresses knowledge of formal aspects of the language, such as its syntax. However, if we believe that actually being able to use this language is central to knowing it, then we are more likely to be inclined towards approaches to teaching and learning that stress the communicative nature of language. Indeed, this distinction has informed a major shift in formal language education, from a focus on form and structure to more of an emphasis on language as a communicative skill.

Following on from the fundamental question of what constitutes knowledge of a language is the other half of the epistemology equation: how is this knowledge transmitted? This question concerns beliefs about how best to teach and learn a language. One such belief relates to whether language is transmitted from teacher to learner. Individuals who believe in a unidirectional transmission of knowledge are more likely to believe in the authority of the language teacher and the legitimacy of that teacher as a model for learning or source of the target language. Meanwhile, someone who regards language proficiency as something that emerges through interaction will probably have very different expectations of both teachers and learners.

People tend not to have a single overarching set of beliefs that spans all domains of learning; our beliefs may differ greatly across domains. For example, a student may approach the study of literature in a very critical fashion, ready and eager to challenge the teacher's pronouncements. Yet the same individual may approach language learning in a very uncritical manner, accepting the teacher's expertise and authority. The finding that beliefs can differ across domains and that even within a single domain, such as language learning, beliefs may vary across sub-domains, such as writing and speaking, is an important one. Another feature of epistemological beliefs we need to take into account is that their effects are not always direct or obvious. For example, a greater trust in authority figures can lead language learners to display a greater reliance on L1 when learning a foreign language (Mori, 1999). As epistemological beliefs essentially deal with the nature of knowledge and how we learn, they are central to how we see ourselves and the world around us. Like all beliefs, they can be facilitative and debilitative, but as they are so central, it is unlikely that they can be immediately modified. However, there is a distinct possibility that learners' epistemological beliefs might be modifiable in the longer term.

Implicit beliefs and mindsets

A further key issue concerning beliefs and learning is individuals' awareness of their own beliefs. Sometimes we are conscious of our beliefs and able to articulate them; these are known as **explicit beliefs**. For example, an individual may have a strong belief in the dangers of global warming and the need to take action to prevent it. Such an individual is likely to have some awareness that this is not universally accepted and that others may not share the belief. However, it is often the case that people are unaware of some of their most deeply held beliefs; these are known as **implicit beliefs**. For example, consider an individual who strongly believes that luck plays a significant role in the outcome of human endeavours and that there are lucky days and unlucky days. This belief may be a key factor in behavioural decisions; this person may be more willing to take risks on a lucky day. Yet the individual may not be aware that this is a belief at all, instead assuming it to be knowledge shared by everyone. As such, this belief is likely to remain impervious to counter-arguments.

We all hold implicit beliefs in various areas of life, including language learning, and these beliefs can have far-reaching effects on how we approach learning tasks. Within educational psychology, the work of Carol Dweck (1999, 2006), along with various colleagues, has played a leading role in exploring the relationships between implicit beliefs and learning. Dweck identifies two core sets of beliefs about learning: an **entity theory** and an **incremental theory**. Individuals holding an entity theory tend to believe that human qualities, including intelligence and the capacity to learn, are fixed within the individual. They believe that we are endowed with the talents that we are born with and there is little we can do to change this. In contrast, incremental theorists believe that human nature is malleable, and, in the case of intelligence and learning, this means that people are capable of developing their intelligence and talents through focused practice and effort. A more accessible terminology for these implicit beliefs is mindsets: we refer to an entity theory as a **fixed mindset** and an incremental theory as a **growth mindset**. It is generally believed that a growth mindset is more likely to facilitate learning since it helps individuals to see that with effort they can improve and become more competent.

There are several factors that contribute to the formation of mindsets of language learners (see Mercer & Ryan, 2010). One of these is the notion that the capacity to successfully learn a language is dependent on an innate talent. A person with a strongly fixed language learning mindset may believe in a 'gift for languages'—that some people are simply naturally good at learning languages, and that those who do not possess this gift are unlikely ever to succeed. However, language learning mindsets are not solely dependent on beliefs relating to a natural talent for languages. We also hold beliefs about other factors we feel play a role in successful language learning. For instance, a person may believe that personality plays a significant role. If this is accompanied by the belief that our personalities are essentially fixed, then that individual is likely to tend towards a fixed language learning mindset. Language learning mindsets result from learners' beliefs about what qualities are desirable in successful language learning combined with a further set of beliefs concerning the malleability of these qualities (see Ryan & Mercer, 2012).

Growth mindset

Mindsets are both complex and powerful, and their significance in language learning is only just being recognized. Mindsets link to a range of other issues, such as goal-setting and motivation, providing an underlying framework for approaches to learning. For example, someone holding a fixed mindset is likely to set goals that avoid risks and possible failure, as such failure would expose the limits of any innate talent. Meanwhile, someone with a growth mindset is more likely to set challenging goals, as this presents an opportunity for learning.

Clearly, mindsets can both help and hinder learning, and perhaps the most exciting finding from research into mindsets is that, despite their deeply held nature, they can change, and teachers have a role to play in encouraging growth mindsets. A fixed mindset may impede learning, but a growth mindset can function as a powerful resource, influencing learner motivation, the setting of goals, and how learners respond to the setbacks and 'failures' that are an essential part of language learning. In the educational psychology literature, there is evidence that pedagogic interventions can encourage growth mindsets in learners, which are, in turn, likely to lead to more successful learning outcomes. For example, Lisa Blackwell, Kali Trzesniewski, and Carol Dweck (2007) designed a series of activities to encourage a group of New York children to regard the brain as a muscle like any other that could become stronger the more it was exercised, and to believe that intellectual growth was something they could influence and control through their own efforts. The research showed that these children subsequently showed a marked improvement in both their grades and their motivation. Although the concept of mindsets has yet to be fully explored within the field of language learning, the research conducted in mainstream educational psychology suggests that nurturing growth mindsets may be a particularly productive strategy for teachers looking to foster more facilitative language learning beliefs.

Attributions

Closely linked to mindsets is the way in which we perceive our successes and failures. On winning a silver medal at the 2012 Olympics, rower Mark Hunter said, 'We gave everything, we tried everything. We wanted to win so badly … we just feel we let everyone down by not winning.' This quotation is interesting in that it provides some insight into how the mind of a dedicated athlete works and it also reveals how the concept of success and failure is relative. For most of us, participating in the Olympics would represent a huge achievement, yet this athlete feels he has let people down by coming second, and he sees this as a failure. Success and failure are highly subjective terms; one individual's success may be another's failure.

Individuals' perceptions of their own successes or failures and the reasons they provide for those successes and failures are known as **attributions**. Attribution theory is concerned with the question 'To what do individuals attribute their perceived successes and failures?' The word 'perceived' is important here; as the above example shows, we all perceive success and failure differently. This can be due to our different expectations of success (see Chapter 6 on expectancy–value theory); different opinions of our ability to succeed in a task (our self-efficacy, as discussed in Chapter 3); our interpretation of our previous experiences; and our sense of how important achieving the task is.

Attribution theory originated in the work of Fritz Heider in the 1940s. Heider claimed that it was how people perceived events, rather than the events themselves, that influenced behaviour (Heider, 1958). Later, Bernard Weiner (1980, 1986) developed this theory further. Weiner was particularly concerned with reasons people gave for their successes and failures in academic and other achievement situations. He originally suggested that people saw their successes or failures as being due to one of four possible causes: effort, ability, task difficulty, or luck. He further suggested that these could be seen on two dimensions, which he termed **attributional dimensions**. The first is the internal/external dimension, which Weiner referred to as **locus of causality**. Ability and effort are normally seen as internal—they are believed to come from within us—while task difficulty and luck are usually seen as being external to us. A second dimension is that of **stability**, that is, whether the factor is seen as fixed or changeable—in other words, can it change or is it something fixed? So effort would normally be seen as changeable, while ability can be seen as fixed or as changeable, depending on whether we believe ability to be something static (a fixed mindset) or something that can change (a growth mindset). Weiner, however, put it in the stable category. The relationship between these four attributions is shown in Table 4.1.

		Locus of causality	
		internal	external
Stability	stable	ability	task difficulty
	unstable	effort	luck

Table 4.1 Matrix of the four main attributions (adapted from Weiner, 1986)

A third dimension is that of controllability, that is, whether we feel the element is within our control or not. For example, most people would feel that the amount of effort they put in is within their control, but there are considerable differences in views about whether ability is controllable. In school situations, the difficulty of the task tends to be seen as being out of one's control; however, if we see ourselves as capable of breaking a task down into manageable subtasks, we might view it as within our control.

The important point is that individuals perceive success and failure differently, they give different reasons for their perceived successes and failures, and they view these reasons in different ways. Thus, it is how individuals see these aspects that leads to different behaviours among learners. This has considerable implications for teachers in the way they interact with their students. For example, if students firmly believe they are doing badly because they are no good at languages, and see this as a fixed factor that is not within their control, they are unlikely to make any effort to improve, believing this will make no difference. It is then important for the teacher to help these individuals to see that they can, in fact, get better at languages, and that they can take control of their progress by using appropriate strategies and putting in effort. Students who believe they are doing badly because the teacher has it in for them—an external locus—and feel that there is nothing they can do about the situation, seeing it as uncontrollable, are unlikely to make any effort to learn. However, students who believe that they are doing badly because their friends distract them—also an external locus—could see the situation as controllable, and sit in a different place or ignore the distractions.

It is important to note that attributions are situation-specific, so one's attributions in language learning might be very different from those in sport or music. Similarly, one's attributions for speaking in an L2 might be different from those for reading or writing in the L2. People also tend to develop different attributions for success and failure, often to protect their sense of **self-worth** (Covington, 1992). Many people attribute failure to external sources. For example, not getting a job might be attributed to unfairness or a preference for an internal candidate, rather than to not being good enough. Research has shown that men tend to externalize failure more than women. This tendency to attribute success to oneself and failure to external factors is known as a **self-serving bias**. It seems that women are likely to have lower expectations of themselves and tend to attribute their successes to external factors more than men do.

Although research into attributions has mainly focused on sport psychology, a few studies have been carried out in the domain of language learning. For example, Williams and Burden (1999) found evidence that as primary school children get older, they become more internal in judging how well they are doing in a language task. However, this trend appears to reverse in secondary school, with pupils judging their successes mainly by external factors such as marks or grades. A far broader range of attributions for perceived successes and failures in language learning is given by older children. These include peer influence ('Friends distract me', 'My friends help me'); task difficulty ('The work's too hard'); ability ('I'm no good'); and poor teaching, as well as mood, circumstances, and materials. Clearly, attribution theory is broader than Weiner's original four reasons, and there is evidence of developmental pathways in the types of attributions learners make as they mature (Williams & Burden, 1999).

Other attributions for success that have been reported include the use of the right strategies, the teacher, interest in the subject, and liking the tasks—for example, computers, videos, or games. Reasons for failures tend to include lack of interest, bad behaviour, and the teacher. In addition, girls appear to be more internal in their attributions for failure than boys (Williams, Burden, Poulet, & Maun, 2004).

Activity 4.3   Exploring reasons for failure

Below are some reasons learners gave for not doing well in a language activity in a secondary school setting in the UK (Williams et al., 2004). Give each statement a label such as 'ability', 'effort', 'interest', 'the teacher', or 'behaviour'. Then say whether each of the attributions is more internal (I) or external (E).

Statement	Label	I/E
'The teacher doesn't like me.'		
'I'm thick.'		
'I don't do my homework.'		
'I can't be bothered.'		
'I mess about.'		
'I'm lazy.'		
'The teacher doesn't control the class.'		
'I'm rubbish at German.'		
'I don't concentrate.'		
'Learning German is more boring than watching paint dry.'		

Photocopiable © Oxford University Press

As a teacher, how would you interact with your class if they gave these attributions? What strategies would you use for dealing with these kinds of attributions?

Working with beliefs in the classroom
Beliefs about how to teach and learn

It is important to point out that many individuals are not simply either teachers or learners; it is possible—and indeed relatively common—for a person to be both a teacher in one context and a learner in another. When we speak of teacher and learner beliefs, we are referring to the beliefs individuals hold in their roles as teachers or learners. In fact, recalling our earlier discussion about the highly situated nature of beliefs, it is conceivable that the same individual may subscribe to different, even apparently incompatible, sets of beliefs as a teacher and as a learner. As an illustration, Jo McDonough (2002) provides a fascinating account of the internal conflicts she experienced learning Greek while working as a teacher of English. For example, a teacher may encourage learners to tolerate variation and to discover answers for themselves in the classroom during the day, and then, in the evening, while attempting to learn another language, implore the teacher to give simple and unambiguous answers. Such an example highlights one of the most intriguing aspects of human belief systems: our beliefs are not always consistent and it is not uncommon for individuals to subscribe simultaneously to incompatible or even contradictory beliefs.

Several studies (for example, White, 1999; Loewen, 2007) have examined the potential mismatch between what learners and teachers believe about the processes of language learning and teaching. A broad conclusion of those studies is that differing expectations brought about by these beliefs can cause considerable problems for the effective management of the classroom and the rapport between the teacher and learners. One commonly cited example of a conflict of beliefs concerns the broader educational culture in which language learning is taking place. Teachers believing in more communicative versions of language education often experience difficulties when attempting to implement these beliefs in contexts where learners are either not familiar with or do not value such a communicative approach.

Activity 4.4   **Reflecting on success and failure in the classroom**

1   Ask your students to get together in groups. First, ask them to think individually of something specific in language learning that they did well recently and to write it down. It could be doing a role play, completing an activity successfully, or communicating with someone successfully, for example. Under this, ask them to write the reasons they did well. The group then collects the reasons together and tries to sort them into groups. Assemble these reasons on the board, grouping those that are similar together. Some examples might be working hard, feeling confident, liking the teacher, or finding the topic interesting. Ask which of these aspects they think are important for success. Ask the students to choose an aspect to work on developing and to write it as an aim in their journals, for example: 'In the next two weeks I shall try to work on/improve …'.

2   Ask your students to think of something they did not do well in respect to language learning. Again, ask them to write this down, along with reasons they did not do well, and then collect and group these reasons on the board. Then ask them which of these reasons they could do something about—in other words, control—and how they would do this. For example: 'I could spend half an hour more on my homework' or 'I could get to class on time'. If there are any that the students do not think they can do something about, then ask them to consider how they could control these aspects. Once again, ask the students to choose an area to work on and write it as an aim: 'In the next two weeks, I shall … .'

3   Record all the reasons your students gave for doing well and not doing well. What sort of differences can you see? What do these tell you about your class? For example, do they lack confidence? Do they tend to see themselves as no good? Do they lack interest?

4   After two weeks, put them in groups so that students each report on their progress. Ask groups to prepare a summary of their discussion and plan how to present it orally to the class. What have you learned? How can you work with the class to help them develop more positive attributions?

The various beliefs that teachers hold can be considered a part of what are known as **teacher cognitions** (Borg 1999, 2006). Teacher cognitions refer to the unobservable mental side of teaching—what teachers think, know, and believe—and research in this area has explored how all of these impact upon teaching practice. What is particularly interesting about this view of teaching is that it shifts the focus away from teachers' actions to the various beliefs, theories, and assumptions that inform those actions. Conventional educational research has tended to focus on the behaviour of teachers, with the implicit assumption that this behaviour in itself constitutes teaching and 'produces' learning. Furthermore, the assumption was that these behaviours and practices were interchangeable between individual teachers; when one teacher used a particular activity, it was essentially the same as when it was carried out by another teacher. Thinking about teacher cognitions and how they affect teaching suggests that it is really the personal beliefs underlying our practices that make us unique as teachers.

Beliefs about each other

Some of the most fascinating beliefs in any classroom are those that teachers and students have about each other. A teacher may come to believe that a particular learner is fundamentally lazy and that any efforts spent helping this individual are likely to be in vain. Learners also have beliefs about teachers. For instance, they may feel that a certain language teacher lacks mastery of the target language and this may make them less receptive to input from that particular teacher. Others might feel that a teacher does not actually like them and this might make them reluctant to make any effort. The beliefs we hold about each other can have a profound effect on how we interact in the classroom.

As teachers, it is important that we strive to generate in our classrooms a culture of beliefs that are as facilitating as possible for language learning. We can influence the beliefs that our learners come to hold by our actions and interactions in the classroom. Essentially, we serve as role models and send messages about the nature of language learning through our own behaviour and especially the ways in which we talk about language learning. One way in which teachers transmit their values about learning is through their use of feedback in the classroom. One type of feedback is praise and it is possible to identify two broad categories of praise: ability praise and effort praise. Ability praise highlights both the end product—a successfully accomplished task—and the abilities of the individual, whereas effort praise emphasizes the process of achieving success and the efforts made by the individual learner. There is a broad consensus in the literature (Dweck, 2007; Kamins & Dweck, 1999) that effort praise tends to be more conducive to successful learning because it helps learners to see progress as within their control.

The example of praise in the classroom illustrates how teachers may indirectly or unintentionally influence the beliefs of learners through their use of language or behaviours. However, there may be times when teachers wish to focus on learner beliefs in a more explicit fashion. A key first stage in achieving this is to engage in awareness-raising tasks involving explicit reflection on and discussion of beliefs.

This can be achieved through journal writing, group discussion, or the use of mind maps, for example. Through reflection, beliefs need to be brought to the surface, articulated, and recognized as beliefs before any processes of change can be contemplated. We can also keep an eye out for instances of dissonance in beliefs within the classroom— such as when elements of doubt or differences in opinion emerge—and exploit the potential in these opportunities for discussing beliefs explicitly in the group.

Summary

We all hold beliefs about teaching and learning, and these influence our actions as teachers or learners. Our beliefs are influenced by contexts and cultures, and also evolve over time. We hold some beliefs more strongly than others, and these strongly held beliefs can be difficult to change. Some beliefs facilitate learning, while others do not. The messages that teachers convey to their learners through praise, feedback, and methods used will influence the beliefs of those learners, and strong differences between the beliefs of teachers and learners can lead to conflict. We are aware of some of our beliefs, while unaware of others. We can have beliefs about whether our abilities as a language learner or teacher are fixed or changeable; these are known as fixed mindsets and growth mindsets. In addition, the reasons we attribute to our perceived successes and failures will have a profound influence on our learning and motivation.

Questions for reflection

1 What beliefs do you think your choice of materials, methodology, and activities are conveying to your learners?
2 What kind of feedback do you give your learners? What messages does your feedback convey to your learners? What sort of feedback do you think you should ideally give?
3 How can you help your learners see their attributions for success and failure as within their control?

Suggestions for further reading

Kalaja, P., & **Barcelos A. M. F.** (2003). *Beliefs about SLA: New research approaches.* Dordrecht: Kluwer.
An essential volume for anyone with a serious interest in beliefs and language learning. The collection of chapters here marks a clear break with past thinking on the role of beliefs in language learning, and ten years after its initial publication, it still sets the theoretical and research agenda in the field.

White, C. (2008). Beliefs and good language learners. In C. Griffiths (Ed.), *Lessons from good language learners* (pp. 121–130). Cambridge: Cambridge University Press.
An accessible yet comprehensive discussion of some of the concepts discussed in this chapter. It provides a concise historical overview of how thinking about the role of beliefs in language learning has developed, and this serves as a background to considering some of the implications for practice.

Dweck, C. S. (2006). *Mindset: The new psychology of success.* New York, NY: Random House.
Although not directly related to language learning, this book discusses some of the concepts covered in this chapter in a highly accessible and informative manner. Theoretical concepts are illustrated throughout by examples of well-known public figures or discussions of the author's personal experience in a way that makes for a both powerful and enjoyable read.

5

AFFECT

Introduction

In this chapter, we consider how feelings and emotions connect to language learning. In the past, discussions of language teaching tended to be dominated by concerns relating to cognitive knowledge of the target language, specific techniques involved in teaching the language, and the mental processes and capacities required to learn it. While these remain important issues, the field has begun to recognize how all aspects of learning are also coloured by the complex web of emotions and feelings involved in learning and using a foreign language. As LeDoux (1998) explains in his book *The Emotional Brain*, 'Minds have thoughts as well as emotions and the study of either without the other will never be fully satisfying' (p. 39). In this chapter, we will use the umbrella term **affect** to cover all the emotionally related aspects of language learning, whereas cognition will be the term used to refer to a range of mental processes such as memory, attention, or thinking. Although we have separated emotional aspects of language learning in this chapter, these are, of course, intimately connected with our cognitions, beliefs, sense of self, motivations, etc. In reality, it is impossible to truly separate the affective elements of our psychology from other facets of our minds and from interactions with contexts and other people. Therefore, throughout this chapter, we will seek to highlight the links with other themes described in this book and show how our feelings and emotions influence the whole of our psychology.

We will begin the chapter by considering what we understand by affect, emotions, feelings, and moods, as well as why these are so very important for successful learning. The next section will explore the work that has already been carried out on the role of emotions and affective states in language learning. We will then turn our focus to the specific affective factor that has perhaps received the most attention, namely **anxiety**. In this chapter, one of our primary aims is to illustrate that emotions also have a facilitatory role to play in language learning; while negative emotions can impede learning, positive emotions can promote and enhance learning. In order to discuss the constructive role of emotions, we will consider aspects of psychology that have been less frequently examined in respect to language learning, such as positive emotions, positive psychology, and the role of emotional intelligence in teaching.

| **Activity 5.1** | **Positive and negative language learning experiences** |

Think about some of your own positive and negative experiences of learning and using a foreign language. Can you remember how you felt at the time and how you feel about the experience now? Make a note of the first words that come to mind.

	Positive experiences of learning and using a foreign language	**Negative experiences of learning and using a foreign language**
Then		
Now		

Photocopiable © Oxford University Press

It is likely that many of the words that you wrote down in this activity reflect a range of emotional responses. You may have come up with words like 'frustrating', 'boring', or 'stressful' for your negative experiences, or you may have thought of words such as 'fun', 'exciting', or 'pleasurable' to describe your positive experiences. This shows us that language learning, and also language use, can be an emotionally charged experience. It also draws our attention to the fact that emotions are more than just a response to an event at a single moment in time; the emotional tone of an experience can stay with us for some time and can also change.

What is affect?

Affect is an abstract concept and an umbrella term that covers emotions, feelings, and moods. The distinction between these particular terms is rather fine-grained and has been the cause of much debate within the psychology literature. We have taken the view that emotions refer to conscious emotional responses to an event. Typically, we can recognize and often even label emotions such as 'happiness', 'anger', 'joy', or 'remorse'. Feelings are different from emotions as they tend to be more specific and refer to our private and subjective reactions to events; so, for example, feelings of disappointment in ourselves for not performing well in a class are likely to be different from our feelings of disappointment when learners similarly fail to live up to expectations in class. There are a limited number of recognized emotions, but the number of ways in which we can feel is infinite. An emotion can be the product of several different feelings. If we think of love as an emotion, then it may comprise feelings of companionship, trust, physical desire, and excitement. Moods are understood as being emotional states that last for longer periods of time and which are generally believed to be less intense than feelings or specific emotional responses to events. Sometimes we may not be able to identify what has caused our mood. For the purposes of this chapter and our emphasis on pedagogy, it is sufficient to note that affective states can vary in terms of their intensity, duration, identifiable cause, and whether they are more private or public in their expression.

Why are emotions so important?

One of the pioneers of modern psychology, William James, described a world without emotions as one where

> [n]o portion of the universe would then have more importance than another; and the whole character of its things and series of its events would be without significance, character, expression, or perspective.

(James, 1902, p. 150)

Very few of us would want to live in such a world. A world without any emotion would be cold and colourless. Think about emotions in relation to the experience of learning a language. Everybody who attempts to learn a language experiences feelings of embarrassment at making basic errors in front of other people; and yet the same language learners can also encounter tremendous feelings of elation at successfully performing even the simplest tasks in the target language. These emotional reactions are integral to the learning experience. At a most fundamental level, emotions mediate our learning, our use of language, and our behaviours and attitudes towards the language, the class, the materials, and even ourselves.

It can be difficult to predict how individual learners may respond emotionally to tasks, materials, and events in class; however, knowing something about our learners as individuals and their interests and motivations can make this a little easier. We know that emotional reactions occur when individuals are involved in situations or activities that they feel have relevance to themselves. For example, somebody with a keen interest in Formula One Grand Prix racing may experience an intense roller-coaster ride of emotions while watching a race, but another individual—one with no such interest—is likely to feel indifference watching the same event. The nature of the emotional reaction, the intensity of that emotion, and, indeed, whether there is any response at all, depends on the meaning a particular situation or event has for an individual (Gross, 2007).

Activity 5.2	**How learners react to classroom activities**

Look at this list of activities from a language classroom. Imagine you are a teacher announcing each activity to the class. What emotional reactions might you anticipate from different learners? Why might learners respond differently to these activities?

1 singing a song in the target language
2 a short vocabulary quiz about fashion-related language
3 watching a clip from a news programme in the target language
4 individual presentations on famous actors
5 a role play about a business meeting
6 reading poetry in the target language.

Most teachers would have produced quite an extensive list of possible reactions for each activity. In the case of the song, for example, some students may feel a sense of excitement or anticipation about an activity that seems fun or a little different, whereas other students—those with no interest in music—may feel a sense of anxiety, embarrassment, or even resentment. The news programme might be seen by some as challenging, real-world relevant, and interesting, while others might regard it as intimidating, daunting, or boring. A teaching activity does not itself produce an emotional reaction; the nature of any emotional response to our materials and activities is dependent upon the interactions between an individual, the task, the setting, and the meaning of the situation for the individual.

The nature of emotions

For teachers who want to get to know their learners better, it can be helpful to understand the nature of emotions. An emotional reaction is often described as having three essential components: a physiological element, expressive behaviour, and subjective feeling. Subjective feelings refer to how an individual interprets a particular event. For example, two language learners may do an activity together that they both find enjoyable and rewarding. Yet although they share the same emotional response, their personal experience of that emotion is unlikely to be the same. Expressive behaviour refers to how we externally express our emotions; an illustration of this could be a learner in a classroom blushing with embarrassment after making a mistake in front of others. In simple terms, we are talking about the body language that communicates our emotions. The physiological aspect of an emotional reaction refers to those physically measurable changes in the body, such as an increased heart rate, that occur when we are in a particular emotional state. As a teacher, it can be useful to become aware of and attentive to learners' facial expressions and body language in order to interpret their emotional responses to classroom life (Gregersen, 2003).

| **Activity 5.3** | **Positive and negative emotions in the classroom** |

Take a look at this list of emotions commonly encountered in language classrooms.

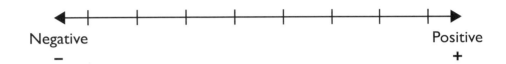

boredom   joy   excitement   frustration   anger   amusement   irritation   anxiety

Where would you rank them on the continuum below from 'positive' (facilitative) to 'negative' (inhibitive)?

Negative — ⟵———————————————⟶ Positive +

Are there any emotions that you found especially difficult to place on the continuum? Are there any that you thought could be both positive and negative?

Learners' emotional responses can be better understood through an examination of some of the workings of the brain and how it processes emotions. In recent years, greatly assisted by technological advances, we have come to know a lot more about the functioning of the brain through an academic discipline known as **neuroscience**. This refers to the scientific investigation of the brain and the nervous system. We would like to offer a very brief discussion here of some of the key insights from this field and show how they may support teachers' understandings and observations of their learners.

John Schumann has long been a pioneer of research into the neuroscience of second language learning (1997, 1999). Some especially interesting findings in this area relate to how the brain processes affect in language learning situations and how language learners' brains evaluate external stimuli leading to emotional responses. These evaluations are known as **appraisals** and it is possible to identify five broad dimensions in which our brains evaluate events. (See Table 5.1.) An understanding of these appraisals can offer teachers a systematic framework that may help them both anticipate and understand learners' emotional reactions.

Novelty	the extent to which something is familiar or unfamiliar
Pleasantness	the extent to which something is appealing or otherwise
Goal conduciveness	the extent to which something is in harmony with one's current purpose or objectives
Coping potential	the extent to which one feels able to cope in a particular situation
Self-compatibility	the extent to which something is in harmony with social and cultural norms, or with one's current or ideal self-concept

Table 5.1 Framework for understanding stimulus appraisals and emotional responses (adapted from Schumann, 1999)

If we look at the first appraisal dimension, novelty, it is not simply the case that novel equals good while familiar equals bad; the emotional response stems from the individual's appraisal of something, whether one sees it as positive or negative. So, for example, a teacher may come into the class armed with a new activity that none of the learners have encountered before. Some learners may feel stimulated or refreshed by the change, while others may feel threatened or overwhelmed by it. When we add the other appraisal dimensions, then the picture becomes even more complex and interesting. Let us go back to the teacher's exciting new activity and look at it in the light of the framework above. The vast majority of the students in the class may be attracted by its novelty and they may also regard it as fun and appealing. However, the timing of the activity may be problematic if some of the students have a very important test the next day. If they see this 'fun' activity as incompatible with their immediate goals, it may lead to feelings of frustration or even anger. This framework can thus be a useful tool for understanding the various—and often unpredictable—emotional reactions we may encounter in the classroom.

Understanding emotions is especially important for teachers because the brain prioritizes emotional reactions. By this, we mean that when we experience a strong emotional reaction, it can often override other cognitive processes as the brain allocates its resources to this reaction. Emotions can both facilitate and inhibit learning. It is possible, for example, for a highly motivated student to be in a class immediately after having had a fierce quarrel with a classmate. In such a case, despite normally displaying high levels of motivation, the student may be continually distracted by feelings of anger and resentment, and thus be unable to focus on the activity at hand. This example shows us that it is impossible to describe motivation in a truly meaningful manner without acknowledging an emotional component and the context in which it arises. In fact, the same applies to most of the constructs we discuss in this book. If we think about beliefs, a language learner may subscribe to a particular belief and usually act in a manner consistent with that belief. Yet there may be occasions when certain emotional reactions override that belief, resulting in very different behaviour. Imagine a language learner who holds a strong explicit belief in the value of taking risks and not being afraid of making errors, but who makes a mistake while speaking and encounters an unexpectedly strong negative reaction from someone she esteems. This experience, and its attendant emotional resonance, may make this individual reluctant to take further risks in respect to making mistakes.

Just as emotions are complex in their formation, they tend to be complex in their effects. Imagine a young man learning Spanish after falling in love with a girl from Spain when visiting the country. He makes great efforts to learn the language, hoping to impress her and gain her approval. Unfortunately, one day they quarrel and she decides to end the relationship. What happens to his motivation to learn? We might expect him to lose interest in the language, but it is also conceivable that his anger and resentment may, in fact, fuel a desire to learn the language, to somehow prove her wrong. Although understanding our learners' emotional states can help us to anticipate some of the behavioural consequences, we also need to take care not to apply an overly simplistic, cause-and-effect relationship between emotion and behaviour. Emotion and affect are a significant part of all learning processes, but there is an argument that they play an especially prominent role in language learning, a long-term endeavour consisting of numerous emotional highs and lows. In the next section, we focus our attention on how emotion and affect have been considered in connection to foreign language learning and teaching.

Activity 5.4

Exploring learners' feelings about using the language

1 Draw the following diagram on the board, with one big circle in the middle and six circles branching from it.

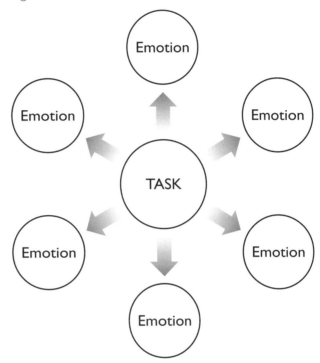

2 In the central circle, write down an activity the class did recently. Ask the students to reflect on what their feelings were when they did the activity, for example, 'anxious', 'bored', or 'excited'. In each of the adjoining circles, write one of the feelings the students reported.

3 Ask your students to copy the circle diagram four times. Ask them to think of four things they have done recently in the foreign language and write the name of the task or activity in the central circles. In the adjoining circles, they should write the feelings they had while doing the activity. Explain that they do not need to fill in all the outer circles but should try to think of at least two feelings they had while completing the task. Get them into groups and ask them to explain why they had those feelings. Ask for some feedback from the groups about the types of feelings people experienced during specific activities and why.

4 Collect in the circles, which students can give you anonymously if they like. What have you learned about your students? What have you learned about the activities you give them? What surprised you, if anything? Does this suggest you need to change anything about how you teach? How can you incorporate a consideration of students' feelings into your teaching?

Affect in language learning

As we mentioned at the beginning of this chapter, the field of second language education—just like most other areas of education—has been dominated by a concentration on the cognitive side to learning. One of the earliest and most influential acknowledgements of the central role of affect in language learning was Stephen Krashen's **affective filter** (Krashen, 1985). Krashen was interested in the distinctions between language learning in formal educational settings and natural acquisition of the language by being immersed in a setting which uses it. His basic position was that natural acquisition processes, especially those used by children learning their first language, were the ideal way to acquire a language. Thus, the aim was to replicate such processes in the classroom by maximizing the amount of comprehensible input— input of language that can be understood—available to learners. This was known as the **input hypothesis**: the more comprehensible input learners were exposed to, the more effectively they could acquire language. He generated a model to describe these processes and one component of his model of relevance to this chapter was called the affective filter. According to Krashen, when the language learning/use situation contains a lot of negative emotions or feelings, the affective filter is raised. This means learners are blocked mentally through the negative emotions, which reduces the amount of comprehensible input reaching the learner. Conversely, with a high degree of positive emotions, the affective filter would be lowered and so learners would be more open to receiving and engaging with comprehensible input. Although this is naturally a somewhat simplistic model of language learning, it is also valuable in recognizing that emotions matter. Essentially, the model provides us with a useful rule of thumb: negative affect tends to impede language learning, while positive affect can facilitate it.

Activity 5.5 **Exploring language learners' emotions**

Read the following statements made by secondary school pupils about their experiences of studying foreign languages in England (Atherton, 2005). Which do you think express the most negative emotional reactions and which the most positive? Why do you think each learner responded in this way? How would you, as their teacher, try to help these pupils overcome their negative emotional responses?

1 'I think it's interesting. It's fun … a little hard now and again.'
2 'It gives me a sense of self-esteem and sense of achievement. I really enjoy learning another language; it's different.'
3 'It's getting harder now, but it's enjoyable and satisfying when you feel that you have achieved something.'
4 'When I get it wrong I used to get embarrassed because everyone used to listen. So it feels like you get a bit gutted.'
5 'Sometimes it's quite fun to learn; it's different, and sometimes it's boring … . It kind of just drags on and on and I just don't get it.'
6 '[S]ometimes I think "Oh no, French is next", and I think "Oh, it's really difficult and I'm not going to be able to do it"'.'
7 'It's a completely new subject; you've never done anything like it, and it's really, really scary.'
8 'I was dreading it before I started but now I enjoy it.'

Anxiety

One specific affective factor which has received a lot of attention within SLA is anxiety. Anxiety is a negative emotion associated with worry and nervousness. Imagine a situation in which you have felt highly anxious. Would the people around you have known that you were anxious? How did you know that you were anxious? Often anxiety is accompanied by physical reactions such as a racing heartbeat, tension, sweating, and increased blood pressure. We may find ourselves pacing around, furrowing our brow, wringing our hands, and tensing our muscles and shoulders. While some people may tend towards being generally anxious individuals, there is a specific form of anxiety known as **foreign language anxiety**, which is related to using or learning a foreign language (Horwitz, Horwitz, & Cope, 1986). Even though a person might not otherwise be especially prone to anxiety, it is possible that in the context of learning or using a foreign language, that individual suddenly becomes highly anxious.

So why does learning a language induce so much anxiety in some people? Using a foreign language is closely connected with self-expression and if we feel limited in our ability to communicate personally meaningful messages, then we may feel that we are not projecting what we consider to be an accurate reflection of ourselves. This limited and restricted form of self-expression and the ensuing frustration can be extremely face-threatening and can undermine our sense of self, confidence, and feelings of security. Imagine someone using a foreign language in a business environment. Despite being a confident, respected, and authoritative figure in his first language (L1), this individual may struggle to articulate ideas adequately in the L2 and therefore feel frustrated, uncertain, and anxious. At a more basic level, even the most apparently trivial aspects of language learning can cause anxiety, such as a learner feeling embarrassed about using an unfamiliar word or sound in front of classmates. The fear of being laughed at and judged negatively by others can cause a high degree of anxiety, especially for teenagers, who are often especially sensitive to threats to their identity, self-esteem, and social standing. Williams and colleagues, for example, found that secondary school boys were embarrassed to speak in a French accent in class for fear of sounding feminine and being laughed at. As one participant explained, 'French is the language of love and stuff' (Williams, Burden, & Lanvers, 2002, p. 520).

Obviously, as teachers, we do not want our learners to be in the position of feeling such negative emotions and discomfort, and we are intuitively aware of the detrimental effect this can have on their motivation and willingness to use the language. However, anxiety is also problematic in terms of language acquisition and achievement, as it can cause learners difficulties in language comprehension, processing, and production. In other words, it can prevent learners from understanding what other people are saying; it can limit their ability to store and retrieve language from memory; and it can inhibit their capacity to communicate their own ideas in both speech and writing. Even in the most stress-free environments, communicating in a foreign language can put an enormous strain on our mental resources as we work hard to decipher utterances, process their meaning, and formulate our responses. The problem is that when learners feel anxious, they expend too much of their mental energy on worrying about their own performance or how they are being perceived by others, carefully evaluating their own output and monitoring the reactions of the people around them. The unfortunate consequence of this is that they are often left with insufficient mental capacity to carry out the communicative task at hand and their performance suffers accordingly. In such situations, even the most basic, formulaic utterances become potential minefields. Of course, a perceived poor performance can also produce even higher levels of anxiety, anxiety being both a cause and a result of poor performance and perceived failure. As a teacher, other learner behaviours that you may recognize as symptomatic of anxiety include suffering from mental blocks, freezing up during an activity, withdrawing from class participation, or offering limited, monosyllabic responses. In some cases, learners may also act the fool or deliberately disengage by using self-handicapping strategies (see Chapter 3) to protect their sense of self, hiding their anxiety behind disruptive behaviours.

A specific form of anxiety that has also been the focus of a large body of research is **test anxiety**, which is the form of anxiety closely associated with test-taking, such as before and/or during a test. There are few of us who relish taking a test or an exam, but for some learners, it is an exceptionally anxiety-inducing experience. This anxiety can lead them to perform badly on tests as they struggle to recall items of language, understand instructions, or produce text of any kind. It is perhaps unsurprising that those who anticipate a poor result and who may be weaker learners suffer most frequently from test anxiety. However, even learners who typically perform well on tests may put themselves under excessive pressure, especially if they tend towards **perfectionism**, and suffer from anxiety in test situations (Gregersen & Horwitz, 2002). Meanwhile, for other learners, tests may bring out the best in them, and in the test situation they may perform at their peak, bringing off one of their best performances just at the critical moment.

All this points to a vital distinction in discussions of anxiety, namely, the distinction between **debilitative** and **facilitative anxiety**. All of our discussion so far has focused on debilitative anxiety—in other words, the negative anxiety that hinders and debilitates language learning and performance. However, researchers have found that a certain degree of anxiety can actually facilitate or even improve performance, and this is referred to as facilitative anxiety. Consider a learner who, for part of his final grade for the school year, has to do an oral presentation in class about his favourite singer. He may be anxious—especially given the importance of the presentation for his overall grade—but he works hard, prepares well, and is interested and motivated to talk about the topic. Before the talk, he may 'psych' himself up using positive **self-talk** and envisaging a successful run-through of his performance. It is, of course, likely that this learner will be anxious, but it is possible that this anxiety may work together with the other factors to help him give his best performance. What this example also shows is that anxiety depends on a range of other contributing factors, such as self-confidence, personality, beliefs, expectations about tasks, and motivation, as well as the stakes involved in a particular activity.

While different levels of anxiety may be facilitative for some and debilitative for others, it is nevertheless important for us, as teachers, to seek to reduce anxiety for all learners in order to ensure that there is as little impediment as possible to successful language learning and use. Many of us know from experience how important it is to foster a positive group atmosphere and a sense of trust, security, and community in the classroom. (See also Chapter 2.) Learners need to feel at ease, comfortable, safe, and unthreatened, and to be in a group setting in which peers support rather than judge and evaluate each another. One factor that can contribute greatly to the group atmosphere is how we deal with mistakes and the kind of feedback we offer to learners, as well as the manner and tone in which we give that feedback. We can work consciously at modelling a positive attitude of growth and learning in which mistakes are seen as a healthy, normal part of the process of language learning. We can also encourage learners to take risks and push themselves and their language use to the next level. (See also Chapter 4.)

Another problematic behaviour that can cause anxiety is when learners focus on their flaws and the inherent risks of failure, rather than on their strengths and their potential for growth and achievement (Gregersen & MacIntyre, 2014a). Therefore, we need to help learners focus on the positives and consider their progress and achievements. Ideally, we want to help them to develop positive **mindsets** and beliefs about learning, and to make facilitative **attributions**. (See Chapter 4.) It may be useful to discuss anxiety explicitly with learners, getting them to consider the roots of their anxiety and what they can do to overcome it. We can explore strategies for learning and using the language to help them to feel empowered to cope with language learning and thereby alleviate feelings of anxiety. We can also work with explicit strategies for regulating emotions, such as breathing and relaxation techniques or discussing anxieties with others and seeking support from them. Regarding goals, learners need to feel that these are realistic and potentially attainable. This means we need to work at scaffolding tasks to ensure the right degree of challenge and at helping learners develop their sense of agency and their ability to manage a task. (See Chapter 7.)

In respect to tests, we can work with learners beforehand to help them to feel prepared for the test and ensure that they know what to expect. Where possible, we can prepare a test at the right level of difficulty, with instructions that are clear and easy to understand and with explicit assessment criteria. We can also teach our learners about test-taking strategies, for example:

- getting sufficient sleep beforehand
- learning to manage and plan their time in the run-up to and during the test
- concentrating on their own exam and not what others in the room are doing
- using breathing exercises
- employing calming self-talk
- using techniques such as taking sips of water, sucking sweets, or wriggling fingers and toes to energize themselves and keep calm.

Finally, should we, as teachers, be present during a test, we can offer our learners a genuine smile. We know that our emotions can be contagious and so sharing a supportive smile with a learner at a critical moment can inspire some positive emotions to hopefully help counterbalance any negative feelings the learner may be experiencing.

Activity 5.6 **Anxiety in language learning**

In 2007, Han-Min Tsai interviewed college students in Taiwan to see if they felt anxious when writing in English and, if so, what caused this anxiety. His interviewees gave some powerful responses, showing the complexity of the causes of anxiety. Here are the words of four of his students, each with a very different story. For each student, decide what the causes of anxiety might be, and how you, as a teacher, could help.

1 'Some of my group members are really good at English writing. They always have good ideas and write quickly. This makes me feel anxious. My mind is always blank. The thought of my classmates being better than I keeps intensifying my anxiety level and mind blankness. It is a vicious cycle. I have told myself many times that I should give up this course.'

2 'I think it is related to my personality. I am a person easily getting worried. I think my childhood experience intensified such personality. In my primary school my sister and I were often blamed by my mother because of our poor performance in studies. My mother always thought other kids were better than her daughters. In her eyes my sister and I had few merits. So I have little confidence since then. Although I think my writing ability is worse than my present co-workers', I have a strong desire to make my English writing better. Such a desire for getting better has further intensified my anxiety level.'

3 'Another factor influencing my writing tests anxiety level is the importance of the subject concerned. English writing is very important not only for our department but also for my future, so I am greatly concerned about whether I can get good grades in it.'

4 'As an EFL student we do not write English every day, so when it comes to English writing we will naturally feel anxious in grammar and word usage … My past experiences tell me that whenever I got my composition back there would be numbers of red marks from the teacher indicating that I made numerous errors in these aspects.'

You have probably come up with a number of suggestions for removing the barriers to these learners' writing. A clear practical implication of this line of research is that by developing activities which allow learners to write or speak about their feelings of anxiety, we may learn more about those feelings—while at the same time providing language practice—and be able to prepare future classes in ways which lower anxiety levels among those learners.

Positive emotions

So what about the role of positive emotions? Much of the research into emotions in educational psychology and in SLA has tended to focus on the negatives, typically looking at anxiety. As a result, there has been less work examining the positive emotions that can facilitate and promote learning. In recent years, there has been a move within educational and social psychology towards what is known as **positive psychology**. In the post-war period, psychology tended to focus on fixing psychological problems, which, of course, remains an important goal. However, advocates of positive psychology argue that psychology has an equally important role to play in understanding human strengths and in promoting positive psychological states and well-being. One of the key goals is to understand what we can do to help people 'flourish' (Seligman, 2011). In SLA, only very recently have scholars—such as Peter MacIntyre and Tammy Gregersen (MacIntyre & Gregersen, 2012; Gregersen & MacIntyre, 2014a)—begun to consciously engage with the developments in positive psychology and consider their implications and relevance for language learning.

We have already considered the potentially face-threatening, anxiety-inducing situations that language learning can engender, but we must also remember that it can provide feelings of achievement, self-worth, enjoyment, and interest, as well as facilitating positive relationships and interactions with others. As with most things in life, learning a language is likely to involve a mixture of both types of emotions and neither should be denied. It is the appropriate balance between the two that is important and positive emotions can counter some of the effects of negative emotions, ensuring the positivity/negativity ratio is in proportion. However, positive emotions have other benefits beyond merely redressing the effects of negative emotions. In ways perhaps reminiscent of Krashen's affective filter—where negativity limited one's ability to take on board the language and positivity opened the mind to engage with new language—the psychologist Barbara Fredrickson (2009, 2013) has proposed a '**broaden-and-build**' theory of positive emotions. This suggests that positive emotions broaden people's attention and the way they think and act, in contrast to negative emotions, which narrow down people's thinking and wish to act. This means that individuals with more positive emotions are able to think in more diverse, creative ways and are more likely to actively explore and approach a topic or area, thereby tending to have minds more open to new experiences and learning. With this broadened range of thinking, individuals become able to build up a repertoire of skills, enabling them to become creative, more resilient to stress and setbacks, and also to build positive relationships with others. All of these, in turn, act as valuable resources to help people to enjoy more positive experiences in the future. A fundamental point here is that positive emotions not only constitute an indicator and response of a happy existence but can also lead to well-being and positivity. This implies what Fredrickson calls an upward spiral of positivity, in which having positive emotions can lead to further, increased positivity in the future.

One of the key issues that positive psychology has addressed is the concept of happiness. This is a surprisingly complex term as used in the literature and it involves multiple dimensions. Firstly, it refers to the more traditional understanding of the word in terms of positive emotions such as joy, love, and contentment—in other words, the 'pleasant life'. This involves happiness gained from pleasure at maybe brief moments in time, a form of happiness that is potentially the most short-lived. But happiness can also refer to leading a purposeful and meaningful life. It has two dimensions. Firstly, there is the 'engaged life', when you use your strengths to engage deeply with challenges in a way that helps you grow and develop. This is exemplified by the concept of **flow** (Csikszentmihalyi, 1990). Flow can occur when people become utterly absorbed in tasks that are not too easy but involve the perfect degree of challenge for their current abilities. The second dimension of happiness is understood as the 'meaningful life' (Seligman, Gillham, Reivich, Linkins, & Ernst, 2009). This is when people engage in activities and actions that have a greater meaning than personal gratification, serving a purpose beyond the individual and contributing to something larger than themselves, such as the environment, social organizations, or future generations. Clearly, teachers are potentially in a position to have such meaning in their lives, given their inherent role in supporting the learning and growth of future generations and of others.

For teaching, it becomes apparent that if we wish to have 'happy' learners, we must go beyond simplistic views equating happiness with momentary joy and fun. While these remain important dimensions to incorporate into our classroom lives—such as through the use of learning games, cooperative tasks, and humour—happiness also stems from being sufficiently challenged and able to develop one's strengths. This means we need to support learners in becoming aware of their strengths and finding ways to employ them meaningfully in the pursuit of language learning. For example, learners whose strength is their sense of humour and playfulness can be encouraged to write a humorous story, act out a comedy version of a role play, or transform gap-fill sentences with humorous additions. It also suggests learners may reap benefits from approaches in which they use the foreign language through projects for social good. An example might be working on a project about a particular social cause and creating a magazine about the topic, which is then sold and the proceeds donated to a relevant charity.

The notion that happiness is associated with feeling challenged or able to realize one's potential suggests that it stems from a purposeful life. This means that happiness is not gained from owning things, such as an expensive car or the latest smartphone—although they certainly bring momentary pleasure for many—but that real, lasting happiness comes from spending time wisely on positive experiences, positive social relationships, and in acts of kindness to others. The implication for the classroom is that we need to focus on language learning in terms of the positive experiences associated with it and the positive social relationships surrounding those experiences—inside and outside of class—as well as through a cooperative, positive community within a group. (See Chapter 2.)

One more dimension of the positive psychology movement that we wish to draw attention to is the concept of **optimism**. This links to our discussion of mindsets and attributions in Chapter 4. Optimism is concerned with positive expectations for the future and confidence about one's goals and future outcomes. In contrast, pessimists are often full of doubt and uncertainty, tending to anticipate negative outcomes. As optimists expect positive future outcomes, they generally work harder, are less likely to give up in the face of challenges, and are more resilient to setbacks. The idea that we can change our position on the optimism/pessimism scale is reflected in the title of a book by one of the leading figures of the positive psychology movement, Martin Seligman (1990): *Learned Optimism*. Although we do not wish learners to be unrealistically optimistic, we would certainly want to promote a positive outlook and set of expectations while acknowledging that these must also remain realistic.

Let us think for a moment about two learners preparing to go on an exchange trip to a foreign country. One of the learners, Luis, is full of fear and anxiety, anticipating failure, embarrassment, and frustration at all the language challenges he is about to face. Ideally, he would like to avoid the trip, and he feels daunted by the prospect of using the language in any circumstances. On the other hand, Sami is full of excitement, curiosity, and interest, anticipating opportunities to have new experiences, meet new people, and try out his language skills. Naturally, Sami is also aware of the possible problems he might encounter in expressing himself, but, as an optimist, he tends to be aware that the consequences of making language mistakes in this setting are unimportant and that somehow he will get by. Ultimately, Sami might envisage being able to laugh about such instances, instead of dreading them and seeing them as major stumbling blocks. While Luis may hopefully change his feelings and attitudes during his stay, it is clear that Sami is in a better position at the outset to benefit from the experience.

So, as teachers, how can we work at helping our learners to be optimistic about their language learning while remaining realistic? Certainly, it can be beneficial to have some explicit discussion about learners' anxieties, putting them into perspective. Seligman (2011) presents a three-stage model for thinking about feared negative events. He suggests thinking about the worst, best, and most likely scenarios and then considering how to manage the most likely scenario. Another way of promoting optimism is by having learners reflect on their explanatory styles—in other words, how they explain their experiences in language learning. Pessimists tend to blame negative events on permanent aspects of the self and any positive events on temporary factors not related to themselves. If we find learners using such explanatory styles, we can challenge their thinking, asking them what other ways this experience could be explained and how they can influence future events in a positive way. (See also Chapter 4.) We can also prompt learners to reflect on their positive experiences in using and learning the language, and to identify their personal strengths. We all have strengths and weaknesses (see the discussion later in this chapter on self-knowledge) and while it is important to be aware of our weaknesses and to work on improving them, it is vital also to reflect on our strengths, considering how we can build on them and use them wisely for positive future outcomes. As teachers, we need to remember to comment on learners' strengths, rather than solely focusing on weaknesses, in order to model a culture of positivity.

Each learner is unique and what will help our students to feel positive and flourish in our classes is likely to be diverse and highly personal, varying across cultural and contextual settings. Yet, while we cannot easily prescribe what individual learners need to do to promote their well-being in class, we can seek to lead by example. If we work at developing our own positive attitudes, emotions, and behaviours in respect to language learning and use, then we can expect that our own optimism and happiness will promote similar positivity in our learners.

Activity 5.7	**Raising awareness of individual strengths and weaknesses**

Consider the various learners in the classes you teach. Think about some of the strengths and weaknesses you perceive in those learners. For example, one learner may tend to lower his voice or mumble unclearly when he is unsure of the language he is using. In contrast, another learner may be particularly good at using the language she already knows to compensate for unfamiliar items of vocabulary. Now consider the following points:

1 How aware are your learners of their own weaknesses in respect to language learning?
2 Can you specify which weaknesses they are aware of?
3 Now think about how aware they are of their strengths and identify which strengths they might be aware of.
4 Finally, think about how you can get your learners to play more to their strengths in your classes.

Emotional intelligence

We have stressed that one of the roles of teachers is to promote a supportive learning environment in which learners flourish and feel positive. An important skill for teachers is how to interpret the emotional reactions of the learners in their classrooms. One useful concept that is now beginning to attract attention within the field of language education is that of **emotional intelligence**. In this discussion, we will be guided by Goleman's (1998) definition of emotional intelligence as 'the capacity for recognizing our own feelings and those of others, for motivating ourselves, and for managing emotions well in ourselves and in our relationships' (p. 318). In this section, we will highlight some of the defining aspects of emotional intelligence, while considering what it has to offer language teachers.

The first element of the definition above is important, though often overlooked. This refers to what is known as **self-knowledge**. In order to understand and interact with others, we need to understand ourselves, realize our strengths and weaknesses, and feel comfortable within ourselves. This is something that is very difficult to achieve alone, so for teachers, it requires actively seeking candid feedback from both colleagues and learners. Self-knowledge requires both listening to direct and indirect feedback from others and being honest with ourselves. Without adequate self-knowledge, none of the other aspects of emotional intelligence we discuss are possible. (See Chapters 3 and 7 on the self and self-regulation.)

The second feature of emotional intelligence is known as **self-management**. Self-management is essentially concerned with how we manage and control our emotions. A unique trait of humans is that they are able to control their emotional responses to various external stimuli. People have the ability to assess a particular situation, manage reactions, and control their behaviour in accord with their immediate goals. So, when we are anxious, we may decide that the best strategy is to conceal the anxiety and act confidently—such as during a job interview. Humans are, to some extent, always evaluating and managing their emotional reactions. Emotionally intelligent self-management occurs when individuals are able to manage their emotions in a way that takes into account the concerns of others.

Many language teachers have, at times, felt undervalued by their institution and frustrated or even angry with students. It is important that teachers consider how they process their emotions and manage them in the classroom. As teachers, we tend to exercise caution in our choice of words in front of students, but sometimes our body language can be revealing in ways we do not intend. It is possible to imagine a language teacher experiencing great frustration at a particular learner who continues to make the same error and does not appear to be learning from those mistakes. The teacher may go to great efforts to conceal the frustration through supportive words, but those feelings may be betrayed by an inopportune sigh or shake of the head. In such a case, all the teacher's words of support are likely to be undermined by the non-verbal communication. Correspondingly, teachers need to be able to interpret the various means of non-verbal communication used by learners (Gregersen, 2003), such as eye contact, facial expressions, and hand movements.

Related to this is the next element of emotional intelligence: **social awareness**. Social awareness is concerned with our ability to interpret what other people are experiencing and thinking—our capacity to 'read' people. To a certain extent, reading others involves entering their world, seeing the world through their eyes. Sometimes this requires teachers to look at themselves from the point of view of their learners. A particular challenge that many language teachers face is that they are often dealing with learners from different cultural backgrounds, who hold different core values. Language teachers need to be sensitive to these values and reflect upon how their own behaviour or values may be in conflict with the expectations of the learners in their classes. (See Chapter 2.)

The final component of emotional intelligence we need to consider is **relationship management**. For teachers, this is a huge consideration because our role in the classroom is pivotal; teachers can be the focal point, setting the general mood and influencing the emotional reactions of others. Successful learning is greatly dependent upon how we manage the various social relationships that occur in the classroom. Key amongst these are the relationships between the teacher and the class as a whole, and the teacher's various relationships with the individuals that make up that class.

We have probably all, at some time in our lives, had negative experiences with a teacher, perhaps a teacher who seemed cold, intimidating, and uninterested in the lives of learners. The chances are that such teachers were lacking in emotional intelligence, unaware of how others perceived them, the effects of their presence, and the importance of social relationships in the teaching context. On the other hand, most of us have encountered teachers who appeared able to manage people and events efficiently without resorting to overt displays of authority and who showed empathy for and interest in their learners. This is usually the sign of a teacher with high levels of emotional intelligence, and the product of this emotional intelligence is that teachers and learners are able to work together in a pleasant and productive learning environment.

Summary

In this chapter, we have tried to show the importance of the emotional side of learning and teaching, and, indeed, that the emotional side at times overrides logical cognition. Our thoughts and actions are just as much a function of our emotions as they are of logical reasoning. We have shown that negative emotions—such as anxiety—can, at times, have a debilitating effect on language learning and use. In contrast, we have also discussed how positive emotions can enhance learning. Understanding and managing emotions in the classroom is a fundamental, though sometimes overlooked, responsibility for teachers. The basic guidelines for teachers have not changed since the time of Krashen's affective filter: negative emotion generally inhibits learning, while positive emotion facilitates it. The clear task for teachers is to create a classroom environment in which positive emotions may flourish. Of course, this is far more easily said than done. We have carefully avoided providing any form of prescriptive list of activities or strategies for encouraging positive emotions in the classroom because we remain acutely aware that everyone is different and that what works for one student or teacher in a particular context may not work for another.

Questions for reflection	1 Think of an activity you have done with a class recently. What emotional responses to this task did you encounter from learners? What was your own response? What cues did you use to evaluate learners' emotional reactions? How can you use this information in an emotionally intelligent way in the future?
	2 In what ways would you consider yourself an emotionally intelligent teacher? In what areas are your strengths and what areas do you perhaps need to work on?
	3 Have you had any teaching experiences in which you have experienced anxiety? Can you think of incidents when your anxiety was debilitative and when it was facilitative?

Suggestions for further reading

Seligman, M. (2011). *Flourish*. London: Nicholas Brealey Publishing.
In this book, the man who is widely considered to be the founder of the positive psychology movement offers a highly accessible overview of what positive psychology has to offer. Of particular interest to teachers may be the stories of positive psychology in action in educational contexts.

Arnold. J. (Ed.). (1999). *Affect in language learning*. Cambridge: Cambridge University Press.
This edited volume may be regarded as essential reading for anybody with an interest in the area of affect in second or foreign language learning. Though written over 15 years ago, the wide range of scholarly papers in the book still feel highly relevant to a present-day audience.

Gabrys-Barker, D., & **Bielska, J.** (Eds.). (2013). *The affective dimension in second language acquisition*. Bristol: Multilingual Matters.
This book provides an up-to-date perspective on theory and research relating to affect and emotion in language learning. It may be of particular interest to teachers because not only does it discuss learner affect but considerable attention is also given to how teachers experience affect in their own professional contexts.

6

MOTIVATION

Introduction

Of all the concepts discussed in this book, motivation is perhaps the most familiar and the one that has attracted the most interest from both researchers and teachers. We encounter discussions of motivation in various walks of life, from sport to education to the business world, and we all feel we have some understanding of what the term means. Across the psychology literature, descriptions of motivation have been varied and the focus of inquiry has inevitably shifted over time. The diverse nature of the various conceptualizations of motivation can be partially explained by the sheer scope of the topic; the study of motivation seeks to explain nothing less than why people behave as they do. In this chapter, we do not have space to cover the whole spectrum of motivation theory; instead, we will limit our discussion to those theories of motivation that have been most closely connected with foreign language learning.

What is motivation?

In this section, we will look at some of the main theories of motivation that have appeared in the psychology literature. We do this primarily because although we often discuss motivation, it is not always clear what we mean when we use the term, nor do we always share a common understanding of what motivation is. To give an example, consider what might be meant when a teacher says 'This student is motivated'. To some teachers, this might mean that the student carries out activities and achieves outcomes that the teacher selects. For others, it might mean that the learner has identified specific goals and makes efforts to realize them. These differing views can be explained by different theories of motivation.

Before moving on to the next section, take some time to think about Activity 6.1, below. After you have completed the activity, keep your answers in mind as you read on through the chapter.

| Activity 6.1 | **Different approaches to 'motivating'** |

Let us step back a little from language learning for a moment and consider motivation more generally. Imagine, for example, a young child learning to play the piano. Which of the following do you think would motivate the child?

1 offering a reward or treat each time the child performs well
2 not allowing the child out to play with friends until he has completed his daily practice
3 adopting a policy of constant praise and encouragement, regardless of actual performance
4 scolding the child when he makes a mistake
5 allowing the child the freedom to choose when and how long to practise
6 setting clear goals for the child
7 regularly discussing progress and future goals with the child
8 making a fixed schedule so that the child practises regularly at the same time every day
9 asking the child to make a schedule for his practice
10 encouraging the child to believe that he is more gifted than those around him.

Think about the strategies that you thought were motivating. Why did you think so? How about those you did not consider motivating? What were your reasons?

Teachers have different ideas about their role in motivating students and the best ways to go about doing this. If we look at the various strategies listed in Activity 6.1, we see a diverse range of approaches, and individual teachers would probably have different opinions as to their relative effectiveness and appropriateness. However, these strategies share a common characteristic: they all assume that motivation is externally directed—that a teacher has the power to motivate a student. What we regard as motivating greatly depends on how we understand the concept of motivation. And a fundamental aspect of this is where we see the origin of this motivation: does it come from outside the learner or from within?

Without a clear understanding of what we mean by motivation, we cannot say whether a particular strategy is motivating or not. Teachers readily acknowledge the importance of motivation in language learning, but there is often little explicit consensus as to what is meant by the term. A robust working definition of motivation is surely an essential in any language teacher's toolbox.

Defining motivation

Before we explore some of the descriptions of motivation found in the psychology literature, we need to think a little about everyday, lay understandings of the term, as these have a significant effect on how teachers regard motivation in the classroom. The word 'motivate' itself can be unhelpful. If you pick up a dictionary, you are likely to find a definition that categorizes the word as a transitive verb, accompanied by an illustration referring to somebody or something 'motivating' another person to do something. For example, the *New Oxford English Dictionary* (1998) offers the following:

> Stimulate (someone's) interest in or enthusiasm for doing something: it is the teacher's job to motivate the child at school.

The verb 'motivate' suggests that motivation is very much an external entity and this is reflected in many of the strategies that teachers have conventionally adopted to 'motivate' their students. Many familiar educational practices, such as rewarding or punishing behaviour, are based on this premise that motivation is linked to the teacher controlling learners or guiding them in a particular direction. Such practices are often informed by the behaviourist theories we discussed in Chapter 1, which regard human behaviour as a consequence of external stimuli and imply that the teacher's role is to provide the appropriate stimuli. In the motivation literature, there is a closely related concept known as **push-pull**. According to push-pull theories of motivation, individuals are either pulled by external stimuli, such as rewards and incentives, or pushed by subconscious forces or drives within themselves. For many, basic understandings of motivation are a combination of behaviourism and push-pull theories of motivation; thus, they come to regard the role of a teacher as navigating the learner towards learning outcomes through the provision of various stimuli.

Push-Pull theories of motivation

Early descriptions of motivation focused on the human tendency to either approach pleasure or avoid pain—in other words, on basic needs. In the field of education, Hull's (1943) **drive theory**, for example, attempted to explain learning and motivation in terms of precise scientific formulae, where certain needs or deficits create drives which, in turn, direct human behaviour. Such an approach was typical of its time, but from these simple beginnings the study of motivation gradually became more sophisticated; Eccles, Wigfield, and Schiefele (1998) trace the development of motivational theory as moving away from a needs base towards the cognitive perspective which dominated the latter part of the twentieth century. This move represented a major shift in conceptualization as we moved from seeing motivation as externally controlled to viewing it as something that comes from within the individual. This shift has considerable implications for language teachers. A view of motivation that emphasizes its external nature places the teacher in a central, controlling role. However, a view that focuses on the internal nature of motivation—as a cognitive perspective does—puts the learner in that central role and thus suggests a whole different set of challenges for the teacher. Since the cognitive perspective is the one that has had the greatest influence on how we understand language learning motivation, we will now focus our discussion on it. (See also Chapter 1.)

Cognitive theories of motivation

Cognitive theories of motivation are concerned with how our thinking shapes our behaviour. In the field of education, they refer to the mental processes that direct learning. In other words, learners make decisions about their own learning. Central to this theoretical framework are what are known as **expectancy–value** theories. These describe how behaviour results from whether a person expects success in a particular activity and the perceived value for that person of success in that activity. Imagine, for example, that a tall adult tempts a small child by holding out some treat. The child is unlikely to make a sustained effort to obtain that treat if it is held at an impossible height for her. The child will soon realize that effort is futile and give up, as she does not expect to succeed. Similarly, if the child regards the actual treat as not especially desirable, then she is unlikely to devote much time or energy to the task of getting her hands on it—the child does not value the object that would result from her efforts. On the other hand, if the child sees that treat as highly desirable and it is placed at an attainable height, then we are likely to observe an intense and probably sustained burst of activity in pursuit of that treat. Expectancy–value theories describe behaviour in terms of ongoing mental cost–benefit calculations and, over the years, researchers have theorized motivation in many different ways based around the expectancy–value framework. This is something language teachers, or even educational institutions, need to take into account when they promote the pragmatic or material benefits of learning a language. For example, if learners are being encouraged by the prospect of economic rewards associated with successfully learning a language, then those learners may make the calculation that the actual likelihood of success and the amount of effort required are not justified by the scale of those rewards. Learners may have a low expectancy of success and place little value on that success. Teachers and institutions may need to find other ways to encourage learners, ways that acknowledge the expectancies and values of learners. It is important that teachers make efforts to understand the particular value learners place on learning language and help them to see long-term purpose in the venture. Additionally, teachers can play a role in enhancing motivation by encouraging learners to understand their own abilities in a way that increases the expectation of success.

Achievement and competence

An influential early model of motivation was known as **achievement theory** (Atkinson & Birch, 1978; McClelland, Atkinson, Clark, & Lowell, 1953). In its earliest forms, achievement theory described motivation in terms of a personality characteristic resulting from a basic human need to improve and strive for excellence. However, in more recent years, the focus has shifted away from achievement to the idea of **competence**. In areas such as music and sport—where so much of the motivational psychology originates—it makes sense to think of effort being directed in the pursuit of excellence. Yet for the majority of us, as we go about our normal, everyday lives, excellence is not usually our primary consideration; we are typically much more concerned with simply getting by, hence the term 'competence' (Elliot & Dweck, 2007). Competence is considered a basic psychological need and is essentially concerned with feeling capable at a given activity. From a motivational perspective, it is important for teachers to foster in learners a sense of competence and also challenge them to develop it further; doing this requires a skilful balancing act when planning and designing learning activities. If learning tasks are beyond current competence, then learners may become demotivated or give up altogether; however, when learning tasks do not push the limits of competence, then learners are unlikely to feel challenged or motivated to improve.

Goals

A central concept within cognitive-based theories of motivation is that of goals. We all have goals and make efforts to achieve them, but we make greater efforts to realize some goals than others. The term 'goals' can refer to anything from a simple to-do list pinned on a desk at the start of the working day to something more significant, such as a deeply held long-term ambition. Understandably, goals have been discussed in many different ways, but one highly influential contribution to our understanding of how people create goals for themselves and work towards those goals was Locke and Latham's (1994) **goal-setting theory**. Goal-setting theory considers three key aspects to the goals we set ourselves: their specificity, their perceived difficulty, and our degree of commitment. Individuals are more likely to commit to a particular action when the likelihood of successfully achieving a goal is high—which means the level of difficulty of a particular task is appropriate to the abilities of the individual in question—and when the goal is clearly expressed in specific, concrete terms. Echoing the earlier discussion of competence, all of this indicates a clear motivational role for teachers in the tasks that they set learners. In order to be motivating, tasks must be appropriate to the current proficiency of the learner—meaning that the goals must include some element of challenge—while the nature and aims of the task must also be clear. If learners do not feel capable of carrying out a particular task or if they are not sure what they are supposed to do or why, then they are unlikely to invest much time or effort in that task. In addition, it is important that teachers encourage learners to set their own goals in language learning, both long-term and short-term. This can be an interesting activity and one which can be carried out in the target language. Learners could be asked to identify their long-term goals of learning the language and discuss these in groups. They could also be asked to set more short-term goals such as: how many words they will learn this week; how many books in the target language they will read; how they will practise speaking the language; or how many television programmes they will watch in the language.

A further important distinction in the nature of goals concerns what is known as the orientation of the goals people set for themselves: the distinction between mastery and performance goals (see Ames, 1992; Dweck, 1999; Woodrow, 2012). Learners with a **mastery goal orientation** are motivated by the satisfaction of successfully learning to perform specific tasks, whereas individuals with a **performance goal orientation** engage in tasks to show their worth in relation to others. As an illustration, imagine two amateur musicians who belong to a local orchestra. They are both accomplished and dedicated musicians who practise diligently. However, the reasons they practise are very different. One of them does so because she genuinely loves playing the cello and wants to become the best cellist she possibly can, while the other practises hard because he derives great pleasure from performing on stage in front of an audience. Although their actual behaviour is the same, one of them is motivated by a mastery goal—simply to become a better cellist—while the other is motivated by a performance goal—to be respected and admired by an audience. The performance-oriented musician is principally concerned with how he looks in front of other people, so he is unlikely to make efforts without the threat, or promise, of evaluation by others.

Additionally, referring back to the discussion of self-esteem in Chapter 3, self-esteem can, for some people, become contingent on the praise they receive. The evaluations of others can therefore assume a significant role in how we feel about ourselves and, as a consequence, how we behave. What is particularly interesting about the second musician in the example above is that he is not especially concerned with his proficiency as a cellist; he would be happy so long as other people thought he was good. In contrast, the evaluations of others are not the main concern of the first musician, the mastery-oriented person. She is more focused on improving her ability to play the cello, and it is for this reason that mastery goals are generally considered to have more beneficial long-term motivational effects and, in turn, be more likely to lead to improved performance. The crucial practical implication for language teachers is that learners should be encouraged to aim to master the language rather than merely to score higher grades than their peers or impress others. In environments where learners have little opportunity to use the target language outside the classroom, language education can become strongly associated with competitive testing and, in such environments, students may tend to measure their language development in terms of test scores and how they perform in relation to others. Teachers need to encourage learners to value mastery of the language. However, in doing so, they may find themselves in conflict with the values of their institution or even the broader societal educational values. (See Chapter 7 for further discussion of goals.)

Activity 6.2	**Thinking about performance-oriented and mastery-oriented behaviour**

Read the following descriptions. Which do you think suggest more performance-oriented behaviour and which more mastery-oriented?

1 a committed gamer who often forgets the time while absorbed in playing online games late into the night
2 somebody who plays online games casually but is determined to get the top score visible on the scoreboard for a particular game
3 a runner determined to beat his own personal best time
4 a student working hard in order to become top of the class in a test
5 a business traveller in a foreign country engaging in conversations with locals to practise the language
6 a person practising the guitar, wanting to play it just like a particular musical hero
7 an ambitious student signing up for a summer workshop because some of the high-performing students in the class have also signed up
8 a child practising reading a poem for a poetry-reading competition the next day
9 an amateur tennis player trying to perfect her serve.

One consideration in distinguishing between mastery and performance goals is the role of other people. If, as in the second example above, the individual is primarily concerned with how he performs in relation to others, then this is performance-oriented behaviour. On the other hand, when there is no concern with how others perform or may evaluate the individual, as in the third example in the activity, then this is mastery-oriented behaviour. When we talk of evaluations by others, we need to be careful not to oversimplify what we mean. These evaluations are not only about competition or receiving praise; considerations such as the desire not to feel foolish in front of others can also be factors. Imagine a group of language learners meeting for a short intensive course with people they have mostly not met before. At the beginning of the course, the learners are streamed into classes according to scores on a placement test. One learner is placed in the high-proficiency class and is worried that his classmates will be much better than him, making him look foolish. These concerns may inhibit his behaviour so that he becomes focused on avoiding making embarrassing mistakes in front of others; this is known as an **avoidance orientation**. Meanwhile, another learner may be placed in a lower-proficiency class and may feel that this is a great chance to show everybody how good she is, even though she is not actually learning much; this is known as an **approach orientation**. When learners are overly concerned with their performance in relation to others or with how other people are evaluating their performance, this can steer their approach to learning in an unhelpful direction.

Of course, an essential aspect of being a good language learner/user is developing an awareness of others and their proficiency. However, teachers need to take care that this awareness does not lead them to overemphasize competition in the classroom, which could encourage performance-oriented behaviour. (See also Chapter 2 for other effects of competition on group dynamics.)

Self-determination theory

At the beginning of this section, we referred to a behaviourist view of motivation as a function of external threats and rewards. However, as we have seen, motivation is also internally driven, and **self-determination theory** (Deci & Moller, 2007; Deci & Ryan, 2002) seeks to explain how people manage both external and internal factors. Key to self-determination theory is the idea that people are constantly trying to manage three core psychological needs: autonomy, a need to feel in control of one's own actions; relatedness, a need to belong or feel connected to other people; and competence, a need to feel capable or accomplished. People do not simply act in response to external stimuli like animals in laboratory experiments; they make and sustain efforts more successfully when they feel competent, when they feel in control of their actions, and when they feel valued by and connected to others.

Self-determination theory is often understood in terms of a simplistic dichotomy between **intrinsic** and **extrinsic** motives. However, this would be a misrepresentation of self-determination theory, and one reason behind this misunderstanding is the slightly confusing terminology involved. The terms 'intrinsic' and 'extrinsic' are often conflated with 'internal' and 'external'; however, it is important to understand the distinction between these terms. Basically, one is intrinsically motivated if one carries out an activity for the enjoyment or satisfaction it provides. One is extrinsically motivated if one does something in order to achieve another goal that is not related to the activity itself. An example would be someone studying for an exam to gain a promotion or more money; if the promotion or the money were not there, then the individual would not want to study for the exam. As another example, think of someone who strongly dislikes running but who decides to run a long distance to raise money for a charitable cause that has deep personal significance for him. How would we explain the motivation to run in such a case? It is extrinsic, since the individual actively dislikes running; in this case, the effort is directed by his own belief in the value of the charitable cause, which is an internal factor. So, we can say that the motivation is extrinsic and internal. However, over time, this person may come to enjoy the physical sensations associated with running and look forward to the feelings of satisfaction or even exhilaration that come from a long run. Now the motivation is both internally directed and intrinsic.

The internal/external distinction can be a very useful one in helping us to better understand the motivation of learners. However, we need to exercise great care not to apply the distinction too broadly or rigidly. What may be an internal factor for one learner may be an external factor for another, and what may be an external factor for an individual learner at one point in time may become internal at another, and vice versa. Nevertheless, as a useful rule of thumb, we can say that motivated behaviour tends to be more focused and sustained when the motives are internal to the learner.

Although self-determination theory is often understood as a dichotomy, it is much more accurate to think of a continuum from the strongly extrinsic to the strongly intrinsic. Unfortunately, in the real world, discussions of extrinsic/intrinsic motivation tend to be oversimplified, often portraying extrinsic as 'bad' motivation while intrinsic is seen as the 'good' kind. The reality is more complex and for teachers, the important thing to realize is that the distinctions between the internal and the external, and the intrinsic and the extrinsic, are not always clear, and neither are they static. People are constantly changing, and central to self-determination theory is the idea of internalization—the degree to which someone comes to feel that a perhaps once external motive belongs to them in the sense that it now feels internal.

For a language teacher, it can be helpful to acknowledge that there may be certain activities that very few learners ever find intrinsically rewarding, and it may be very difficult for teachers to change this. However, teachers are able to influence how learners understand the purpose of these activities. If learners understand these activities as being connected to outcomes that they value, that are internally valid, then they are more likely to make sustained efforts towards such ends. It is important, therefore, that teachers explain the purpose of the activities they present so that rather than simply carrying out tasks because the teacher tells them to, learners approach tasks with clear aims in mind.

In the field of language education, perhaps the clearest manifestation of self-determination theory has come in the area of learner autonomy. (See also Chapter 7.) Language learner autonomy is concerned with how language learners are able to take charge of and direct their own learning (see Benson, 2011; Murray, Gao, & Lamb, 2011; Ushioda, 2011). Somewhat coincidentally, self-determination theory was emerging at the same time that the field of language education was beginning to expand the provision of independent learning facilities and self-access learning centres (Dörnyei & Ushioda, 2011). As a consequence, the notion of autonomy has, perhaps a little unfairly, become associated with the notion of learners studying independently in self-access centres. This is a narrow and unhelpful view of learner autonomy, which is an altogether much richer concept that attempts to explain how learners take responsibility for setting their own learning goals, how they assess their successes and failures, and how they attribute those successes and failures to their own strategies and efforts.

Activity 6.3   **Investigating what motivates your learners**

1   Ask your class to consider the following questionnaire.

Which of the following factors do you think make you work harder at something or make a big effort? Which don't make you work hard?
Give each one a score of 1, 2, or 3.

1 = This demotivates me.

2 = I don't have any feelings about this./This doesn't affect how I work.

3 = This motivates me to work hard.

☐ getting a high mark for some work

☐ liking the teacher

☐ being with classmates I like

☐ being interested in the topic of the lesson

☐ receiving praise

☐ feeling happy

☐ seeing other people doing better than me

☐ working in groups

☐ working in pairs

☐ finding the work easy

☐ feeling uncomfortable, such as too hot or cold

☐ feeling confident that I can do something

☐ thinking the teacher is interested in me

☐ having clear goals for the lesson

☐ having clear rules about how we work together in class

☐ sitting still for a long time

☐ being in a bad mood

☐ feeling that I have some choice in what I do

Photocopiable © Oxford University Press

2 Ask students to compare their answers with two other students and see if there are any similarities or differences.

3 Collect the questionnaires and examine them. What have you learned about your class? What can you do differently in the future?

Emotions and context

Cognitive theories of motivation provide a solid framework for understanding behaviour, but they do not tell the full story. Although we may like to think of ourselves as logical, rational beings, there are many occasions when our actions are informed by more than cold, cognitive calculations. We have all done things in our lives that have been difficult to explain—things that may not have made sense from a purely rational perspective and that may even have been considered bad for us. Emotional responses to a situation can be immediate, powerful, and often unpredictable. As an illustration, think of an ostensibly highly motivated learner making efforts to use the target language outside the classroom. Instead of the anticipated supportive reaction, the learner encounters indifference and even a little hostility as the people she tries to use the target language with ignore her efforts and reply to her in her first language. The implication is that she is just not good enough to communicate in the target language. She finds this experience very frustrating and a little embarrassing. Rationally, she understands the value of practising the language outside the classroom, but the accumulation of frustration means she just cannot put herself in that situation again, and, even worse, it is affecting her approach to learning the language in general. As teachers, we need to take this emotional dimension of motivation into account.

Activity 6.4

Exploring irrational decision-making

Consider the following three cases, familiar from everyday life. In each scenario, the individual chooses a course of action that cannot be simply explained by rational thought. Think about each case and consider some of the reasons why the different individuals choose to act in the way they do.

Case 1

This individual lives in the centre of a busy and congested city. The roads are in semi-permanent gridlock and cars are taxed very highly in order to discourage ownership. Additionally, parking is almost impossible at times and, even when it is possible, it can be prohibitively expensive. Fortunately, the city has an excellent and affordable public transport system. It simply makes no sense to own a car here, yet this particular individual chooses to do so despite not being especially wealthy.

Case 2

This individual is in early middle age and has been experiencing a few worrying health issues—nothing major yet, but the kind of thing that is regularly publicized in awareness campaigns as being a possible indicator of something very serious. He is aware of this and a few people close to him have encouraged him to see a doctor, yet he stubbornly refuses to do so.

Case 3

This individual is a secondary school teacher who recently had to take some time off due to personal and stress-related issues. Her school and all her colleagues have been both understanding and highly supportive, doing their best to help her through a difficult time. Nevertheless, she has developed a tendency to be the first in school every morning and one of the last to leave in the evening.

Now think about your own experiences as either a teacher or a learner. Can you recall any occasions when you took a course of action that was difficult to explain by simple logical reasoning? Can you remember some of the factors that influenced your actions?

One characteristic of thinking about motivation in the twenty-first century is a growing awareness of the need to develop multi-level models of motivation that take into account more than cognitive factors (Ryan, 2007). Our physical and emotional states can often override cognitive processes. (See Chapter 5.) The particular context in which an activity is taking place is also a crucial factor in determining how people act. If we think about a contextual factor as apparently trivial as the weather, this can have a huge impact on our eagerness to learn. Imagine being a student in a class in a hot, humid climate, where everybody around you seems to be drained of energy and the sound of the constant heavy rain makes it almost impossible to hear what the teacher is saying. These considerations are probably a much more significant factor in your immediate motivation to learn than any higher-level motives. Earlier theories of motivation regarded these unpredictable emotional or contextual factors almost as inconveniences or distractions, but these factors can play a huge role in shaping our behaviour and teachers cannot afford to ignore them.

Review

In this section, we have presented a brief overview of developments in motivation theory with the aim of encouraging teachers to work towards their own working definitions of motivation in language learning. We have seen that motivation is a term we all know and use, but it can be understood in different ways and there are numerous different facets of motivation. As teachers, we influence learner motivation both directly and indirectly, through obvious means—such as the types of goals we present or the learning tasks we set—and through less obvious means—such as how we interact with students in a class. Motivation is complex and difficult to pin down; learners can be motivated by deeply held internal goals or by seemingly unimportant contextual factors. The huge challenge for teachers is to understand how all of these factors come together within the motivation of a learner.

Key developments in foreign language learning motivation theory

Historical origins

Let us now turn our attention to how motivation has been discussed within the specific context of foreign language education. In order to do this, we briefly need to consider the historical development of theories of foreign language learning motivation, as it is difficult to understand current discussions of language learner motivation without some knowledge of previous controversies.

There has long been a belief that foreign language learning is essentially different from other educational pursuits, and this has certainly influenced how the motivation to learn a foreign language has been discussed (Ushioda, 2012). For a very long time, prior to the 1990s, L2 motivation theory was dominated not by theories from educational psychology but by the ideas of two Canadian social psychologists, Robert Gardner and Wallace Lambert (1972). Starting in the late 1950s, Gardner and Lambert pioneered the systematic investigation of language learning motivation and, in many respects, the focus of their research was influenced by a uniquely Canadian perspective on learner attitudes to a target language, its culture, and its people.

The **socio-educational model**, as it later became known (Gardner, 1985), posited two key orientations that shaped the motivation of language learners: an **integrative orientation**, concerned with feelings of identification with the speakers of the target language, and an **instrumental orientation**, connected to the material rewards associated with acquiring the target language. The socio-educational model of L2 motivation hypothesized that an integrative orientation—the desire to be liked and accepted by speakers of the L2—was more likely to lead to sustained motivated language learning behaviour. This model proved intuitively appealing to both researchers and teachers, with its apparently clear dichotomy between those learners who felt some kind of connection with the target culture and those who were learning for pragmatic, material reasons.

From a twenty-first-century perspective, it is easy to underestimate the significance of Gardner and Lambert's work. Prior to Gardner and Lambert, language learning success was seen very much as a function of learner aptitude allied to teaching methods. Little attention was paid to learners or the effects of some of the attitudes they may have held; recognizing the role of learner attitudes towards the language and learning was a major breakthrough that we now take for granted. However, the social psychological approach to language learning motivation was primarily concerned with understanding broad trends across large population groups. Although this approach offered some genuinely fascinating insights, it had little to say to teachers about what was happening with a particular student in a particular class at a particular time (Ushioda, 2008).

Moving away from social psychology

From the 1990s, the focus of language learning motivation research began to shift towards the actual events occurring in the classroom (see Crookes & Schmidt, 1991; Dörnyei, 1994; Oxford & Shearin, 1994). The general trend within L2 motivation research over the last twenty years or so has been to move away from the kind of investigations favoured by social psychologists that describe broad patterns across large populations towards interpretations of motivation that are situated more within education. This growth in 'education-friendly' accounts of language learner motivation has served to make research in the area more relevant and accessible to practising teachers.

Motivation over time

An approach that was deliberately and clearly education-friendly was the model of learner motivation proposed by Williams and Burden (1997), which describes how social and contextual factors influence the development of motivation within language learners. Williams and Burden recognized the importance of the distinction between internal factors and external factors that we discussed earlier in this chapter and argue that motivation needs to come from within if it is to be meaningful. They take an essentially constructivist approach, seeing motivation as involving learners making their own decisions about what to do and how much effort to expend based on their own understanding of a situation. (See Chapter 1 for a discussion of constructivism.)

A further important aspect of Williams and Burden's model is that it introduced a specific temporal dimension that distinguishes between initiating motivation and sustaining it. Motivation is often seen as initiating—getting learners interested or turning them on. However, motivation is also concerned with sustaining effort over time. The reasons a student embarks on a particular activity should not be confused with how that student sustains efforts. For example, a young person may be attracted to a particular language out of admiration for a certain figure from popular culture, but this admiration is unlikely to sustain efforts to learn the language over an extended period of time. In fact, the young person's admiration for that figure may soon fade while the efforts to learn the language persist, influenced by considerations other than those that stimulated the initial efforts to learn. Williams and Burden point out the dangers of conflating these separate stages. For language teachers, there is a clear need to be aware of this distinction when trying to understand the motivation of their students and to pay attention to sustaining motivation in what is a long endeavour.

Motivation as a process

Dörnyei & Otto (1998) further explored the temporal dimension to L2 learning motivation in their **Process Model of L2 Motivation**. This model identifies three stages of motivation: the preactional stage, the actional stage, and the postactional stage. The preactional stage corresponds to initiating motivated behaviour and relates to the choices individuals make when setting particular goals. The actional stage explains how motivation is sustained in the pursuit of those goals set at the preactional stage. The postactional stage relates to how people evaluate their execution of a particular task and this evaluation, in turn, feeds into the preactional stage of a subsequent action. So the process described in this model is one of making choices to act in a particular way, acting on those choices, and then evaluating those actions in a way that informs future behavioural choices. As an illustration, let us consider a recently retired person who decides that she would like to use some of her new free time to study a language. Since she also greatly enjoys reading, she decides to begin by reading some graded readers in order to improve her vocabulary. At the outset, the preactional stage, she makes a plan of how many books to read and decides to keep an accompanying vocabulary notebook. She later goes to the library full of enthusiasm and borrows as many books as possible. She starts to read some of the books; we can consider this the actional stage. After some time has passed, she realizes that her vocabulary notebook entries are a little inconsistent, with some books requiring almost every other word to be entered and others none at all. She also feels a noticeable drop in her enthusiasm for the project. She reflects on why this may be: the postactional stage. As a result of this reflection, she concludes that she initially took out too many randomly selected books and decides that a better future course of action would be to borrow fewer books and limit the books she chooses to particular reading levels. She then goes to the library again, with her initial enthusiasm retuned, thus starting the next round in the process.

The process model acknowledges that actions do not occur in isolation; they have both antecedents and consequences. Language learning is a long-term endeavour usually characterized by many ups and downs, and over the course of learning a foreign language, any learner is likely to encounter many fluctuations in enthusiasm and commitment. For a model of motivation to be educationally meaningful, it needs to help teachers and learners themselves understand some of these motivational ebbs and flows. Importantly, it makes clear that we must be careful not to simplistically label learners as being either motivated or not. Motivation can change over time and is a more complex set of emotions, thoughts, and behaviours than such binary thinking would suggest.

Considering context

One of the greatest recent changes in thinking about foreign language learner motivation is that we no longer consider motivation as an individual trait, i.e. a fixed attribute a person possesses. We no longer think of motivated or unmotivated learners; we prefer to think of learners who are motivated at a particular time or place to do a particular thing:

> Motivation is less a trait than a fluid play, an ever-changing one that emerges from the processes of many agents, internal and external, in the ever-changing complex world of the learner

(Ellis & Larsen-Freeman, 2006, p. 563)

Of course, people have individual goals and aspirations, but they are also motivated through their relationships with others and their environment. They can be demotivated by these too. Think of a young person joining a new school and being full of enthusiasm for learning a foreign language for the first time. In the first few lessons, this individual is brimming with excitement and curiosity, but he gradually begins to notice that few of the forty other people in the classroom share this enthusiasm, and that this is not helped by the fact that the teacher is barely audible above the general buzz of conversation. If we were to isolate such a person from this particular context in order to investigate his motivation, we may come up with a very positive picture. However, this would be almost meaningless given the actual context in which learning is taking place.

When we think of the learning context, it is necessary also to think beyond the walls of the language classroom. As a language teacher, it is easy to forget that language learners do other things in addition to learning languages. They have other interests, roles, and responsibilities, and they do not simply abandon these other aspects of their identity when they enter the language classroom. Motivation to learn a language is connected to other ongoing behaviours. For example, teenage language learners have other social identities—they may be sons or daughters, musicians, athletes, or countless other possibilities—and these are not entirely separate from the language learning experience. At times, these other identities may be competing with identities as language learners. For example, a learner may feel that too much effort in the cause of learning a foreign language threatens her identity as a dedicated athlete. And, at other times, these other identities may reinforce language learning behaviour. Consider how the prospect of an overseas trip connected to the sport at which this individual excels may serve to inspire and energize her language learning. In order for language teachers to fully understand the motivation of their students, it is necessary for them to look not only at the 'language learner' but at the person as a whole (Ushioda, 2009). This implies that it can be useful for teachers to get learners to write or talk about their lives outside of the language classroom. In doing so, learners may discover various links between competing identities and ways of connecting or harmonizing them.

Motivation as self-realization

Dörnyei's L2 Motivational Self System

At the present time, the dominant model of language learning motivation is Zoltán Dörnyei's **L2 Motivational Self System** (Dörnyei, 2005, 2009). This is a conceptualization of motivation that accommodates contextual, personal, and temporal dynamics, and considers motivation as a part of self-realization, as a part of becoming the person we would like to be. The L2 Motivational Self System is based upon the concept of **possible selves** (see Markus & Nurius, 1986; Oyserman, Bybee, & Terry, 2006), which refer to the various images we have of who we might become. These may be positive, aspirational images—'hoped-for selves'—or negative images of the person we hope to avoid becoming—'feared selves'. This conceptualization provides a framework for understanding how we all have some idea of the person we are, the type of person we would like to be at some point in the future, and the kind of person we are afraid of becoming. Within this framework, we are guided to make efforts to move from our current state towards becoming the person we hope to be and to protect ourselves from becoming the feared self.

We all have visions of ourselves in some possible future state and these visions reflect assessments of our potential, our expectations, our hopes, and our fears. The L2 Motivational Self System is concerned with the L2-specific dimension to these visions and how they direct efforts to learn a language. The model proposes two principal sets of self-guides: the **ideal L2 self** and the **ought-to L2 self**. The ideal L2 self represents the person we would like to become if we could use the L2. The learner also develops an ought-to L2 self, which emerges from perceived obligations and responsibilities to others as a language learner. These can come from a variety of sources, such as parents, teachers, and even peer pressure. A third, experiential, component, the **L2 learning experience**, is included and this dimension of motivation stems from our interaction with the learning environment as well as from our perceptions of past language learning successes and failures.

The main driving force in the motivation to learn a language comes from the perceived discrepancies between one's current sense of self in the L2 and one's ideal L2 self, and it is the strength and intensity of these visions that are crucial in initiating and sustaining learning. These visions derive much of their motivational power from the unique human capacity to 'experience' events in our imagination. Possible selves are more than simple goals or mere internal representations of ourselves in some future state; they contain some degree of experienced meaning and relevance to the current self-concept. An illustration of this might be a young graduate student whose ideal L2 self-concept involves giving presentations at academic conferences in English. For this individual, visions of the future self might include some of the nervousness experienced at the beginning of the presentation, feeling lost for words or intimidated by the large audience, as well as some of the elation felt when the audience bursts into applause at the end. The nervousness shows that the vision is realistic and sufficiently close to the individual's current self-concept; a vision in which the individual gives a perfect presentation smoothly and without any difficulty is likely to be implausible fantasy having no motivational effect. Mental imagery enables the learner to 'experience' through the power of the imagination the emotional highs and lows associated with achieving the ideal state, feeling competent, and preparing the coping strategies necessary to achieve this ideal. Since the human brain processes imagined events in the same way that it processes actual events, learners are able to feel that they have already lived the experience through their ideal L2 self visions, and thus feel prepared, competent, and motivated.

Activity 6.5   **Considering mental imagery in context**

Look at the following cases of language learners and their mental imagery. In which cases do you think the mental images are likely to lead to motivated learning behaviour? Can you think of reasons why any of these visions might not result in sustained learning effort?

Case 1

A man in his mid-twenties sometimes imagines working in a section of his company that does a lot of business overseas. The transfer will probably happen one day anyway, but it would be a good idea for him to learn a foreign language in order to speed up that move.

Case 2

A woman in her early thirties is enthusiastically attending language classes, at her employer's expense. The deal with her employer is that she must achieve a certain score on a standardized test within a fixed period of time. At home, she sometimes finds herself dreaming about using the language to travel around the world by herself. However, these thoughts are usually interrupted by one, or both, of her two young children.

Case 3

A young woman is in her final year at school and is currently considering her options for university. She has always wanted to learn English and see the world working as a flight attendant and this is a big factor in her thinking. However, although her English is not bad, she is aware that it may be difficult for her to find her dream job because she has always been quite a short person.

Case 4

A group of three friends start their own small company shortly after university. For most of the time, it has been more of a labour of love than a successful business, based around a shared interest. However, they recently received a large order from China that has the potential to make the business very successful. One of the three partners visited China and found that he enjoyed trying to use the language. He also realized that the ability to use the language may be essential to the future success of their company. Since returning, he often finds himself imagining using Chinese in both business and social situations.

Visions on their own are not sufficient to generate motivated behaviour and certain conditions need to be met to enable the motivating power of these self-guides. We all have visions of our future selves, but not all of these visions lead to motivated behaviour. If we look at Case 1, we can see that his vision does not seem radically different from his current self and is likely to happen at some point anyway, without the extra effort. In such cases, it is unlikely that an individual will exert much effort to realize something that does not represent a sufficient contrast to the existing situation. Furthermore, both his imagery and his future prospects appear rather vague, yet in order for mental imagery to be motivating, it needs to be highly specific and detailed. In Case 2, we can see that the visions of travelling around the world alone are likely to conflict with her ought-to L2 self as represented by the demands of her employer and also with other elements of her self-concept, such as her responsibilities as a mother of two young children. Additionally, in this case, since her thoughts are often interrupted by her children, these mental images are unlikely to be either vivid or regularly activated within the current working self-concept. In Case 3, there is an issue of plausibility. She is unlikely to get much taller, and since there is a height requirement for her dream job, she knows that there is very little possibility of her ever meeting this requirement. An ideal L2 self must be plausible in order to energize learning. Visions in isolation may simply lead to daydreaming or fantasies, which can be very pleasant but which do not energize learning. It is the visions operating under certain facilitating conditions that create a motivating ideal L2 self. We see this best illustrated in Case 4, where the individual's visions of being a successful language user exist in harmony with other aspects of his life, and his professional activities are, in fact, likely to activate and develop those visions. Importantly, there are also negative consequences associated with a failure to realize these visions.

Motivation in the classroom

Motivation and successful language learning

So what do any of these theories of motivation have to say to teachers in language classrooms? One thing we need to be wary of is oversimplifying the relationship between motivation and language learning success. There are many studies that show strong correlations between motivation and proficiency, but this is far from saying that motivation necessarily leads to high proficiency. It may simply be the case that proficient learners feel more motivated because they are engaged in something they are good at. Although we cannot claim that motivation directly leads to proficiency, we can be more confident in putting forward the argument that low levels of motivation impede successful learning. For this reason alone, an awareness and understanding of motivation must be a priority for teachers.

Motivation, unpredictable learners, and unpredictable learning

One of the joys—and sometimes one of the frustrations—of being a teacher is how unpredictable the job can be. For example, a certain activity may work wonderfully well with one group of learners, but when we try it again with another, perhaps even very similar, group it may fall flat. At the beginning of the chapter, we discussed the early attempts of psychologists to describe learning behaviour in terms of precise formulae, but teachers soon find out that learners and their learning do not follow exact, linear patterns. Sometimes people can behave in the most unexpected ways and this is something teachers must bear in mind when thinking about how students motivate themselves and about their own role in that process. Teachers need to be wary of settling upon a one-size-fits-all approach to motivational strategies. Activities that work in one case may not work in another, something one learner may find motivating may demotivate another, and something that may motivate an individual learner at one time may have the reverse effect at another.

| **Activity 6.6** | **Exploring the unpredictable side of motivation** |

Look at the following list of episodes that may happen to a language learner. Try to think of ways in which the episode may be motivating for the learner. Next, think of ways in which the same episode may be demotivating.

1   getting a surprisingly high score on an important test
2   getting a disappointingly low score on an important test
3   finding an authentic listening activity surprisingly easy
4   seeing a classmate do something impressive in the target language
5   falling in love with a speaker of the target language
6   breaking up after a serious relationship with a speaker of the target language
7   being praised by the teacher for excellent pronunciation
8   being moved by a film in the target language
9   being in a class where very few people seem interested in learning the language.

No event is inherently motivating in itself; learners are primarily motivated through their own interpretations of an experience. So if we look at one of the episodes mentioned in Activity 6.6—say, the case of seeing a classmate do something impressive in the target language—a possible outcome is that the other learners would feel inspired by witnessing this, believing it is also within their potential to achieve such a feat. Another possibility is that some of the learners may feel disheartened by or even resentful of their classmate's success. The result in this case could be demotivation, frustration, and a subsequent resistance to learning the language. We simply do not know how any individual is going to react to a particular experience, and this suggests that it makes more sense for teachers to think in terms of motivational contingencies. By this, we mean that teachers should think more about a range of possible or typical outcomes. A further practical illustration of this idea could be a teacher planning to introduce a musical activity into a class with younger learners. There is a sound and coherent rationale behind this choice of activity, as young learners tend to be stimulated by musical activities. However, there are some young people who intensely dislike such activities, and if these individuals are influential within a particular class, then attempting to force such an activity on unwilling learners could meet with disaster. Motivation comes not only from the activity itself but also from the group of learners, the particular context in which it is taking place, and the personal interpretations of that activity by the individuals involved.

Furthermore, as discussed in Chapter 2, the learning group and the various sub-groups operating within it constitute a crucial element of the learning context. In order for teachers to understand the motivation of individual learners, they also need to be aware of and understand how the group dynamics work within their classes.

Motivation and the teacher

One of the issues recurring throughout this chapter is that of the role of the teacher in motivating learners. However, we also need to consider the motivation of teachers themselves. Many of the general principles of motivation—such as the fundamental psychological need to feel competent and autonomous that we described earlier in this chapter—apply as much to teachers as they do to learners. Nevertheless, it is still possible to identify particular motivational characteristics of being a teacher. We can point to two broad areas in which teachers derive pleasure and satisfaction from their work: one is their interest in the subject matter and the other is the appeal of the educational process itself, interacting with learners and feeling a part of their development. Obviously, individual teachers differ in the degree to which they feel satisfied or motivated by these aspects of the teaching process, but there is a clear implication that factors threatening opportunities either to engage with the subject or to feel a part of learners' development may demotivate teachers. Since language learning can be a long and arduous process, many teachers are not around by the time their learners develop into proficient L2 users. A particular motivational challenge for language teachers is therefore to stay positive and enthusiastic without having immediate access to the rewards of their efforts.

A further factor to consider is the context in which teaching is taking place. Like learners, teachers are affected by the immediate physical environment; they may approach a lesson full of energy and enthusiasm on a beautiful spring day, but very differently when the weather is less inspiring. Teachers are also motivated—and demotivated—by groups; they often look forward to and make extra efforts for teaching certain groups of learners yet feel apprehensive about teaching others. Finally, we need to recognize the huge influence the institutional context can have on the motivation of teachers. When teachers are working in a context that does not reflect their own values and aspirations as educators—at the micro-level of a particular institution, the macro-level of the broader educational system, or both— then they are likely to become demotivated. On the other hand, teachers working in a supportive context tend to make greater and more sustained efforts to help their learners.

Teacher motivation is an important issue in itself, but a particular interest for us is the connection between teacher motivation and learner motivation. Perhaps the most important motivational task for teachers is that of serving as a role model for learners. Teachers are constantly sending motivational messages through their own behaviour and interactions with learners. When teachers show enthusiasm and passion, students pick up on this and it can be contagious. Expertise in a subject and pedagogic 'technique' can be great assets in the classroom but, according to Csikszentmihalyi (1997), it is a passion for teaching and commitment to a class that learners really pick up on. When teachers are passionate and enthusiastic, and when they demonstrate this to their classes, students are encouraged to develop a similar passion for learning.

Summary

Understanding the motivation of students and playing a part in enhancing that motivation is surely one of the most rewarding aspects of being a teacher. The first step towards achieving this must be to understand motivation itself, and a crucial part of this is acknowledging that teachers can only do so much. Teachers do not motivate learners by trying to control them or direct them towards particular outcomes; motivation comes from within learners themselves. Attempting to force learners into directions they do not wish to go in is an approach doomed to failure and one that can only result in stress and disaffection all round. On the other hand, working with learners, getting to know them and their dreams, and helping them to realize those dreams must surely be one of the most rewarding occupations available.

Questions for reflection	1 What role, if any, can teachers play in motivating students to learn a language?
	2 What can you do as a teacher to help learners set goals and develop motivating visions?
	3 As a teacher, your own motivation will fluctuate over time. What are the specific things that cause you to feel demotivated? What can you do to combat these feelings of demotivation?

Suggestions for further reading

Dörnyei, Z., & **Ushioda, E.** (2011). *Teaching and researching motivation, second edition.* Harlow: Pearson Education.
This is the second edition of the standard work in the field. This book provides a general overview of theories of motivation from educational psychology, a detailed account of the various approaches to understanding the motivation of language learners, and a discussion of some of the practical considerations for teachers.

Dörnyei, Z., & **Kubanyiova, M.** (2014). *Motivating learners, motivating teachers: Building vision in the language classroom.* Cambridge: Cambridge University Press.
This is a teacher-friendly summary of new perspectives on motivation, with a particular focus on vision and its motivational role. What is noteworthy about this book is that it pays attention to the motivation of both learners and teachers.

Schunk, D. H., **Meece, J. R.**, & **Pintrich, P. R.** (2014). *Motivation in education: Theory, research, and applications, fourth edition.* Boston, MA: Pearson Education.
The latest edition of this classic text offers a comprehensive yet accessible summary of some of the key themes discussed in this chapter. The book does not address any of the specifics relating to the motivation to learn a language, but it should still be considered one of the most authoritative, and most readable, accounts of motivation in educational contexts.

7

AGENCY AND SELF-REGULATION

Introduction

So far in this book, we have focused on what learners bring to the learning process—their perceptions of themselves, their beliefs, feelings, and motivations, and the significant influences these have on language learning. We now move on to consider how learners actually carry out their learning—the actions they engage in as they navigate their way through learning a language, and the ways in which they regulate these processes and develop a sense of **agency**. As we have seen in previous chapters, agency is the feeling that one can act and have control over one's actions. We first focus on the strategies learners need in order to learn effectively and autonomously, and then discuss other aspects of **self-regulation**, such as goal setting and achieving. Finally, we examine the area of **metacognition**, which involves the processes used to plan and regulate our learning.

Agency

Successful language learning does not depend solely on the teacher, although teachers play a central role in creating the conditions conducive to learning. What is also needed is the activity, initiative, and engagement of the learner (van Lier, 2008). In this respect, learners need to feel a personal sense of agency—a belief that their behaviour can make a difference to their learning in that setting. This feeling of agency emerges from the interaction of many of the psychological facets covered in the book so far.

Firstly, in order to develop feelings of agency, learners actually need to believe that they are capable of learning a foreign language. They need to believe that they have the ability to do it and that this ability can be developed. They also need to see that their attributions for their past successes and failures are within their control. This takes us back to the key role of beliefs, in particular self-beliefs, and how optimistic learners feel in respect to their language learning. (See Chapters 3 and 4.) Secondly, learners need to be willing and motivated to take action to develop their language skills. If learners are motivated to work on their language skills, they need to feel able to do this and view it as a worthwhile undertaking, anticipating some kind of improvement or outcome worth pursuing.

A useful concept here is that of **engagement**. We talk about learners being engaged when they are passionate and enthusiastic about their learning; when they are invested personally in the process; and when they show an inner drive to learn and improve, taking pride and interest in what they do. We all recognize learners who are visibly engaged in their learning, but we must remember that not all learners will 'display' their engagement in the same way. Some may be shyer and more reticent to speak up in class, but this is not to say that they are not interested or do not feel engaged or a sense of agency—they may simply choose not to play an active role in certain tasks or activities. Nevertheless, in language learning, we acknowledge that in general learners improve through practice and using the L2, and so we would clearly want to encourage learners to actively use the language. As teachers, we need to find the balance between pushing all learners to the boundaries of their comfort zones so that new learning can take place but also permitting them a sense of security and comfort by allowing them to take a less visibly active role where appropriate. Fundamentally, we wish to avoid having learners who are disengaged—who, in other words, lack a connection to language learning and are apathetic, overly passive, anxious, or bored.

Agency and engagement are also interconnected with contextual factors, as already outlined in Chapter 2. Being engaged or feeling a sense of agency are not solitary, individual experiences; rather, they are social and contextually situated. This means our sense of agency can stem from feelings within a group or from our relationships with peers or teachers. We can become more engaged when sharing ideas and working with others, 'catching' their enthusiasm and motivation through processes of **contagion**. The setting we learn in, both physical and psychological, can also promote or inhibit our sense of agency and engagement. Some settings may be perceived as offering more resources and more opportunities for personal choice and freedom than others.

The idea of Maslow's hierarchy of needs (see Chapter 1, page 13) is helpful in understanding how learners' agency and engagement can be promoted. Learners are most likely to feel a sense of agency when they are able to reach their full potential or a state of self-actualization—finding meaning in what they do and expressing their sense of self. Certain settings and teaching approaches are more likely than others to arouse learners' curiosity and interest, prompting them to become more engaged, think more deeply, and relate more personally to the learning experience. Key pedagogical strategies here include ensuring that learners experience a variety of input and activities, but without overdoing this and causing sensory overload. For example, as teachers, we can vary resources, media, task types, language skills practised, thinking skills required, topics, pace of tasks, working formats of classes, etc.

In this context, an additional concept from Chapters 1 and 2 worth revisiting is that of **affordances**. Van Lier (2004) explains that contexts represent latent potential until learners interact with them—in other words, it is how learners interpret and relate to contextual factors and resources that generates their potential for learning. This is a perspective which emphasizes the idea that learners make their own sense out of what they encounter and use affordances in ways that are personally meaningful and relevant to them as individuals. Therefore, learner agency depends on learners' individual psychology and how they bring this to bear in interpreting affordances in their contexts, within and outside of class. It is learners' perceptions of resources and contexts—as opposed to any inherent characteristic of a particular resource—that contribute most to their agency.

Activity 7.1	**Interacting with resources in the environment**

Think about the following foreign language learning resources. You may like to focus on those that are available in your own setting. Think also of a class of learners you have worked with. Can you imagine how two or three different types of learners might engage differently with each of these resources? What aspects of their psychology might explain these differences? How might you help learners to broaden their range of potential resources for language learning?

1 blogging
2 the teacher
3 a school library
4 index cards for vocabulary
5 a collection of foreign-language music
6 peers in class
7 a social networking site for those learning the language
8 a vocabulary app for a mobile phone
9 an online grammar quiz
10 a foreign-language drama group.

So, for example, one student might use the school library to read a lot of fiction, another might use it as a quiet place to do homework, while another might look up references on the dangers of water pollution for a project. However, others might see it as a place to keep warm in the school break, a place to escape, or somewhere to go to think quietly. It all depends on learners' preferences, styles, mindsets, confidence, motivation, interests, etc. as to what resources they use and in what ways.

Strategies

If learners believe they have the capacity to learn the language, and assuming they are motivated and willing to take an active role in learning, they then need to know what action to take to learn that language. Among other things, this requires a knowledge of **strategies**. Strategies are the conscious actions that learners use to help them to learn or use a language. A strategy might be a technique a student uses to learn a word, structure, useful phrase, or how to ask the way. Let us illustrate this by looking at the actions taken by some different learners in their endeavours to learn a language. The first learner tries to remember a word by finding a word that sounds similar in her first language and linking the two. Another rehearses ways of asking for items in a shop in his head so that he can buy what he needs. Yet another notices how something is expressed by a native speaker and tries to remember this in case she finds a chance to use the same phrase later. These are examples of **cognitive strategies**, which are mental processes learners use to memorize and retain information, rehearse what will be said, analyze how language works, and retrieve information from memory when needed. However, learners also need other types of strategies. When the second learner enters the shop, he might also need to use **social strategies** to help him to communicate with the shopkeeper. These might include asking for clarification of something said—such as the price or the weight of an item. In addition, he might need to use strategies to make up for a lack of language he needs to express himself—such as asking the shopkeeper to tell him the name of an item, or using mime, gesture, or pointing to get a meaning across. Such actions are known as **compensation strategies**, as they compensate for a lack of knowledge of the language. Another group of strategies are called **affective strategies**. These are strategies that learners can use to regulate their emotions, such as breathing deeply to lower their anxiety or encouraging themselves through positive self-talk to make an effort to initiate conversation with a stranger. A final important group of strategies are known as **metacognitive strategies**, and are used to regulate and control the learning process. These might involve learners planning what to do, monitoring their progress, and noticing how they are coping with the process of learning.

The appropriate use of strategies can enhance both learning and using a language. Strategies for learning would include such actions as noticing and analyzing how a language works or memorizing words and chunks of language to retrieve for use in the future. Strategies for use involve learners in using the language that they have at their command—however limited this might be—to achieve a particular goal. Of course, the strategies for use can also result in learning; they may lead to further input of language from the interlocutor, who may provide a missing word or phrase. Thus, there can be considerable overlap between use and learning, although the distinction can be helpful in developing our understanding of different types of strategies.

So what is a strategy? One helpful definition is that strategies are

> thoughts and actions consciously chosen and operationalized by language learners, to assist them in carrying out a multiplicity of tasks from the very onset of learning to the most advanced levels of target-language performance.

(Cohen, 2012, p. 136)

This definition is useful in a number of ways. First, for action to be strategic, Cohen feels that it must involve the conscious use of strategies, although there is some controversy in the literature as to how conscious actions need to be in order to be classified as strategies. It is perhaps helpful to think about behaviours being 'deliberate', which is the term Oxford (2011) uses instead of 'conscious'. Secondly, Cohen's definition focuses on choice, because, as he says, 'this is what gives a strategy its special character' (p. 136). Individuals choose strategies that suit them and their particular purposes. Thirdly, Cohen suggests that we use strategies at all levels of proficiency, meaning that it is not just beginner learners who need strategies; advanced learners still employ strategies, albeit perhaps different ones.

The strategies individuals use are personal to them, and the ways in which they are used can be creative. If you think about the strategies that you employ to learn and use a language, they are probably personal to you and consciously chosen by you. Moreover, they are probably different from someone else's strategies; they may be linked to your culture, your reason for learning, your personality, or your learning style. Hakki Erten's data from students in the UK memorizing English words illustrate the personal nature of strategy choice. Erten (1998) gave his participants several words to remember, and asked them to tell him what they did to remember them. He asked a student to memorize the word 'sibling', and the student found a strategy that linked the meaning of the word to its spelling: 'Sibling, yeah, *SIB* the beginning of sister *SI* and *B* in brother, sibling, brothers and sisters.' Another participant was asked to memorize the word 'immerse' and said: 'Immerse I think of the sea because in German it is *mere* so diving into the sea.' The student was using a strategy which involved linking the new word to a word he knew in another language that sounded similar and then creating a mental picture to link the two.

Berry (1998) provides a striking example of the individual nature of strategies in describing how Hong Kong Chinese children struggled to adapt to a UK boarding school environment. A student describes using the following strategy:

> I remember once I learnt how to use the word 'pardon'. After my teacher had said something I said 'Pardon' to see her reaction. She repeated what she had said. I said 'Pardon' again. This time I was told off because she had already repeated herself and explained things very clearly. By seeing her reaction I knew I had used 'Pardon' correctly.

(Berry, 1998, p. 266)

Activity 7.2   **Analyzing strategies**

The following statements were made by Hong Kong Chinese children studying at a school in the UK (Berry, 1998). Decide whether they are **cognitive**, **social**, **affective**, or **compensation** strategies.

1 'I tried to analyse what people said.'

2 'I introduced Chinese food in front of many people. I started speaking in a trembling voice … I looked at the teachers I knew, which was something I always did in the lessons. I didn't look at the students. I would be very afraid if I did so. I didn't want to see their facial expressions.'

3 'I could point to the objects and say this or that to make people understand what I wanted.'

4 'I tried to be with the English boys as often as possible. I didn't stay with the Chinese students at all.'

5 'I started to notice that the *K* sound is not necessarily represented by the letter *K*. *Ch* may take the *K* sound as well. All in all, the *K* sound can be represented by different letters.'

6 'When I got stuck in expressing myself I explained it to them in other words. They guessed what I wanted and supplied the missing words for me.'

7 'I sometimes asked the English girl sitting next to me for help. For example, I would say "What's going on now?"'

8 'I would recall these words. When I succeeded in recalling them from my memory I told myself I could remember them.'

What types of strategies do you notice your learners using? How could you engage your learners in reflecting on the range of strategies that they use and in exchanging ideas with each other?

However, strategies do not always fall neatly into these categories and there is considerable overlap between them. For example, you may have labelled the last statement as affective, as it is concerned with telling oneself that one has succeeded, but there is also a cognitive aspect to it, as it is also to do with recalling words. When discussing strategies with learners, it is worth remembering that the strategies they use are likely to involve elements of different types as well as being highly personal.

Another way in which strategies have been classified is as direct or indirect. In her book *Language Learning Strategies: What Every Teacher Should Know*, Rebecca Oxford (1990) includes memory strategies, cognitive strategies, and compensation strategies under direct strategies. These strategies deal directly with the language itself, such as remembering, retrieving information, understanding and producing the language, and using the language when there are knowledge gaps. Indirect strategies include affective, social, and metacognitive strategies, and are thus concerned with controlling the emotions, maintaining social relations, and regulating the learning process rather than relating directly to the language itself. Once again, it is worth pointing out that there is a substantial amount of overlap between these groups, but the distinctions help us to become aware of the wide range of strategies that learners can use when learning a language.

Studies on learners' use of strategies show that they rarely use individual strategies in isolation but generally combinations of strategies. Erten (1998) provides an example of a Swiss student trying to learn the word 'bulk', having been given a definition and an example of its use in the sentence 'I've finished analysing the bulk of my data'. She explains her thought processes:

> … the most, the most things … bulk, bulk, bulk. The bulk, the ball, bulk, ball, sounds similar. It means it is not finished all, but mostly, most of the things but not all of them.
>
> (Erten, 1998, p. 219)

First, she defined the word for herself, saying 'the most, the most things'. Next, she repeated the word, 'bulk, bulk, bulk', and then found a phonemic association between 'bulk' and 'ball'. Finally, she modified her definition as 'most of the things but not all'. Thus, this learner combines several strategies in attempting to learn the word.

Unhelpful strategies

It is important to point out that not all strategies that students use are beneficial to learning. People develop strategies in order to manage a particular situation or cope with a specific problem. Students soon assess the characteristics of a setting and work out ways to survive in it. So, for example, in education systems where passing tests is important, learners will learn to use strategies to pass tests, rather than strategies to learn; these are strategies that are appropriate for 'surviving' in this setting. In a class where correct answers are valued at the expense of critical thinking, children will develop strategies to help give the right answer, rather than strategies of thinking and working things out. In his influential and thought-provoking book *How Children Fail*, John Holt (1982) provides striking examples of the ways in which school children become skilled at employing strategies that are important to their survival in a classroom situation. He calls these 'narrow and defensive strategies'. These are brought into play by pupils to try to make sense of what is going on in the classroom and meet the demands that are made of them. An example is the 'mumble an answer' strategy that he observed children using: believing that teachers are tuned in to hearing the correct answer, pupils mumble a response in the hope that the teacher will think it is correct. Another strategy he observed was children waving hands in the air to make the teacher think they knew the answer even if they did not, since the teacher would pick on those who did not have their hands up. Holt argues that children will often use coping strategies to complete the daily tasks they are given and notes that the really able thinkers in our classes are those who do not feel a strong need to please grown-ups at all costs but who work to improve their skills and abilities. In our teaching, we clearly wish to encourage critically reflective learners who are driven by the desire to learn for themselves and for the pleasure of improving and becoming more competent.

The role of context

As has been stressed throughout the book, the contexts in which learners find themselves influence many different aspects of the learning process, and these include the learning strategies that they use. Teachers therefore need to establish an environment in which there is an emphasis on learning rather than on correct answers—where learners are encouraged to work things out for themselves, ask questions, take risks, and learn from errors. We need to emphasize the importance of analyzing how the language works; of understanding what is behind a text rather than simply being able to answer factual comprehension questions; and of seeking ways of using the language even with limited competence. In this way, learners will be encouraged to employ strategies that foster learning. The choice of strategy will also be influenced by the social setting of the learners. For example, if they are in a country where there are many speakers of the target language, they might be able to use many more social strategies, whereas in an environment offering few such opportunities, they might tend to use social media, films, newspapers, or television.

Pedagogical implications

We have stressed that strategies should be selected and used appropriately. Learners need to choose strategies that are suitable for tackling the task at hand and that suit them as individuals, and they need to use these strategies effectively in combination. Learners who are unsuccessful may use many strategies but not select the most appropriate ones or be flexible in their use. If learners employ strategies appropriately, they can take more control of their own learning and greatly enhance the process in an independent way. Teachers can play an active role in helping learners to become aware of and experiment with a range of strategies. They can engage learners in discussions about the strategies they use, encouraging them to share these with classmates and try out new ones. This can lead to further discussion about how using the new strategies went. Learners can also observe the strategies their peers or teachers use and discuss each other's experiences.

Coping strategies

One useful way of getting students to reflect on and discuss their strategy use is to give them a questionnaire that lists different strategies and ask them to reflect on how often they use certain strategies. Examples of this type of questionnaire are provided in Oxford (1990) and Cohen and Chi (2002). Questionnaires such as these serve as a good starting point for discussions about different strategies, learners' own preferences, and other strategies and types of strategies they may wish to explore. As language educators, one of our goals is to help our learners to know how to learn a language and to become independent in doing so. It is in this respect that some form of 'strategy training' can be useful in empowering learners by equipping them with a range of strategies for tackling the complex task of learning a foreign language.

An area related to this is the growing field of teaching thinking skills. If people are taught to think critically, analytically, and creatively, to make decisions, and to solve problems, this will equip them to face the demands of the workplace in an ever-changing world and, more immediately, to learn more effectively. Herbert Puchta and Marion Williams (2011) have explored the teaching of thinking through the second language. Through learning to solve problems, make decisions, or recognize cause and effect, learners develop their second language ability at the same time as their thinking ability.

Activity 7.3	**Reflecting on your strategies**

Reflect on your preferred strategies for learning a language. If possible, compare your own responses with someone else's.

1 How do you go about learning and memorizing new words? For example, do you use index cards, imagery, sound combinations, or memory associations?

2 How do you mentally approach language learning tasks? Do you use repetition, look for patterns, compare languages you know, etc.?

3 How do you compensate in a conversation when you don't know a word? Do you paraphrase, use gestures, find a synonym, explore other languages for related words, or use other strategies?

4 How do you organize your learning? For example, do you set specific goals, use a notebook, use online organizers, or evaluate your progress?

5 How do you manage your emotions in learning? Do you try to reduce your anxiety, reward yourself for goals achieved, or talk with others about your feelings when learning a language?

6 How do you engage with other people to help you learn? Do you enjoy working with others? Do you seek out opportunities to use the language? Do you ask others to correct you?

Learning styles

Although there is some controversy surrounding the question of whether we really have individual learning styles, it does seem likely that we each have a broad set of preferences as to how we learn, even if these are not rigidly fixed. For ourselves as teachers, having a learning style preference affects the way we teach and we must consciously remind ourselves that others may approach language learning in quite different ways. This means that we need to consciously seek to accommodate different learning styles in the teaching methods that we employ. No learner style is inherently better than any other; they merely represent different ways of going about language learning. Naturally, styles are closely linked to the strategies we tend to use. Depending on our style preferences, we are likely to select specific strategies for particular tasks.

The number of possible ways of categorizing style preferences is considerable. Many different inventories for classifying styles have been developed, generating a 'quagmire' of style constructs (Dörnyei, 2005). For example, style preferences can be organized according to whether learners prefer visual, auditory, tactile, or more kinaesthetic input; whether they tend to be more active or passive, or more analytic or holistic in their approach; or whether they prefer to use their intuition or depend more on highly organized approaches (for example, Oxford, 1993; Reid, 1987; Willing, 1987). While it can be useful to be aware of our own and our learners' preferences, we must take care not to 'pigeon-hole' learners tightly into fixed categories. Instead, as with strategies, we should seek to encourage learners to remain flexible in adopting different styles for different purposes and experimenting with styles beyond their traditional comfort zones.

Self-regulation

Self-regulation is the overarching focus of this chapter and refers to the processes whereby learners control and regulate their own learning. It involves setting goals; taking actions such as using strategies; monitoring and evaluating learning actions and behaviours; and taking the necessary steps to keep ourselves on course to our goals. Self-regulatory learners are aware of themselves as learners. They know their own strengths and weaknesses as well as their preferred modes of learning. They are aware of what goals they wish to achieve, are motivated to work towards these, and have a plan of how to do it. They are able to observe and evaluate themselves as they go about the job of learning a language. Importantly, they feel a sense of control in their ability to regulate their own learning processes.

As teachers, we can support our students in becoming self-regulated learners by attending to these different stages. This means ensuring that they feel engaged and empowered to take control through feelings of agency and competence. As far as possible, we can encourage students to set their own goals, choose tasks and topics, and manage their own time. We can help them to set appropriate goals by raising their awareness of different types of goals, goal-setting strategies, and ways of monitoring progress towards goals. We can provide opportunities for conscious reflection on various learning behaviours and actions. We can encourage students to reflect on the strategies they use and how these contribute to their own goals. We can promote self-assessment rather than reliance on the teacher's assessment. We can also ask students to think about other behaviour, such as how they engage with and respond to peers, resources, feedback, and tasks.

| Activity 7.4 | **Exploring learning strategies** |

1 Ask your students to tell you some of the strategies they use to learn a language. Then ask them to make a list of the ways in which they personally learn and use the language in three columns:

Ways I learn new language	**Ways I communicate in the language**	**Ways I control my anxieties**

2 When they have finished their personal lists, put students into groups to look at each other's lists. Ask everyone to choose one or two strategies from other people's lists to try out during the next two weeks. Ask them to make notes in a journal about their experiences and bring the journals to class after two weeks.

3 In this next class, ask the students to report back on their experiences to their groups, explaining which strategies they may continue to use and which strategies didn't work for them and why. Ask them to make notes of their group discussion in their journals and submit these journals to you at the end of class.

4 Look through the journals of individual learners' experiences and their discussions. What have you learned about your students and their strategy preferences? Were there any surprises? How can you help them to develop their strategy use further?

Goals

Learners tend to have many goals, of which some may be set by the learners themselves and some by others. They may wish to be popular in school; they may wish to work on a task with a specific peer with whom they want to become friends; they may wish to do well in exams to get a place on a prestigious training programme; or they may wish to conquer a specific challenge such as being able to order a meal in a restaurant on their own. Goals may be more short-term in nature, for example, 'I want to read my first full-length novel in the foreign language', or they may be more long-term, for example, 'I want to become a foreign language teacher working in another country'. As teachers, we want to encourage our learners to achieve their language-related goals; however, it is important to understand that not all goals are desirable. Clearly, we do not wish to support learners towards goals such as failing an exam to spite a parent or cutting one of their peers out of a group activity. Attending to positive, constructive, forward-looking goals is vital. Social goals can be promoted through group cohesion activities, and language goals can be discussed and worked towards with supportive frameworks. A popular acronym used in goal setting is 'SMART goals', which refers to goals which are specific, measurable, achievable, realistic and relevant, and time-bound (Doran, 1981). Attending to these characteristics of goals makes it more likely that we will achieve them and we can work with learners in helping them to explicitly express their specific goals for a course or academic year in these terms.

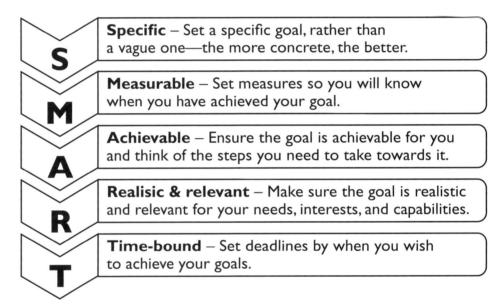

Figure 7.1 SMART goals

An important distinction between different types of goals concerns what are known as mastery goals and performance goals, as we discussed in Chapter 6 in respect to motivation. Mastery goals refer to the types of goals in which a learner wants to 'master' some new skills or knowledge. An example would be a student who wants to be able to understand a favourite TV show in the foreign language and who is willing to work to achieve the idiomatic language frequently used in the show. In fact, this reflects what is known as a **mastery-approach goal**, in which the aim is to 'master' the content for one's own growth and learning. **Mastery-avoidance goals** refer to a learner's desire to master the subject but driven by a need to avoid a possible negative outcome. An example would be a student who wants to learn all the vocabulary in a unit so as not to misunderstand the teacher or the texts and exercises set for homework. Performance goals refer to the kinds of goals in which a learner wants to 'perform' to others. A student who wants to impress her friends on a school trip with how much she can say in an encounter in a coffee shop would be one example. This would also be an illustration of a **performance-approach goal**, in which the aim is to make a good impression on others and show how good one is to one's peers. The other type of performance goal is a **performance-avoidance goal**, in which the emphasis is on the learner not wanting to look bad in front of others. An example could be a learner who wants to learn to speak in a club so as not to make a fool of himself in front of his friends. Naturally, learners' goals can involve a combination of these goal orientations, which are not mutually exclusive.

Metacognition

Another vital component of self-regulatory behaviour is an ability to plan and control how we learn and think about our own learning, and it is this aspect that we turn to next. Let us consider a student trying to read a document about global warming in a foreign language to gain information in preparation for a presentation on the subject. The student gets her vocabulary notebook and her dictionary and sits by a computer so she can look things up if necessary. She thinks about what she already knows about the subject and makes some notes on a mind map as well as writing down some questions she would like answered. She decides first to read the text quickly to try to understand the gist of the passage and see if the text is suitable for her purpose before she reads it more carefully. She writes some of the new words that she might want to use in her presentation in her vocabulary notebook, looks for ways of remembering their meanings, and looks up the pronunciation of some of the words so she can use them correctly. She then writes some more notes on her mind map, ready to prepare her presentation, and thinks of ways to put her message across convincingly to her audience. This student is engaging in what is known as metacognitive behaviour, a crucial aspect of effective learning.

Metacognition is, in essence, an awareness of one's own cognitive processes in learning. It involves thinking about and understanding how we learn, as well as regulating and controlling our learning. Both of these aspects are important features of metacognition. While cognitive strategies are mental processes concerned with processing information in order to learn, metacognitive strategies involve learners looking at their learning from outside, as it were, in order to see how they are approaching it and plan the strategies they will use to learn. It also involves reflecting on and understanding what we know. In other words, metacognition is concerned with thinking about one's thinking and knowing about one's knowing. Our thinking is cognition, while thinking about our thinking is metacognition. This is a vital distinction. If we use our thinking strategically to complete a task, we are acting cognitively. If we understand, regulate, and control our use of learning strategies, we are acting metacognitively.

Metacognition involves different types of knowing. As Flavell—one of the pioneers of the metacognitive movement—identified, it includes knowing about oneself as a learner, knowing about the task, and knowing about the strategies one can use to carry out the task (Flavell, 1979). These three types of knowledge are essential for acting strategically on a task. So, for example, I know I am nervous as a language user and I like to get things right. My task is to buy a train ticket at a busy station in a language I am not very familiar with. There is a queue, so I know I need to be fairly quick about my purchase. I first look up the word 'ticket' in my dictionary, and then select the strategy of rehearsing 'Please can I have a ticket to X?' Next, I go through numbers so that I might understand the price. Finally, I take a deep breath to control my nerves, and ask for my ticket.

Anderson (2012) explains that 'metacognition is the ability to make one's thinking visible. It is the ability to reflect on what one knows and does and what one does not know and does not do' (p.170). He sees metacognition as involving different components or stages. These include planning for learning, deciding when to use strategies, monitoring their use, combining strategies where appropriate, and evaluating their effectiveness. These stages are not linear, but a shifting pattern— moving backwards and forwards from one stage to another—and more than one process might be operating at one time. Metacognition also involves self-assessment and the ability to make changes in how one learns when appropriate. In the example above, the student planned how she was going to work, used different strategies to understand and to learn, and finally reviewed what she had learned. Her mind was engaged in planning and regulating the learning process itself.

There have been many different ways of categorizing metacognitive strategies. Basically, learners first need to focus their attention on the task and the skills required to carry out the task. This involves linking new material with what is already known, a constructivist concept. (See Chapter 1 for a discussion of constructivism.) Next, they need to plan their learning. This includes identifying the purpose of a learning task, organizing their learning, and setting goals. Learners then need to select and use strategies, and for this, they need to understand the range of strategies available. They then monitor their progress and evaluate how effective this strategy was for them.

Clearly, metacognition is a vital component of self-regulation. The evidence from the literature strongly suggests that individuals who use metacognitive strategies are more effective learners, and that training in metacognitive strategies facilitates language learning, as well as developing learner autonomy and agency. It is clear from this discussion that the teacher needs to play a role in helping learners to develop their metacognitive abilities in order to become effective learners. We would argue that empowering learners to know how to learn is every bit as important as imparting subject knowledge. In discussing the role of the teacher, Anderson (2012) stresses that teaching learners to understand and control their cognitive processes is one of the most important skills that teachers can develop in their students. He explains that

> [r]ather than focusing students' attention only on issues related to learning content, effective teachers structure a learning atmosphere where thinking about what happens in the learning process leads to stronger learning skills.

> (Anderson, 2012, p. 172)

Teachers and coursebook writers can integrate a metacognitive component into their language lessons in many different ways. One way is to engage learners in reflecting on how they learn. They can keep learning diaries, where, after completing an activity, they reflect on what strategies they used. They can compare their strategy use with others through discussion and decide whether there are any new strategies they would like to try out and add to their repertoires. They can also assess themselves after an activity; teachers can give students the grading criteria that they will later use themselves. In this way, teachers can get an insight into whether learners overestimate or underestimate their abilities and also into learners' perceived strengths and weaknesses. Such reflections lead to greater learner autonomy and control, and, ultimately, to more effective learning.

Activity 7.5

Managing language learning

The following statements were made by different children from Hong Kong who were settling into a school environment in the UK (Berry, 1998). They all spoke English as a second language. These are descriptions of how they tried to manage their studies in English. What does each statement tell us about the child's metacognitive behaviour? What differences can you see between these children?

1 'I listened a lot. I also read a lot. I read anything such as leaflets, etc. I watched English films.'
2 'I talked a lot with my room-mate. I rehearsed what I wanted to say in my mind before I spoke.'
3 'I only checked those new words which appeared frequently in the book because they might reappear later.'
4 'I chose story books which were only one level above my English standard. Then there were only a few words I didn't know from the text.'
5 'I talked to my room-mates. If they didn't talk to me I would take the initiative and talk to them. I wouldn't just wait for my room-mates to talk to me. Every evening I spoke at least a few times in English.'
6 'I thought about my cousin who is now over 20 years old. I imagined myself as my cousin and tried to see things from her point of view … She should know things better than I do. I could really sort things out.'
7 'I plan to improve my grammar by doing as many English exercises as possible.'
8 'In order to help understand the book, I bought a guide book and watched the film *Romeo and Juliet*.'

So, for instance, the child in Example 1 liked to have language input to process; the child in Example 2 liked to communicate and found that rehearsal was a useful strategy; and the child in Example 7 had plans to study grammar by doing focused exercises. These represent very different, but effective, ways to go about learning.

Summary

In this chapter, we have explored the ways in which multiple facets of learner psychology combine to generate learners' sense of agency. This sense of capability, engagement, and willingness is vital for them to feel empowered to take control and self-regulate their own learning as autonomous learners. We have considered the importance of contextual resources for language learning and the need to understand how learners interpret the relevance of resources, rather than seeing the materials themselves as having inherent beneficial characteristics. We then discussed different types of strategies that learners can employ to learn and use a language, and considered how these strategy choices can reflect style preferences. We also looked at other components of self-regulation, such as goal setting, and the core skills for directing one's own learning that stem from metacognition and using metacognitive strategies. We conclude that teachers need not only to teach their learners the language but also to support them in knowing how to learn and how to manage their learning, equipping them with the skills to become independent and potentially lifelong language learners.

Questions for reflection

1　Consider the classes you teach. How much opportunity is there for learners to exercise agency and feel in control of their learning? Could you make any improvements in this respect within your institutional and cultural constraints?

2　Learners benefit from discussing the strategies they use and trying out and evaluating new ones. What specific ideas do you have for doing this with your students at different levels and ages?

3　In what ways could you help your students become more metacognitively aware in their learning? How can you help them to plan their learning, select how they will go about it, and monitor their progress?

Suggestions for further reading

Mercer, S., **Ryan, S.**, & **Williams, M.** (Eds.). (2012). *Psychology for language learning.* Basingstoke: Palgrave Macmillan.
This edited volume provides an overview of current theory and research in psychology in foreign language learning. In Chapter 10, **Cohen** provides a comprehensible summary of the latest thinking on learning strategies. In Chapter 12, **Anderson** summarizes the subject of metacognition and provides good examples of how to integrate metacognitive training into the curriculum.

Griffiths, C. (2013). *The strategy factor in successful language learning.* Bristol: Multilingual Matters.
This readable book examines the link between strategy use and successful language learning, considering elements such as frequency and choice of strategies. It contains an excellent section exploring pedagogical concerns and discussing how strategy training can be conducted, as well as factors to consider in strategy instruction. It also includes useful questionnaires for student reflection.

Cohen, A. D., & **Macaro, E.** (Eds.). (2007). *Language learner strategies.* Oxford: Oxford University Press.
This collection of papers offers a contemporary overview of key issues in the field of language strategy research. Although the book focuses on an agenda for strategy research, it also indirectly generates rich insights for practice.

8

BRINGING IT TOGETHER

Introduction

Throughout this book, we have emphasized the importance of the connections and interactions between the various psychological constructs, and shown ways in which they are linked together. Nevertheless, for organizational reasons, each chapter has inevitably focused on a specific topic area. In this final chapter, we shift our attention to a more explicit discussion of the interactions that we have alluded to in the earlier chapters.

Teachers know intuitively about the interconnections between different facets of their learners' psychologies and the ways in which these all link to the different social groups their learners move in. Teachers also understand that all these aspects influence learning. Think of the ways in which you and your colleagues discuss learners and issues in your classes. You might make statements such as this:

> Omar got a bad grade on his last test and seems to think that he'll never be able to learn a language, no matter what he does. As a result, he really seems to have no motivation at all right now. In class, he seems bored and uninterested. He won't make any effort or do his homework, and he has no goals or ambitions at the moment. I'm also starting to worry that his low motivation is spreading to his friends, and sometimes even the entire class seems to be struggling under the influence of his negativity.

While this is a fictitious statement, many teachers will recognize the kinds of connections we make between different psychological aspects of our learners as we do here between attributions, motivation, emotions, effort, goals, contagion, and group dynamics.

In this final chapter, we will attempt to bring together the different aspects of learning that we have addressed in the various chapters of this book and to view the psychology of language learning as a whole, rather than in terms of its constituent parts. We show how integrating these aspects can provide a lens through which to view and understand different areas of learning and teaching.

Activity 8.1   **Thinking about different psychological aspects**

Think of a particular individual that you have taught. How would you describe that learner in terms of the different psychological constructs covered in this book? Write them in the table below. If possible, compare your student with a colleague's (without revealing the name of the student). What are the reasons for these differences?

Psychological construct	Description of student
Cultural context	
Ability to work in a group	
Self-concept	
Facilitative or debilitative beliefs about learning	
Mindsets	
Attributions for success and failure	
Positive and negative emotions towards language learning	
Anxiety	
Ability to set goals	
Types of motivation	
Sense of agency	
Strategies used	

Photocopiable © Oxford University Press

Willingness to communicate (WTC)

We will begin by exploring the concept of **willingness to communicate (WTC)** and use this as an example of how the different elements we have addressed come together to influence our learners and ourselves as teachers at any one point in time. In the second part of the chapter, we reflect on the book as a whole and consider what practical lessons we can draw from a holistic consideration of the insights from all of the chapters. We have articulated these in the form of a set of principles, mindful of the need for teachers to critically appraise these as appropriate to their own unique settings and needs.

Activity 8.2

Comparing activities in our first and second language

Look at the following list. Which of these things do you think you would feel comfortable doing in your first language? Which would you feel comfortable doing in a language that you were learning?

	L1 Yes/No	L2 Yes/No
volunteer an opinion in front of a group of people, such as in a class or meeting		
tell a joke or funny story to a small group of people you know reasonably well		
ask for help in buying some unfamiliar item of food in a shop		
offer to help a stranger who appears to be lost		
say something to a child who is misbehaving in a public place		
send a note of condolence to a colleague		
give a presentation on your hobby to a group of strangers		
make a telephone call to check precise details of an order		
ask for directions when lost		
compliment a colleague on what they are wearing		
write a short thank-you email to a friend		
order a meal in a restaurant		
start up a conversation with a stranger next to you in a public place, for example, on a bus or plane		

Photocopiable © Oxford University Press

Were there any major differences between your responses for L1 and L2? How would you explain these differences?

L2 willingness to communicate (**L2 WTC**) combines various aspects of language learning psychology. It was originally conceived of as a personality trait to explain why some people appear to be more willing to communicate than others. The original theory and research related to L1 communication (McCroskey & Richmond, 1987, 1991). However, since communication is an obvious goal of foreign language education, it was not long before researchers began to explore how the concept could be applied to second or foreign language learners. According to MacIntyre (2007), WTC represents the 'probability of initiating communication given choice and opportunity' (p. 567). Fundamental to the notion of L2 WTC is an awareness that when people communicate in a second language, the experiences and associated thoughts and feelings do not necessarily duplicate how they would feel in respect to communicating in their first language. At times, L2 users may feel inhibited by various factors, such as their lack of active vocabulary or unfamiliar settings or interlocutors; however, there may be times when communicating in the L2 can be a liberating experience and individuals actually feel more willing to communicate.

If we reflect on some of the possible factors contributing to our L2 WTC, we can probably think of a host of things, ranging from a simple lack of interest in the immediate task or lesson to deep-rooted anxieties about being able to communicate in a foreign language in front of others. Indeed, our L2 WTC may be influenced by a combination of factors, such as a poor relationship with the interlocutor or dislike of the topic under discussion. Clearly, any meaningful model of L2 WTC needs to acknowledge this range of possible interacting factors. Perhaps the best-known model of L2 WTC is the so-called pyramid model (MacIntyre, Clément, Dörnyei, & Noels, 1998). The pyramid model describes L2 WTC in terms of an array of interacting factors. (See Figure 8.1.) At the base of the pyramid are relatively stable factors, such as personality and what has been called intergroup climate. Intergroup climate refers to the position and status of the target language within the society in which it is being learned. At the apex of the pyramid is actual L2 use in a specific situation. In between these two extremes come a range of situational and contextual factors that combine with learner characteristics like communicative competence and/or L2 self-confidence.

Within this model, a host of contextual and personal factors come together at any one moment to lead to a learner using or not using the L2. This model has elements of the immediate situational level from the nested systems model presented in Chapters 1 and 2, and also elements of the more global macro-level. So, for example, a learner's L2 WTC will be affected at a macro-level by social norms and expectations of behaviour according to age, gender, and power dynamics across social groups in a particular culture, as well as by societal attitudes towards the language being learned. At a micro-level, WTC will be influenced by how learners feel in a specific social situation, how familiar they are with that setting, and their relationships to those they are communicating with. The temporal dimension of the nested systems model also plays a role; other factors determining WTC may be learners' past experiences in comparable situations, what they would like to use the language for in the future, and how important this

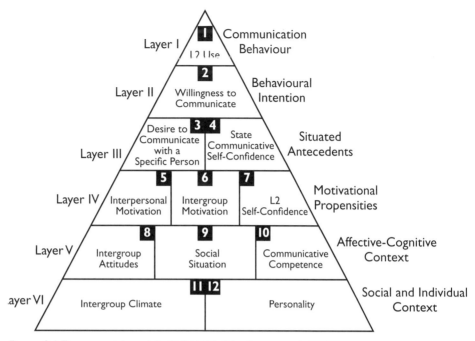

Figure 8.1 The pyramid model of L2 WTC (MacIntyre et al., 1998)

interaction is for them now or in the long term. As with the nested systems model, all of these contextual layers and temporal factors come together and interact with learners and their characteristics at any one time.

Here we are using the example of willingness to communicate to illustrate how the different aspects of psychology discussed in this book can be brought together to explain a particular aspect of teaching. For example, to what do learners attribute past successful and less successful experiences in using the language? What do they believe about the nature of their abilities and how changeable they are? How competent do learners feel they are? How do they compare themselves to others? How motivated are they to interact in this setting? How motivated are they generally to use the language given the opportunity to do so? What emotions does the situation elicit? What mood are they in at that point in time? What communication strategies are they aware of and how comfortable do they feel using them?

While we can acknowledge that the interplay of all these psychological factors at any one moment leads to specific behaviours on the part of the learner, the challenge for us as teachers is not to feel overwhelmed by the complexity and dynamism of all these different aspects. We need to be sensitive to and understanding of the fact that our learners are complex individuals whose behaviour in class will be influenced by a range of factors we may not be aware of. It is often helpful for learners to think about and discuss things that help them to learn or communicate in an L2 and those that inhibit them, to raise their own awareness of these issues, and perhaps to discuss ways to overcome the more negative aspects. Having illustrated how the various aspects of psychology we discuss can be brought together to examine one facet of teaching, we will now attempt to integrate the different aspects and present a set of principles.

A guide to structuring more holistic thinking about psychology

In this section, we suggest a set of principles to help guide our thinking about language learning psychology in practice by clustering key insights from the chapters together into more holistic guidelines. However, in doing so, we are aware that there are no easy solutions to working with the complexity of learner psychology without oversimplifying. We need to outline a few caveats first. It is, to some degree, inevitable that we have to generalize or simplify reality to make it manageable and comprehensible. As we saw above in the case of WTC, it is impossible to account for every aspect of an individual's learning behaviour.

Here we would like to consider four main types of simplification that people may engage in when discussing language learning psychology. The first form of simplification is to reduce the complexity of the interrelatedness between the diverse elements of an individual's psychology and the contexts they act within. As with the organization of this book, a need for clarity often leads writers and researchers to consider individual aspects of a person's psychology in isolation. While this is indeed useful in making the different aspects easier to understand, it does risk painting an incomplete or even inaccurate picture. If, for example, we think about the emotions an individual feels at any one point in a class, they can be influenced by a host of factors, such as the topic, peers, motivation, self-concept, memories of things that occurred earlier in the day, anticipation of an event later in the day, or various combinations of all of the above. We therefore tend to focus on what we perceive as the most salient elements or those that are easiest and most likely to change. Think of how motivated you feel to work today; it is doubtful you can reduce this to a single factor. It is true that one element may play a more dominant role at one time than at another, but it is usually an accumulation or combination of several factors together. A related form of simplification is reducing human behaviour to simplistic cause-and-effect relationships, in which a change in one factor is portrayed as causing a corresponding change in another. However, in reality, our behaviour is typically much more complex than this. What we think and feel affects what we do, but, in turn, what we do affects what we think and feel.

The second form of simplification is a tendency to consider constructs in binary terms—in other words, we classify something as good/bad, high/low, or positive/negative. Such dichotomies can be found in all areas of language learning—for example, native speaker/non-native speaker, learner-centred/teacher-centred, authentic/non-authentic. However, these dichotomies rarely reflect reality, which is not usually so neat and categorical, and which instead tends to contain more blurred boundaries than distinct extremes. For example, if we recall the discussion of mindsets (see Chapter 4), we saw how this is often couched in terms of fixed (bad) and growth (good). The reality is that most people lie somewhere in between the extremes on a continuum and one's actual mindset is often a unique blend of the two. Similarly, we often discuss self-concept in terms of having a positive/high or negative/low self-concept. (See Chapter 3.) Instead, we suggested that it is more appropriate to consider a healthy self-concept, which is realistic and balanced.

A third way in which we simplify learner psychology is to perceive of constructs as fixed and static. In this way, we avoid having to confront the way in which learners' psychology changes across contexts and time. For example, we may talk about a learner being motivated as if that individual were always equally and consistently motivated. However, we know from our own experiences that our motivation may vary within the timeframe of a single class, from day to day, and across the lifespan of our career. Therefore, it helps to remain conscious of the potential for change in learner psychology across micro-timescales of minutes within a class as well as across macro-timescales, such as the course of an academic year. A useful analogy here might be the difference between a still image and a moving picture; when considering or describing language learners and their psychology, we should aim to see them as a moving picture that captures change across time and situations.

The fourth thing people do to make the diversity of the real world manageable is to make generalizations about contexts and cultures. We all make generalizations (see Figure 8.2) and they can be very useful tools at times. However, in some cases, generalizations can lead to the labelling of students, perhaps as a particular 'type' or in connection to certain groups to which they belong. These stereotypes and

Analysing dichotomies

prejudices about a group or culture stem from over-simplification of a complex entity. Groups are very rarely homogeneous and they are usually full of unique individuals, who may vary from whatever is considered to be the group norm. While we may usefully think about typical cultural norms and values in a setting and how these may be influencing a learner's psychology, we must also keep our minds open to the notion that individuals often do not fit these patterns.

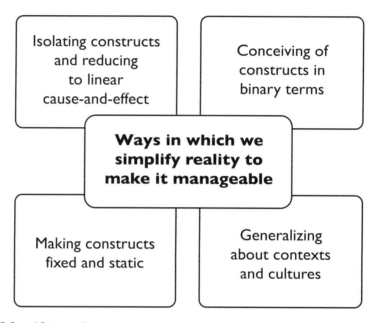

Figure 8.2 Simplifying reality

In the remainder of this chapter, we pull together the issues discussed in the book and suggest some guidelines which combine the insights from across the chapters and relate them to classroom practice. We do not intend these guidelines to be seen as definitive or prescriptive, but rather as a base from which you can reflect on and evaluate their appropriateness for your own specific context.

Principles for practice

So what are some general principles that can help guide our practices in respect to language learning psychology? Naturally, the guidelines we offer here represent our own subjective and selective interpretations of the chapters, and you may take individual points from each chapter that are of particular interest or relevance to you. Nevertheless, we hope this set of guidelines can support you in your teaching and help translate some of the insights from the book into useful principles for practice.

Principle 1: Remember to be group-centred as well as learner-centred.

One of the key points emerging from all the chapters is that individuals are socially situated within groups and cannot be thought of as separate from them. While individual learners affect the group they are part of, the group affects the individual within it too. Therefore, while there has been recognition of the importance of learner-centred approaches in language teaching, we feel that there also needs to be an awareness of the importance of the group and its dynamics. A healthy group atmosphere is vital for effective learning and for the well-being of all in the group, including ourselves as teachers. As outlined in Chapter 2, a positive group atmosphere can be promoted by cultivating a sense of trust, interest, and group belonging and identity among members. We must remember to support positive relationships between the learners in a class and be mindful of their need for social connection and interaction. Nevertheless, we should not lose sight of the individuals and their uniqueness in how we work with our groups. It is important to maintain an appropriate balance between the view of the whole group and its individual members.

Principle 2: Learners' lives beyond the classroom are central to who they are.

Another theme that emerges from the chapters is that learners in our language classrooms can never be separated from the other areas of their lives. When they enter our classrooms, they bring a host of experiences, beliefs, values, and feelings with them, and these can strongly affect how they behave and engage with language learning. Their lives beyond the language classroom are a key part of who they are and what is important to them. When learners are able to connect language learning to other areas of their lives, it can help them to feel valued and respected as individuals and can boost their motivation. Some ways of doing this include asking learners to do projects on hobbies or give presentations on topics that interest them, basing lessons around language that emerges from discussion with learners, discussing learners' aims and aspirations in life, or asking them to write their language learning history. Fundamentally, we need to try to provide ways for learners to incorporate other aspects of their lives that are important to them into their language learning and take an interest in learners as individuals with lives beyond the language classroom.

Principle 3: Ensure open pathways of communication with learners.

Throughout the book, we have stressed the importance of good relationships between members of a group, and here the teacher plays a crucial role. In building positive relationships, the teacher can engage in dialogue with learners, seek their opinions, learn to really listen to them, and give them opportunities to talk and share their perspectives on topics as well as classroom practices. This fosters a sense of agency in learners, helping them to become engaged and feel that their opinions matter. If learners misbehave, we can seek to find out why by opening a genuine, respectful dialogue with those individuals, giving them a chance to share with us their view of events. Being accessible as a teacher and open to dialogue can go a long way towards providing students with a positive and communicative environment in which to learn and use languages.

Principle 4: Promote a belief in the potential for everyone to improve their abilities.

This principle stems from our understandings of mindsets and self-beliefs, as discussed in Chapters 3 and 4. However, it also underpins many other factors, such as motivation, emotions, and self-regulation, making it a hub in learner psychology. Fundamentally, we want all our learners to feel a sense of agency and believe that they can improve their language skills. This does not mean that we want learners to have unrealistic beliefs, but believing that they can improve is central to optimism and positivity about the language learning experience. Nobody is fixed in their abilities, which can always be expanded. This means that all learners can develop their skills compared to where they currently are, given an investment of time and energy together with effective strategy use and self-regulation. We need to work consciously at ensuring learners share this belief by discussing beliefs about language learning explicitly; promoting appropriate attributions; showing by the feedback we give that we believe they can improve; and examining positive role models who exemplify commitment and persistence rather than natural, effortless talent.

Principle 5: Provide opportunities for and encourage self-regulation.

Principle 4 is a prerequisite for this next point. Learners need to feel empowered with a sense of control over their learning. There are many ways for teachers to support learners' agency and self-regulation, as discussed in Chapter 7. These include allowing them freedom and choice where possible; helping them to set appropriate goals; raising their awareness of themselves and how best to learn language; and ensuring they are aware of a range of strategies for language learning and use. Not only can we provide opportunities for learners to self-regulate but we should also be encouraging them to engage with and invest in their language skills beyond the classroom. This can be achieved through projects and tasks that connect with real-world opportunities to use the language, as well as by raising awareness of language learning opportunities inside and outside of the classroom.

Principle 6: Promote positive emotions and reduce anxiety in the language classroom.

We know that fear can inhibit participation and generate negative group dynamics. As language learning can induce anxiety, we must take care not to add any additional fear to the process. For example, the ways in which we respond to learner mistakes can influence the level of anxiety in a language classroom. We all recognize that mistakes are a healthy part of the learning process and we need to ensure our responses, feedback, and classroom behaviour convey that message too. In addition—rather than just focusing on reducing the negative—we also need to promote positive emotions, such as enjoyment, pride, and curiosity. Basically, we want our classrooms to be positive places in which to encounter and use language with others, and working on the emotional climate is a central factor contributing to that positivity. With an absence of anxiety and a healthy set of positive emotions, learners are ideally placed to be motivated and engaged, feel safe to take risks, and push themselves to develop their skills.

Principle 7: Plan with motivation in mind.

As teachers, we intuitively recognize the centrality of learner motivation in successful language learning—including positive attitudes towards the language and its teaching. Many of the other principles will ultimately lead to enhanced learner motivation when learners feel a sense of agency, competence, positive emotions, interest, and a supportive group climate. However, we can also ensure, when organizing our classes, that we plan with motivation in mind. This means that when working on our lesson plans, we can explicitly consider the content, tasks, overall goals, methods, etc. from the perspective of how motivating they are for our specific learners in terms of interest, relevance, challenge, variation, potential to set and evaluate goals, and scope for creative and critical thinking and autonomy.

Principle 8: As teachers, we should seek to serve as positive role models for learners.

Finally, we know from our discussions of mindsets, attributions, self-concepts, group interactions, use of strategies, etc. that learners benefit considerably from positive modelling of these and from examples to emulate. As teachers, we have the potential—alongside peers and parents—to serve as influential role models for our learners. We need to be careful about the kind of language we use when talking with students about their work, abilities, and behaviour, as well as about language learning itself. We can work on exemplifying growth mindsets towards language learning through the way we talk about mistakes, successes, goals, and the processes of language learning. As we saw in Chapter 6, learners soon pick up on their teacher's passion and enthusiasm for teaching, and this means that we should not be afraid to display our own enthusiasm, curiosity, and love of learning to learners. Additionally, we can share our willingness to learn and accept mistakes as a healthy part of the learning process.

Summary

The central message of this final chapter, and of this book as a whole, has been that there are no one-size-fits-all recipes for successful language teaching, and that learning is dependent upon an ever-changing, complex interaction of factors. We are all different: what works with one student may not work with another; what works in one class may not work in another; what works for one teacher may not work for another. We hope you, the reader, will reflect critically on these principles and the contents of this book, evaluating them in the light of your own beliefs, values, and preferred teaching styles, as well as according to the particularities, characteristics, and needs of your own setting.

Language teaching is a complex, challenging, but hugely rewarding profession. Clearly, as language teachers, we need knowledge of the target language itself and we also need to know about the nature of language—how it is learned and specific methods for teaching various aspects of language. Yet we must remember that language learning and use are inherently social undertakings. We need to appreciate the highly emotional nature of learning a language, which can be so closely tied to our sense of self and to our ability to present ourselves to others. For these reasons, we are convinced that a central skill in any language teacher's toolkit is an understanding of the psychology surrounding the experience in order to ensure we acknowledge the emotional, social, and motivational, as well as cognitive and metacognitive, dimensions of learning a language. It also means recognizing the importance of individuals as social human beings and, consequently, the centrality of the relationships we form with learners in the course of teaching. Teaching languages is rarely a straightforward job, but we hope the perspective presented in this book can offer some insights to add to your repertoire of skills and help you to teach with an understanding of the special human and social dimensions of the language classroom in mind. Most of all, we hope you have enjoyed this book; we hope that you feel reading it has enhanced your teaching and inspired you to learn more about this fascinating dimension of teaching and learning.

Suggestions for further reading

McCombs, B. L., & **Miller, L.** (2007). *Learner-centred classroom practices and assessments: Maximizing student motivation, learning and achievement.* Thousand Oaks, CA: Corwin Press.
An excellent book that is based on research from educational psychology. Despite the title, it does not only focus on individuals but presents a broad, psychology-based approach to creating an effective and positive learning environment and offers practical strategies for practice.

Gregersen. T., & **MacIntyre, P.** (2014b). *Capitalizing on language learners' individuality: From premise to practice.* Bristol: Multilingual Matters.
Written in a highly accessible style, this book covers many of the same topics addressed the current volume. The authors are ambitious in the ways that they successfully bridge theory and practice. Each chapter provides a succinct theoretical overview of a particular learner characteristic and this is supplemented by a related series of practical classroom activities.

Dörnyei, Z., & **Ryan, S.** (2015). *The psychology of the language learner revisited.* New York, NY: Routledge.
This is the second edition of what has become a classic text in the field of language learner psychology and would be particularly recommended for readers interested in further explorations of the theoretical dimension. In this new edition, the authors not only update the original text but also engage in a critical dialogue with it. This provides a useful insight into how thinking on the psychology of the language learner has changed in recent years, and how it continues to do so.

GLOSSARY

accommodation: Piaget's term for modifying existing knowledge to include new input.

achievement theory: A theory of motivation that describes how people have differing needs for achievement, and how these needs lead to action.

affect: An umbrella term covering emotions, moods, and feelings.

affective filter: The processes through which negative emotions can filter out language input and thus impede language acquisition.

affective strategies: Strategies used to regulate emotions, such as breathing deeply to lower anxiety.

affordances: The perceived resources in the environment that learners can interact with in order to learn.

agency: A feeling held by individuals that they have control over their actions.

anxiety: Feelings of nervousness and unease that can have physical manifestations, such as shortness of breath or increased heart rate.

appraisals: The evaluations individuals make of a particular situation, which, in turn, lead to a particular emotional response.

approach orientation: An orientation to engage in activities as a means of achieving a desired outcome, for example, engaging in learning a language to develop one's proficiency in the language or to master a task.

assimilation: Piaget's term for combining new information with existing knowledge.

attention: Concentration of mental effort and filtering out of distractions.

attributional dimensions: A way of classifying attributions that refers to the extent to which individuals explain outcomes as being due to factors that:
1 are within their own control
2 are internal or external
3 may change over time.

attributions: An individual's explanations of the reasons for particular outcomes, such as perceived success and failure experiences.

audiolingual method: An approach to language teaching based on a behaviourist theory of learning, which views learning a language as habit-formation, typically involving repetition or substitution.

avoidance orientation: An orientation to engage in activities as a means of avoiding unwanted or undesirable outcomes, for example, learning a language to avoid miscommunication in a multilingual work environment.

behaviourism: A theory of psychology which claims that learning takes place through habit-formation.

big-fish-little-pond effect: The effect that can occur when individuals in groups organized according to ability develop a self-concept that reflects comparisons with others in this restricted group, instead of with others from the bigger social group. Typically, an individual in a group of relatively low ability (little pond) gains an unduly high self-concept (big fish).

broaden-and-build: A theory of positive psychology which holds that positive emotions can help individuals to develop skills and the capacity to learn.

cognitive approach: An approach to learning which focuses on mental processes and emphasizes the value of the human mind being actively engaged in learning.

cognitive strategies: Conscious mental processes learners employ to learn and use a language, such as memorizing words or analyzing language features.

collective agency: A belief that as a group or team we have the ability to direct and control our actions to achieve our goals.

collective efficacy: A belief that as a group or team we have the ability to achieve our goals.

collectivist culture: Cultures which are believed to emphasize group goals and values.

community of practice: A group of people who work together, engaging in common activities and sharing practices in a specific domain.

compensation strategies: Strategies used to compensate for a lack of knowledge of the language, such as using mime or gesture.

competence: A fundamental psychological need to feel capable of performing a given task or of functioning in a particular situation.

complexity perspectives: An umbrella term for a range of different perspectives that are all based on systems thinking (see also *systems thinking*).

conditioning: A process of getting animals or humans to respond to a stimulus in a desired way and reinforcing the behaviour so it happens more frequently.

constructivism: A psychological approach concerned with how individuals develop their personal understandings of the world.

contagion: Anything that is contagious. In the psychology literature, the term is often used in connection with emotions and describes how feelings such as enthusiasm or motivation can be caught from others.

debilitative anxiety: Feelings of anxiety that can impede or hinder performance or learning.

debilitative beliefs: Beliefs that can impede or hinder successful learning

downward social comparison: When learners compare themselves with others they perceive as less competent.

drive theory: A theory of motivation which holds that people are 'driven' to meet internal needs, such as hunger or thirst.

ecological psychology: A psychological theory which argues that individuals must be understood within the context of their environmental systems.

emotional intelligence: The ability to recognize or understand one's own and other people's emotions.

empathy: Understanding the world from someone else's perspective and being able to put oneself in that person's shoes.

engagement: A personal investment in the learning process and an inner drive to learn and improve.

entity theory: A belief that aspects of the human condition such as intelligence or ability are fixed and therefore cannot be changed or developed.

epistemological beliefs: Beliefs about the nature of knowledge and learning.

expectancy beliefs: The belief that we have the capacity to do something specific in respect to using or learning a language.

expectancy–value: A concept of motivation which describes how people are motivated to act based upon the value they associate with a given act and the perceived likelihood of success.

explicit beliefs: Beliefs we hold that we are fully aware of and able to articulate.

extrinsic motivation: Motivation to engage in a particular activity as a means to some external outcome or reward.

facilitative anxiety: Feelings of anxiety that can enhance performance or learning.

facilitative beliefs: Beliefs that contribute to successful learning.

fixed mindset: A set of beliefs and assumptions formed around the notion that aspects of the human condition cannot be changed or developed.

flow: A feeling of being fully immersed or involved in doing a particular activity.

foreign language anxiety: A particular form of anxiety associated with the use of a foreign language.

formal operational thinking: One of Piaget's stages of development, during which individuals begin to use abstract reasoning.

goal-setting theory: A theory which considers goals in terms of their specificity, perceived difficulty, and our degree of commitment.

Golem effect: Where teachers' negative evaluations of learners can function as strong impediments to learning.

growth mindset: A set of beliefs and assumptions formed around the notion that aspects of the human condition can be changed or developed through focused effort.

holistic learning: Learning which considers the whole person.

humanism: An approach to psychology which emphasizes the importance of feelings and emotions.

ideal L2 self: A possible future self deriving from an individual's dreams and aspirations as an L2 learner and user.

identity: How we view ourselves in relation to specific contexts and groups.

implicit beliefs: Beliefs that we hold but may not be fully aware of or able to articulate (also known as implicit theories).

incremental theory: A belief that aspects of the human condition, such as intelligence, can be developed by the individual through focused effort or practice (see also *growth mindset*).

individualist culture: Cultures which are believed to emphasize individual goals and independence.

information processing: A branch of cognitive psychology which is concerned with how we take in information and the mental processes involved in learning.

inner speech: The speech people use in their minds without any articulation to regulate their thoughts.

input hypothesis: A theory of second language acquisition which holds that learners make progress by being exposed to linguistic input slightly beyond their current level of proficiency.

instrumental orientation: A concept from the socio-educational model of motivation which explains how people are motivated to learn a language by the material rewards associated with success.

integrative orientation: A concept from the socio-educational model of motivation which explains how people are motivated to learn a language by feelings of identification with the people and cultural values associated with a target language.

intrinsic motivation: Motivation to engage in a particular activity deriving from engaging in the act itself rather than from external outcomes or rewards.

L2 learning experience: The experience of learning a language arising from our interaction with the environment as well as from our perceptions of our successes and failures.

L2 linguistic self-confidence: Confidence in one's ability to communicate in a second or foreign language.

L2 Motivational Self System: A leading framework of language learner motivation. It is associated with concepts such as the ideal L2 self, the ought-to L2 self, and the L2 learning experience (see also *ideal L2 self, ought-to L2 self,* and *L2 learning experience.*).

L2 willingness to communicate (L2 WTC): How willing individuals are to communicate with others in their second language when they have the opportunity to do so (see also *willingness to communicate*).

leadership style: The way in which those in authority exercise leadership, for example, whether they are autocratic or *laissez-faire* in style.

learner autonomy: A readiness to take control of one's learning—independently or in cooperation with others—to achieve one's learning purposes.

locus of causality: The extent to which an individual feels that a certain outcome is due to internal or external causes (see also *attributional dimensions*).

logical positivism: A philosophical movement which views knowledge as factual and holds that knowledge can be discovered through controlled experiments.

mastery-approach goal: A goal where the aim is to master something for one's own growth and learning.

mastery-avoidance goal: A goal driven by one's desire to master something in order to avoid getting things wrong or being misunderstood.

mastery goal orientation: An orientation to learn through a desire to develop competence or mastery of a particular task. Within education, this usually reflects an interest in the subject and in learning itself.

metacognition: The processes of thinking about our thinking, which are used to plan and regulate our learning (see also *self-regulation*).

metacognitive knowledge: Knowledge of how we think and learn.

metacognitive strategies: Strategies used to think about our thinking and learning in order to regulate and control the learning process.

mindset: A set of beliefs and assumptions that can exert a powerful effect on approaches to learning (see also *implicit beliefs*).

near-peer role model: A peer who is close in age or proficiency and who is seen as representing attainable goals.

nested systems: Systems embedded in other systems, each affecting the others.

neuroscience: The scientific study of the brain and nervous system.

optimism: An outlook, sometimes described as a disposition, in which the most positive outcome is expected in a particular situation.

ought-to L2 self: A possible future self deriving from an individual's perceived obligations as a language learner and the expectations of others, such as parents, peers, and teachers.

perfectionism: A tendency to want to be perfect and thus to want to avoid all mistakes or errors.

performance-approach goal: A goal where the aim is to achieve something to impress others.

performance-avoidance goal: A goal where the aim is to achieve something so that one does not look bad in front of others.

performance goal orientation: An orientation to engage in tasks to demonstrate one's competence or ability in relation to others.

peripheral participation: When a new member of a group spends time observing the group from the edge and participating in minor roles.

personal construct theory: A theory associated with constructivism and concerned with how we create our own understandings of the world—constructs—that are personal to us and differ from other people's understandings.

positive psychology: A field of psychology concerned with promoting personal well-being, as opposed to the negative, problematic aspects of psychology.

positivist approach: An approach which maintains that knowledge can be discovered through carefully controlled experiments (see also *logical positivism*).

possible selves: Visions of one's self in future possible states. These visions can involve both desirable and undesirable images and may direct behaviour either towards realizing desirable visions or away from becoming the undesirable version of one's future self.

private speech: The speech used when people verbalize their thoughts by speaking aloud, which helps them to regulate their behaviour.

Process Model of L2 Motivation: A language learning model that attempts to explain the various stages of motivation, from the initial decision to act, through to the execution of the act, and finally on to an evaluation of the act.

push-pull: A model of motivation that explains human behaviour in terms of internal 'pushes' and 'pulls' from external factors.

Pygmalion effect: Where a teacher's strong belief in the potential of a learner encourages the learner towards high achievement.

relatedness: A psychological need to feel connected to people.

relationship management: The ability to maintain and develop good interpersonal relationships.

scaffolding: Collaborative talk that provides support for learners to carry out a learning activity or to communicate.

self-actualization: A state in which we have reached our potential and feel completely fulfilled.

self-concept: Our beliefs about our competence in a specific domain, including both cognitive and affective aspects.

self-determination theory: A theory of human behaviour based around the balancing of three basic psychological needs: autonomy, relatedness, and competence.

self-efficacy: Our belief about our ability to succeed in specific situations.

self-esteem: Our overall evaluation of ourselves and our worth.

self-fulfilling prophecy: When someone believes something about us, that person may treat us in a way that conveys that evaluation to us, which, in turn, influences both our beliefs about ourselves and how we behave.

self-handicapping behaviours: Actions taken by learners—such as not revising or not making an effort—that they can then blame for any anticipated failure rather than having to attribute it to a lack of ability or any other personal characteristic.

self-knowledge: An understanding of our own capabilities or emotions and how these may affect thought and behaviour.

self-management: The ability to control our own impulses and behaviour in ways that lead to successful relationships with others.

self-regulation: The processes whereby learners control and regulate their learning, such as setting goals, using strategies, and evaluating progress.

self-serving bias: When individuals explain their successes as being due to internal, personal factors, while attributing failures to external factors.

self-talk: This can be considered as an inner voice, or our mind speaking to us. Self-talk can be both positive and negative.

self-worth: Our evaluation of our worth.

sensory-motor stage: The first of Piaget's stages of development from childhood to adulthood, during which infants explore the world through their basic senses.

social awareness: The ability to understand the needs of others and to be able to identify non-verbal cues and power dynamics within social situations.

social comparison process: A process whereby we compare ourselves to others to gain a sense of our competence and abilities.

social strategies: Strategies used to communicate with someone.

socialization: The processes by which individuals become aware of and acquire the practices of the communities to which they belong.

sociocultural theory: A psychological theory which sees learning as first social and then individual. Learners first construct knowledge through communication and this knowledge is then internalized.

socio-educational model: A model of language learning motivation in the social psychological tradition. It is associated with integrative and instrumental motivation and with the role of social contexts in motivational processes.

stability: The extent to which an individual believes that the causes of a particular outcome may change over time (see also *attributional dimensions*).

strategies: Conscious actions learners use to help them learn or use a language.

symbolic tools: Devices people use to organize and control their mental processes, such as lists or mind maps.

systems thinking: A perspective which argues that in order to understand something, we need to look at all the parts of the system to which it belongs and their various interactions.

teacher cognitions: What teachers think, know, and believe about learning and teaching.

test anxiety: Feelings of anxiety that are aroused by taking examinations or tests.

tools: Devices we use to organize and influence the world (see also *symbolic tools.*)

upward social comparison: When learners compare themselves with others they perceive as being more competent.

variable: A factor that can be measured and studied in an experiment, such as level of anxiety or achievement.

willingness to communicate (WTC): How willing we are to communicate with others when we have the opportunity to do so.

working memory: The mental system that holds pieces of information while they are processed.

zone of proximal development (ZPD): The difference between a person's current level of ability and the higher potential level that can be achieved with scaffolding.

REFERENCES

Atkinson, J. W., & **Birch, D.** (1978). *Introduction to motivation, second edition.* New York, NY: Van Nostrand.

Ames, C. (1992). Classrooms: Goals, structures, and student motivation. *Journal of Educational Psychology, 84(3),* 261–271.

Anderson, N. J. (2012). Metacognition: Awareness of language learning. In S. Mercer, S. Ryan & M. Williams (Eds.), *Psychology for language learning: Insights from research, theory and practice* (pp. 169–187). Basingstoke: Palgrave Macmillan.

Arnold, J. (Ed.). (1999). *Affect in language learning.* Cambridge: Cambridge University Press.

Arnold, J., & **Brown. H. D.** (1999). A map of the terrain. In J. Arnold (Ed.), *Affect in language learning* (pp. 1–24). Cambridge: Cambridge University Press.

Atherton, L. (2005). Attitudes towards foreign language learning among secondary students in England. (Unpublished Ed.D thesis). University of Exeter.

Babad, E. Y., **Inbar, J.**, & **Rosenthal, R.** (1982). Pygmalion, Galatea, and the Golem: Investigations of biased and unbiased teachers. *Journal of Educational Psychology, 74,* 459–474.

Baddeley, A. (2007). *Working memory, thought, and action.* Oxford: Oxford University Press.

Bandura, A. (2000). Exercise of human agency through collective efficacy. *Current Directions in Psychological Science, 9(3),* 75–78.

Baumeister, R. F., & **Leary, M. R.** (1995). The need to belong: Desire for interpersonal attachments as a fundamental human motivation. *Psychological Bulletin, 117(3),* 497–529.

Benson, P., & **Lor, W.** (1999). Conceptions of language and language learning. *System, 27(4),* 459–472.

Benson, P. (2011). *Teaching and researching autonomy, second edition.* London: Pearson.

Berry, R. S. Y. (1998). A study of the strategies used by Hong Kong Chinese learners in learning English in an independent school environment in the United Kingdom. (Unpublished PhD thesis). University of Exeter.

Blackwell, L. S., Trzesniewski, K. H., & Dweck, C. S. (2007). Implicit theories of intelligence predict achievement across an adolescent transition: A longitudinal study and an intervention. *Child Development, 78(1)*, 246–263.

Bong, M., & Skaalvik, E. M. (2003). Academic self-concept and self-efficacy: How different are they really? *Educational Psychology Review, 15(1)*, 1–40.

Borg, S. (1999). Studying teacher cognition in second language grammar teaching. *System, 27(1)*, 19–31.

Borg, S. (2006). *Teacher cognition and language education: Research and practice.* London: Continuum.

Branch, R., & Wilson, R. (2009). *Boosting self-esteem for dummies.* Chichester: John Wiley & Sons.

Bronfenbrenner, U. (1979). *The ecology of human development.* Cambridge, MA: Harvard University Press.

Bruner, J. S. (1960). *The process of education.* Cambridge, MA: Harvard University Press.

Bruner, J. S. (1966). *Towards a theory of instruction.* Cambridge, MA: Harvard University Press.

Buckler, S., & Castle, P. (2014). *Psychology for teachers.* London: Sage.

Choy, S. C. (2003). An investigation into the changes in student perceptions of and attitudes towards learning English as a second language in a Malaysian college. (Unpublished PhD thesis). University of Exeter.

Cialdini, R. B., Borden, R. J., Thorne, A., Walker, M. R., Freeman, S., & Sloan, L. R. (1976). Basking in reflected glory: Three (football) field studies. *Journal of Personality and Social Psychology, 34(3)*, 366–375.

Clément, R. (1980). Ethnicity, contact and communicative competence in a second language. In H. Giles, W. P. Robinson, & P. M. Smith (Eds.), *Language: Social psychological perspectives* (pp. 147–154). Oxford: Pergamon.

Cohen, A. D. (2012). Strategies: The interface of styles, strategies, and motivation on tasks. In S. Mercer, S. Ryan, & M. Williams (Eds.), *Psychology for language learning: Insights from research, theory and practice* (pp. 136–150). Basingstoke: Palgrave Macmillan.

Cohen, A. D., & Chi, J. C. (2002). Language strategy use inventory and index. In R. M. Paige, A. D. Cohen, B. Kappler, J. C. Chi, & J. P. Lassegard (Eds.), *Maximizing study abroad* (pp. 16–28). Minneapolis, MN: Center for Advanced Research for Language Acquisition, University of Minnesota.

Cohen, A. D., & Macaro, E. (Eds.). (2007). *Language learner strategies.* Oxford: Oxford University Press.

Cooley, C. H. (1902). *Human nature and the social order.* New York, NY: Scribner.

Covington, M. V. (1992). *Making the grade: A self-worth perspective on motivation and school reform.* Cambridge: Cambridge University Press.

Crookes, G., & **Schmidt, R. W.** (1991). Motivation: Reopening the research agenda. *Language Learning, 41,* 469–512.

Csikszentmihalyi, M. (1990). *Flow: The psychology of optimal experience.* New York, NY: Harper & Row.

Csikszentmihalyi, M. (1997). Intrinsic motivation and effective teaching: A flow analysis. In J. L. Bess (Ed.), *Teaching well and liking it: Motivating faculty to teach effectively* (pp. 72–89). Baltimore, MD: Johns Hopkins University Press.

Davis, B., & **Sumara, D.** (2006). *Complexity and education: Inquiries into learning, teaching, and research.* New York, NY: Routledge.

Deci, E. L., & **Moller, A. C.** (2007). The concept of competence: A starting place for understanding intrinsic motivation and self-determined extrinsic motivation. In C. S. Dweck, & A. J. Elliot (Eds.), *Handbook of competence and motivation* (pp. 579–597). New York, NY: Guilford Press.

Deci, E. L., & **Ryan, R. M.** (Eds.). (2002). *Handbook of self-determination.* Rochester, NY: University of Rochester Press.

Donato, R. (1994). Collective scaffolding in second language learning. In J. P. Lantolf, & G. Appel (Eds.), *Vygotskyian approaches to second language research* (pp. 33–56). Norwood, NJ: Ablex Press.

Doran, G. T. (1981). There's a S.M.A.R.T. way to write management's goals and objectives. *Management Review (AMA FORUM), 70(11),* 35–36.

Dörnyei, Z. (1994). Understanding L2 motivation: On with the challenge. *The Modern Language Journal, 78(4),* 515–523.

Dörnyei, Z. (2005). *The psychology of the language learner: Individual differences in second language acquisition.* Mahwah, NJ: Lawrence Erlbaum.

Dörnyei, Z. (2009). *The psychology of second language acquisition.* Oxford: Oxford University Press.

Dörnyei, Z., & **Kubanyiova, M.** (2014). *Motivating learners, motivating teachers: Building vision in the language classroom.* Cambridge: Cambridge University Press.

Dörnyei, Z., & **Ushioda, E.** (2011). *Teaching and researching motivation, second edition.* Harlow: Pearson Education.

Dörnyei, Z., & **Murphey, T.** (2003). *Group dynamics in the language classroom.* Cambridge: Cambridge University Press.

Dörnyei, Z., & **Otto, I.** (1998). Motivation in action: A process model of L2 motivation. *Working Papers in Applied Linguistics, 4,* 43–69.

Dörnyei, Z., & **Ryan, S.** (2015). *The psychology of the language learner revisited.* New York, NY: Routledge.

Dweck, C. S. (1999). *Self-theories: Their role in motivation, personality, and development.* Hove: Psychology Press.

Dweck, C. S. (2006). *Mindset: The new psychology of success.* New York, NY: Random House.

Dweck, C. S. (2007). The perils and promises of praise. *Educational Leadership, 65(2),* 34–39.

Eccles, J. S., Wigfield, A., & **Schiefele, U.** (1998). Motivation. In N. Eisenberg (Ed.), *Handbook of child psychology* (pp. 1017–1095). New York, NY: Wiley.

Ehrman, M. E., & **Dörnyei, Z.** (1998). *Interpersonal dynamics in second language education: The visible and invisible classroom.* Thousand Oaks, CA: Sage.

Elliot, A. J., & **Dweck, C. S.** (2007). Competence and motivation: Competence as the core of achievement motivation. In A. J. Elliot, & C. S. Dweck (Eds.), *Handbook of competence and motivation* (pp. 3–14). New York, NY: Guilford Press.

Ellis, N. C., & **Larsen-Freeman, D.** (2006). Language emergence: Implications for Applied Linguistics. Introduction to the special issue. *Applied Linguistics, 27(4),* 558–589.

Erten, I. H. (1998). Vocabulary learning strategies: An investigation into the effects of perceptual learning styles and modality of word presentation on the use of vocabulary learning strategies. (Unpublished PhD thesis). University of Exeter.

Festinger, L. (1954). A theory of social comparison processes. *Human Relations, 7(2),* 117–140.

Fisher, R. (1995). *Teaching children to think.* Cheltenham: Stanley Thornes.

Flavell, J. H. (1979). Metacognition and cognitive monitoring: A new area of cognitive developmental enquiry. *American Psychologist, 34,* 906–911.

Fletcher, M. (2001). *The development of holistic learning: Celebrating SEAL.* Hythe: SEAL.

Forsyth, D. R. (2014). *Group dynamics, sixth edition.* Belmont, CA: Cengage.

Fredrickson, B. L. (2009). *Positivity.* New York, NY: Three Rivers Press.

Fredrickson, B. L. (2013). Updated thinking on positivity ratios. *American Psychologist, 68(9),* 814–822.

Frijda, N. H., & **Mesquita, B.** (2000). Beliefs through emotions. In N. H. Frijda, A. S. R. Manstead, & S. Bem (Eds.), *Emotions and beliefs: How emotions influence thought* (pp. 45–77). Cambridge: Cambridge University Press.

Gabrys-Barker, D., & **Bielska, J.** (Eds.). (2013). *The affective dimension in second language acquisition.* Bristol: Multilingual Matters.

Gardner, R. C. (1985). *Social psychology and second language learning: The role of attitudes and motivation.* London: Arnold.

Gardner, R. C., & **Lambert, W. E.** (1972). *Attitudes and motivation in second-language learning.* Rowley, MA: Newbury House Publishers.

Gibson, J. (1979). *The ecological approach to visual perception.* Boston, MA: Houghton Mifflin.

Goleman, D. (1998). *Working with emotional intelligence.* New York, NY: Random House.

Gregersen, T. (2003). To err is human: A reminder to teachers of language-anxious students. *Foreign Language Annals, 36(1),* 25–32.

Gregersen, T., & **Horwitz, E. K.** (2002). Language learning and perfectionism: Anxious and non-anxious language learners' reactions to their own oral performance. *The Modern Language Journal, 86(4),* 562–570.

Gregersen, T., & **MacIntyre, P. D.** (Eds.). (2014a). *Studies in Second Language Learning and Teaching: Positive Psychology in SLA Special Issue, 5(1).*

Gregersen. T., & **MacIntyre, P. D.** (2014b). *Capitalizing on language learners' individuality: From premise to practice.* Bristol: Multilingual Matters.

Griffiths, C. (2013). *The strategy factor in successful language learning.* Bristol: Multilingual Matters.

Gross, J. J. (2007). *Handbook of emotion regulation.* New York, NY: Guilford Press.

Hadfield, J. (1992). *Classroom dynamics.* Oxford: Oxford University Press.

Hadfield, J., & **Dörnyei, Z.** (2014). *Motivating learning.* Harlow: Pearson Education.

Hamachek, D. E. (1987). Humanistic psychology: Theory, postulates and implications for educational processes. In J. Glover, & R. Ronning (Eds.), *Historical foundations of educational psychology* (pp. 159–182). New York, NY: Plenum Press.

Harmer, J. (2011). *The practice of English language teaching, fourth edition.* Harlow: Pearson Longman.

Harter, S. (1999). *The construction of the self: A developmental perspective.* New York, NY: Guilford Press.

Heider, F. (1958). *The psychology of interpersonal relations.* New York, NY: Wiley.

Hemmi, C. (2014). Dual identities perceived by bilinguals. In S. Mercer, & M. Williams (Eds.), *Multiple perspectives on the self in SLA* (pp. 75–91). Bristol: Multilingual Matters.

Hofmann, W., **Schmeichel, B. J.**, **Friese, M.**, & **Baddeley, A. D.** (2011). Working memory and self-regulation. In K. D. Vohs, & R. F. Baumeister (Eds.), *The handbook of self-regulation: Research, theory, and applications, second edition.* (pp. 204–226). New York, NY: Guilford Press.

Holliday, A. (1994). *Appropriate methodology and social context.* Cambridge: Cambridge University Press.

Holt, J. C. (1982). *How children fail.* Harmondsworth: Penguin.

Horwitz, E. K., Horwitz, M. B., & **Cope, J.** (1986). Foreign language classroom anxiety. *The Modern Language Journal, 70(2),* 125–132.

Hull, C. L. (1943). *Principles of behavior.* New York, NY: Appleton Century Crofts.

Hyland, K., & **Hyland, F.** (Eds.). (2006). *Feedback in second language writing.* Cambridge: Cambridge University Press.

James, W. (1902). *The varieties of religious experience: A study in human nature.* London: Longmans, Green, & Co.

Kalaja, P. (1995). Student beliefs (or metacognitive knowledge) about SLA reconsidered. *International Journal of Applied Linguistics, 5(2),* 191–204.

Kalaja, P., & **Barcelos, A. M. F.** (Eds.). (2003). *Beliefs about SLA: New research approaches.* Dordrecht: Kluwer.

Kalaja, P., Menezes, V., & **Barcelos, A. M. F.** (Eds.). (2008). *Narratives of learning and teaching EFL.* Basingstoke: Palgrave Macmillan.

Kamins, M. L., & **Dweck, C. S.** (1999). Person versus process praise and criticism: Implications for contingent self-worth and coping. *Developmental Psychology, 35(3),* 835–847.

Kelly, G. A. (1955). *The psychology of personal constructs.* New York, NY: Norton.

Krashen, S. D. (1985). *The input hypothesis: Issues and implications.* London: Longman.

Kumaravadivelu, B. (2006). *Understanding language teaching: From method to postmethod.* Mahwah, NJ: Lawrence Erlbaum.

Lantolf, J. P., & **Poehner, M. E.** (Eds.). (2008). *Sociocultural theory and the teaching of second languages.* London: Equinox.

Lantolf, J. P. (1994). Sociocultural theory and second language learning; Introduction to the special issue. *The Modern Language Journal, 78(4),* 418–420.

Lantolf, J. P. (Ed.). (2000). *Sociocultural theory and second language learning.* Oxford: Oxford University Press.

Larsen-Freeman, D. (2012). Complex, dynamic systems: A new transdisciplinary theme for applied linguistics? *Language Teaching, 45(2),* 202–214.

Larsen-Freeman, D., & **Cameron, L.** (2008). *Complex systems and applied linguistics.* Oxford: Oxford University Press.

Lave, J., & **Wenger, E.** (1991). *Situated learning: Legitimate peripheral participation.* Cambridge: Cambridge University Press.

LeDoux, J. (1998). *The emotional brain: The mysterious underpinnings of emotional life*. New York, NY: Simon and Schuster.

Lewin, K., **Lippitt, R.**, & **White, R. K.** (1939). Patterns of aggressive behavior in experimentally created social climates. *Journal of Social Psychology, 10*, 271–301.

Lightbown, P. M., & **Spada, N.** (2013). *How languages are learned, fourth edition*. Oxford: Oxford University Press.

Little, D. (1999). Developing learner autonomy in the foreign language classroom. *Revista Canaria Estudios Ingleses, 38*, 77–88.

Littleton, K., & **Mercer, N.** (2013). *Interthinking: Putting talk to work*. Abingdon: Routledge.

Locke, E. A., & **Latham, G. P.** (1994). Goal setting theory. In H. F. O'Neil, & M. Drillings (Eds.), *Motivation: Theory and research* (pp. 13–29). Hillsdale, NJ: Lawrence Erlbaum Associates.

Loewen, S. (2007). The prior and subsequent use of forms targeted in incidental focus on form. In H. Nassaji, & S. Fotos (Eds.), *Form focused instruction and teacher education: Studies in honour of Rod Ellis* (pp. 101–116). Oxford: Oxford University Press.

McClelland, D., **Atkinson, J.**, **Clark, R.**, & **Lowell, E.** (1953). *The achievement motive*. New York, NY: Appleton-Century-Crofts.

McCombs, B. L., & **Miller, L.** (2007). *Learner-centred classroom practices and assessments: Maximizing student motivation, learning and achievement*. Thousand Oaks, CA: Corwin Press.

McCroskey, J. C., & **Richmond, V. P.** (1987). Willingness to communicate. In C. McCroskey, &. A. Daly (Eds.), *Personality and interpersonal communication* (pp. 129–156). Newbury Park, CA: Sage.

McCroskey, J. C., & **Richmond, V. P.** (1991). *Quiet children and the classroom teacher*. Bloomington, IN: ERIC Clearinghouse on Reading and Communication Skills.

McDonough, J. (2002). The teacher as language learner: Worlds of difference? *ELT Journal, 56(4)*, 404–411.

MacIntyre, P. D. (2007). Willingness to communicate in the second language: Understanding the decision to speak as a volitional process. *Modern Language Journal, 91(4)*, 564–576.

MacIntyre, P. D., **Clément, R.**, **Dörnyei, Z.**, & **Noels, K. A.** (1998). Conceptualizing willingness to communicate in a L2: A situated model of confidence and affiliation. *Modern Language Journal, 82*, 545–562.

MacIntyre, P. D., & **Gregersen, T.** (2012). Affect: The role of language anxiety and other emotions in language learning. In S. Mercer, S. Ryan, & M. Williams (Eds.), *Psychology for language learning: Insights from research, theory and practice* (pp. 103–118). Basingstoke: Palgrave Macmillan.

Maiklad, C. (2001). The beliefs and practices of Thai English language teachers. (Unpublished PhD thesis). University of Exeter.

Markus, H. R., & **Kitayama, S.** (1991). Culture and the self: Implications for cognition, emotion, and motivation. *Psychological Review, 98(2),* 224–253.

Markus, H. R., & **Nurius, P.** (1986). Possible Selves. *American Psychologist, 41,* 954–969.

Markus, H. R., & **Wurf, E.** (1987). The dynamic self-concept: A social-psychological perspective. *Annual Review of Psychology, 38,* 299–337.

Marsh, H. W. (1986). Verbal and math self-concepts: An internal/external frame of reference model. *American Educational Research Journal, 23(1),* 129–149.

Marsh, H. W., & **Craven, R.** (2002). The pivotal role of frames of reference in academic self-concept formation: The big-fish-little-pond effect. In F. Pajares, & T. Urdan (Eds.), *Adolescence and education, Volume II* (pp. 83–123). Greenwich, CT: Information Age Publishing.

Maslow, A. H. (1954). *Motivation and personality.* New York, NY: Harper.

Maslow, A. H. (1968). *Towards a psychology of being, second edition.* New York, NY: Van Nostrand.

Maslow, A. H. (1970). *Motivation and personality, second edition.* New York, NY: Harper and Row.

Maslow, A. H. (1987). *Motivation and personality, third edition.* New York, NY: Addison-Wesley.

Mead, G. H. (1934). *Mind, self, and society from the standpoint of a social behaviorist.* Chicago, IL: University of Chicago Press.

Mercer, S. (2011). *Towards an understanding of language learner self-concept.* Dordrecht: Springer.

Mercer, S., & **Ryan, S.** (2010). A mindset for EFL: Learners' beliefs about the role of natural talent. *ELT Journal, 64(4),* 436–444.

Mercer, S., & **Williams, M.** (Eds.). (2014). *Multiple perspectives on the self in SLA.* Bristol: Multilingual Matters.

Mills, N., Pajares, F., & **Herron, C.** (2007). Self-efficacy of college intermediate French students: Relation to achievement and motivation. *Language Learning, 57(3),* 417–442.

Mitchell, R., & **Myles, F.** (1998). *Second language learning theories.* London: Arnold.

Mori, Y. (1999). Epistemological beliefs and language learning beliefs: What do language learners believe about their learning? *Language Learning, 49(9)*, 377–415.

Mruk, C. (2006). *Self-esteem research, theory, and practice: Toward a positive psychology of self-esteem, third edition.* New York, NY: Springer.

Murphey, T., & **Arao, H.** (2001). Changing reported beliefs through near peer role modeling. *TESL-EJ, 5(3)*, 1–15. Retrieved January 27 2015 from http://www.tesl-ej.org/ej19/a1.html

Murphey, T., **Falout, J.**, **Fukuda, T.**, & **Fukada, Y.** (2014). Socio-dynamic motivating through idealising classmates. *System, 45*, 242–253.

Murray, G. (Ed.). (2014). *Social dimensions of autonomy in language learning.* Basingstoke: Palgrave Macmillan.

Murray, G., **Gao, X.**, & **Lamb, T.** (Eds.). (2011). *Identity, motivation and autonomy in language learning.* Bristol: Multilingual Matters.

New Oxford English Dictionary. (1998). Oxford: Oxford University Press.

Norton, B. (2000). *Identity and language learning: Gender, ethnicity and educational change.* Harlow: Longman.

Norton, B. (2013). *Identity and language learning.* Bristol: Multilingual Matters.

Norton, B. (2014). Identity and poststructuralist theory in SLA. In S. Mercer, & M. Williams (Eds.), *Multiple perspectives on the self in SLA* (pp. 59–74). Bristol: Multilingual Matters.

Nunan, D. (1988). *The learner-centred curriculum: A study in second language teaching.* Cambridge: Cambridge University Press.

Oxford, R. L. (1993). *Style analysis survey (SAS).* Tuscaloosa, AL: University of Alabama.

Oxford, R. L. (1990). *Language learning strategies: What every teacher should know.* New York, NY: Newbury House.

Oxford, R. L. (2011). *Teaching and researching language learning strategies.* Upper Saddle River, NJ: Longman.

Oxford, R. L., & **Shearin, J.** (1994). Language learning motivation: Expanding the theoretical framework. *The Modern Language Journal, 78(1)*, 12–28.

Oyserman, D., **Bybee, D.**, & **Terry, K.** (2006). Possible selves and academic outcomes: How and when possible selves impel action. *Journal of Personality and Social Psychology, 91(1)*, 188–204.

Pavlenko, A., & **Norton, B.** (2007). Imagined communities, identity, and English language teaching. In J. Cummins, & C. Davidson (Eds.), *International handbook of English language teaching* (pp. 669–680). New York, NY: Springer.

Piaget, J. (1966). *The origins of intelligence in children.* New York, NY: International Universities Press.

Piaget, J. (1974). *To understand is to invent.* New York, NY: Viking Press.

Puchta. H., & **Williams, M.** (2001). *Teaching young learners to think.* Innsbruck: Helbling Languages.

Reid, J. (1987). The learning style preferences of ESL students. *TESOL Quarterly, 21(1),* 87–111.

Rhodewalt, F., & **Vohs, K. D.** (2005). Defensive strategies, motivation, and the self. In A. Elliot, & C. Dweck (Eds.), *Handbook of competence and motivation* (pp. 548–565). New York, NY: Guilford Press.

Rogers, C. R. (1969). *Freedom to learn.* Columbus, OH: Charles Merrill.

Ryan, R. M. (2007). Motivation and emotion: A new look and approach for two reemerging fields. *Motivation and Emotion, 31(1),* 1–3.

Ryan, S., & **Mercer, S.** (2012). Implicit theories: Language learning mindsets. In S. Mercer, S. Ryan, & M. Williams (Eds.), *Psychology for language learning: Insights from research, theory and practice.* Basingstoke: Palgrave Macmillan.

Salmon, P. (1988). *Psychology for teachers: An alternative approach.* London: Hutchinson.

Schmuck, R. A., & **Schmuck, P. A.** (2001). *Group processes in the classroom.* Boston, MA: McGraw Hill.

Schumann, J. H. (1997). *The neurobiology of affect in language.* Oxford: Blackwell.

Schumann, J. H. (1999). A neurobiological perspective on affect and methodology in second language learning. In J. Arnold (Ed.), *Affect in language learning* (pp. 28–42). Cambridge: Cambridge University Press.

Schunk, D. H., **Meece, J. R.**, & **Pintrich, P. R.** (2014). *Motivation in education: Theory, research, and applications, fourth edition.* Boston, MA: Pearson Education.

Seligman, M. E. P. (1990). *Learned optimism.* New York, NY: Simon & Schuster.

Seligman, M. E. P. (2011). *Flourish.* New York, NY: Simon & Schuster.

Seligman, M. E. P., **Gillham, J.**, **Reivich, K.**, **Linkins, M.**, & **Ernst, R.** (2009). Positive education. *Oxford Review of Education, 35(3),* 293–311.

Skinner, B. F. (1957). *Verbal behavior.* New York, NY: Appleton.

Skinner, B. F. (1987). *Upon further reflection.* Englewood Cliffs, NJ: Prentice Hall.

Stevick, E. (1980). *Teaching languages: A way and ways.* Rowley, MA: Newbury House.

Taylor, F. (2013). *Self and identity in adolescent foreign language learning.* Bristol: Multilingual Matters.

Thomas, L., & **Harri-Augstein, S.** (1985). *Self-organised learning: Foundations of a conversational science for psychology.* London: Routledge and Kegan Paul.

Triandis, H. C., Bontempo, R., Villareal, M. J., Asai, M., & **Lucca, N.** (1988). Individualism and collectivism: Cross-cultural perspectives on self-ingroup relationships. *Journal of Personality and Social Psychology, 54(2),* 323–338. Retrieved January 27 2015 from http://dx.doi.org/10.1037/0022-3514.54.2.323

Tsai, H. (2007). Improving a college-level EFL writing class in Taiwan: From understanding students' writing anxiety to the implementation of a process-product approach. (Unpublished Ed.D thesis). University of Exeter.

Tuckman, B. W. (1965). Developmental sequence in small groups. *Psychological Bulletin, 63(6),* 384–399.

Underhill, A. (2013). The inner workbench: Learning as a meaningful activity. In J. Arnold, & T. Murphey (Eds.), *Meaningful action* (pp. 202–218). Cambridge: Cambridge University Press.

Ushioda, E. (2008). Motivation and good language learners. In C. Griffiths (Ed.), *Lessons from good language learners* (pp. 19–34). Cambridge: Cambridge University Press.

Ushioda, E. (2009). A person-in-context relational view of emergent motivation, self and identity. In Z. Dörnyei, & E. Ushioda (Eds.), *Motivation, language identity and the L2 self* (pp. 215–228). Bristol: Multilingual Matters.

Ushioda, E. (2011). Why autonomy? Insights from motivation theory and research. *Innovation in Language Learning and Teaching, 5(2),* 221–232.

Ushioda, E. (2012). Motivation: L2 Learning as a special case? In S. Mercer, S. Ryan, & M. Williams (Eds.), *Psychology for language learning: Insights from theory, research and practice* (pp. 169–187). Basingstoke, UK: Palgrave Macmillan.

van Lier, L. (2004). *The ecology and semiotics of language learning.* Dordrecht: Kluwer.

van Lier, L. (2008). Agency in the classroom. In J. P. Lantolf, & M. E. Poehner (Eds.), *Sociocultural theory and the teaching of second languages* (pp. 163–186). London: Equinox.

Vygotsky, L. S. (1978). *Mind in society.* Cambridge, MA: MIT Press.

Weiner, B. (1980). *Human motivation.* New York, NY: Rinehart and Winston.

Weiner. B. (1986). *An attributional theory of motivation and emotion.* New York, NY: Springer-Verlag.

Weinstein, R. S. (2002). *Reaching higher: The power of expectations in schooling.* Cambridge, MA: Harvard University Press.

White, C. (1999). Expectations and emergent beliefs of self-instructed language learners. *System, 27,* 443–457.

White, C. (2008). Beliefs and good language learners. In C. Griffiths (Ed.), *Lessons from good language learners* (pp. 121–130). Cambridge: Cambridge University Press.

Williams, M., & **Burden, R. L.** (1997). *Psychology for language teachers: A social constructivist approach.* Cambridge: Cambridge University Press.

Williams, M., & **Burden, R. L.** (1999). Students' developing conceptions of themselves as language learners. *The Modern Language Journal, 83(2),* 193–201.

Williams, M., **Burden, R.**, & **Lanvers, U.** (2002). 'French is the language of love and stuff': Student perceptions of issues related to motivation in learning a foreign language. *British Educational Research Journal, 28(4),* 503–528.

Williams, M., **Burden, R. L.**, **Poulet, G. M. A.**, & **Maun, I. C.** (2004). Learners' perceptions of their successes and failures in foreign language learning. *Language Learning Journal, 30,* 47–51.

Willing, K. (1987). *Learning styles in adult migrant education.* Sydney: National Centre for English Language Teaching and Research.

Woodrow, L. (2012). Goal orientations: Three perspectives on motivation goal orientations. In S. Mercer, S. Ryan, & M. Williams (Eds.), *Psychology for language learning: Insights from theory, research and practice* (pp. 188–202). Basingstoke: Palgrave Macmillan.

Woods, D. (2003). The social construction of beliefs in the language classroom. In P. Kalaja, & A. M. F. Barcelos (Eds.), *Beliefs about SLA: New research approaches* (pp. 201–229). Dordrecht: Kluwer.

INDEX

Page numbers annotated with 'g' and 'f' refer to glossary entries and figures respectively.

THE UNOFFICIAL

PRINCESS BRIDE

COOKBOOK

Inspiring | Educating | Creating | Entertaining

Brimming with creative inspiration, how-to projects, and useful information to enrich your everyday life, quarto.com is a favorite destination for those pursuing their interests and passions.

First published in 2022 by Epic Ink, an imprint of The Quarto Group,
142 West 36th Street, 4th Floor, New York, NY 10018, USA
T (212) 779-4972 F (212) 779-6058 www.Quarto.com

Epic Ink titles are also available at discount for retail, wholesale, promotional, and bulk purchase. For details, contact the Special Sales Manager by email at specialsales@quarto.com or by mail at The Quarto Group, Attn: Special Sales Manager, 100 Cummings Center Suite 265D, Beverly, MA 01915 USA.

10 9 8 7 6 5 4 3 2

ISBN: 978-0-7603-7756-7

Library of Congress Cataloging-in-Publication Data

Names: Reeder, Cassandra, author.
Title: The unofficial Princess Bride cookbook : 50 delightfully delicious
   recipes for fans of the cult classic / Cassandra Reeder, the Geeky chef.

Description: New York, NY : Epic Ink, 2022. | Includes index. | Summary:
   "The Unofficial Princess Bride Cookbook celebrates the 35th anniversary
   of the iconic movie with fun trivia and 50 food and drink recipes from
   its most memorable scenes"-- Provided by publisher.
Identifiers: LCCN 2022004681 (print) | LCCN 2022004682 (ebook) | ISBN
   9780760377567 (hardcover) | ISBN 9780760377574 (ebook other)
Subjects: LCSH: Cooking. | Beverages. | Cooking motion pictures. | LCGFT:
   Literary cookbooks.
Classification: LCC TX714 .R4373 2022 (print) | LCC TX714 (ebook) | DDC
   641.5--dc23/eng/20220202
LC record available at https://lccn.loc.gov/2022004681
LC ebook record available at https://lccn.loc.gov/2022004682

Group Publisher: Rage Kindelsperger
Publisher: Delia Greve
Creative Director: Laura Drew
Managing Editor: Cara Donaldson
Cover and Interior Design: Amelia LeBarron
Illustrations: Amelia LeBarron
Photography: Bill Milne

Printed in the United States of America

THE UNOFFICIAL

PRINCESS BRIDE

COOKBOOK

50 Delightfully Delicious Recipes for Fans of the Cult Classic

CASSANDRA REEDER,
THE GEEKY CHEF

EPIC INK

Table of Contents

Introduction

In 2022, *The Princess Bride* and I will turn thirty-five. It is one of the first films I remember seeing. I know that, in ways both big and small, it had a profound effect on me when I was growing up. I also know I'm far from being alone in that.

One of my favorite things about the film is that it elicits pure joy from people of all walks of life. Many societal barriers tend to dissolve once fans start discussing *The Princess Bride*, and I believe this is by design. It is a story about stories: what makes them great and the power they have to "bwing us togevver." Everyone seems to have a different favorite quote, a line that speaks to them. And when you add all these quotes together, you get the movie. William Goldman—the author of both the screenplay and the novel—knew what he was doing.

Food is like that too: a great people-uniter. And while it is true that the film has maybe five food-moments (if you squint your eyes), *The Princess Bride* is full of inspiration for dishes to be shared and enjoyed together. Some of these recipes were born from thoughtful analysis of the film and novel's setting. Many more came from silly puns and from the fact that, like Fezzik, I cannot resist a rhyme. Some recipes are pulled directly from the beloved source material(s), and some were as much of a stretch as Vizzini's deductive reasoning. I have tried to add some "historical" elements to the recipes, so you will see flavors from Medieval and Renaissance era Europe and Scandinavia—but like the film itself, there will be anachronisms and anatopisms aplenty. Most of these dishes are befitting for any castle feast, but they'd also be right at home on your dinner table.

I could quote most of the movie and ace most trivia quizzes before I got the opportunity to do this cookbook. And now I have an even deeper appreciation for it than I'd have ever thought possible. Over these few months, I've immersed myself in this story and the lore of the film, both on and off screen: I listened to Mark Knopfler's phenomenal soundtrack while cooking, and I played the movie

in the background as I wrote. I read the script over and over and over again, and reread Goldman's incredible novel twice. I listened to Cary Elwes' *As You Wish* audiobook each night as I went to sleep, watched every cast interview and featurette I could find, and searched for any new behind-the-scenes info I could glean, everything culminating in an entirely *The Princess Bride*-themed Thanksgiving feast. Even after all that, I'd happily watch the film again tomorrow and enjoy every second of it because the magic is not diminished with time or repetition.

I hope this cookbook comes across as the love letter that it is. As I finish writing it, I can't help but think of Mandy Patinkin's favorite line of dialogue from the film: it's the one about not knowing what to do with himself after completing his quest. Living, breathing, and eating *The Princess Bride* has been a wonderful experience and it's surreal to be done. Obviously, Inigo's quest was much bigger than mine, but I know how much this film means to so many people and I hope I have done it justice.

Drinking Game

TAKE A SIP WHENEVER . . .

- Westley says, "as you wish."
- Ew, kissing!
- Fizzini says, "inconceivable!"
- Fezzik rhymes a word.
- You get used to disappointment.
- Anyone says "true love" or "twu luv."
- Inigo says, "prepare to die."

CHUG WHEN . . .

- "I don't think they exist . . ."
- "Have fun storming the castle!"
- "Booooooo!"
- "If you haven't got your health, you haven't got anything."
- "Mawidge"

FINISH YOUR DRINK WHEN . . .

- Vizzini and Westley drink during The Battle of Wits
- "I want my father back, you SOB."

Booooooze!

Drinks
and
Cocktails

Vizzini's Iocane Fizzini

SERVES 2

In the iconic Battle of Wits scene, the Man in Black challenges Vizzini to deduce which glass of wine is laced with Iocane powder—a deadly poison. Vizzini is a man with sophisticated sensibilities and a knack for drama, and the picnic he prepared was impressive considering the urgency of the situation. However, given more time and resources, he may have made a drink with a bit more flair and panache for such an important occasion, like this sparkling martini enhanced with the flavors of his native Sicily. After all, when you're going up against a Sicilian and death is on the line, a little ostentation is in order. For this drink, you'll want to use confectioners' sugar (assuming you haven't spent the last several years building an immunity to Iocane powder).

INGREDIENTS

3 oz (85 ml) London Dry Gin

1½ oz (45 ml) Martini™ Rosso
   or other Italian-style vermouth

1½ oz (45 ml) blood orange juice

6 oz (175 ml) prosecco

Pinch of confectioners' sugar

Slice of blood orange peel, for garnish

1. Fill a cocktail shaker with ice. Add the gin and vermouth. Shake well!

2. Strain into two serving glasses. Add the blood orange juice, then top off both glasses with the prosecco.

3. Add a pinch of Iocane (confectioners' sugar) to one or both glasses. Give it a quick stir. Be sure your opponent doesn't see which glass was "poisoned."

4. Serve! Let the battle of wits begin!

GARNISH: Slice of blood orange peel
SERVING VESSEL: Wine glass or champagne flute
PAIRINGS: Arancini à la Vizzini (page 52) or "Battle of Wits" Brie and Apple Crostini (page 64)

Fire Swamp Flame Spurt

SERVES 1

Westley and Buttercup's trek through the Fire Swamp begins with a bang—or a "pop!" I should say. The flame spurt is the first of the three terrors that the pair encounters in the Fire Swamp: bursts of flame erupting from the ground catch Buttercup's dress on fire and are promptly extinguished by Westley. To approximate this scorching experience, either mezcal or a peated whiskey will give the drink a smoky taste which will burn going down, and an infusion of chili pepper will add additional heat. For a truly cinematic experience, use citrus oils to create your very own fire spurt!

INGREDIENTS

FOR THE SPICY LIQUOR
1 cup (235 ml) peated whiskey or mezcal
   (see tip)
1 jalapeño or other chili pepper, sliced

FOR THE DRINK
2 oz (60 ml) spicy liquor
4 oz (120 ml) orange juice
½ oz (15 ml) pomegranate syrup
   or grenadine, or to taste
Thick slice of orange peel, for garnish
   (optional)

1. Combine the ingredients in a small, sealable container, such as a mason jar. Let infuse overnight. If you don't have the patience for the chili pepper infusion, add a dash or two of your favorite extra spicy hot sauce.

2. Fill a cocktail shaker with ice. Add the whiskey and orange juice. Shake well. Pour the contents of the cocktail shaker into a glass filled with ice.

3. Slowly pour the pomegranate syrup over the back of a spoon or by trickling it down the side of the glass, allowing it to settle at the bottom. Once settled, give a gentle stir to create a gradient effect.

GARNISH (OPTIONAL): Hold the orange rind over the glass, peel-side facing the top of the cocktail glass. Bring a lighter or match up to the pith of the orange slice. Squeeze the peel and the oils will ignite in a burst of flame, much like a flame spurt—be careful! Afterward, run the charred peel around the rim then drop it into the glass as a garnish.

SERVING VESSEL: Glencairn, tumbler, or lowball glass

PAIRINGS: Roasted R.O.U.S. (page 83) and Lightning Sand Parfait (page 134) for a complete Fire Swamp dining experience.

TIP

If you cannot find mezcal or peated whiskey, substitute rye whiskey or tequila with a drop or two of liquid smoke added after the chili pepper infusion.

Dread Pirate Robert's "No Survivors" Bumbo

SERVES 1

We only get a very brief snapshot of Westley's time aboard the ship *Revenge*, but we can be reasonably sure he indulged in an occasional swashbuckling refreshment from time to time. Bumbo was a sort of rum cocktail favored by pirates in the seventeenth century. Its most basic form contained dark rum, water, sugar, and nutmeg. More ingredients were added over time, such as citrus juice (helpful for preventing scurvy, a common problem for sailors) and other spices, like cinnamon. With the addition of overproof rum, which typically contains a whopping 50% alcohol, this cocktail truly leaves no survivors.

INGREDIENTS

1½ oz (45 ml) dark spiced rum
½ oz (15 ml) overproof rum
1 oz (30 ml) water or pineapple juice
1 teaspoon simple syrup
½ oz (15 ml) lime juice

Freshly grated nutmeg or
    a dash of ground nutmeg
Dash of cinnamon (optional)
Lime wedge and/or pineapple slice,
    for garnish

1. Fill a cocktail shaker with ice. Add the rum, water, simple syrup, lime juice, nutmeg, and cinnamon (if using).

2. Shake well. Pour into a serving cup.

GARNISH: Lime wedge and/or pineapple slice speared with a Jolly Roger toothpick
SERVING VESSEL: Goblet, chalice, mug, or rocks glass
PAIRING: The Pirate Ship *Revenge* Salmagundi (page 95)
VIRGINIZE: Replace the spiced rum with spiced apple cider. Replace the overproof rum with water and a couple drops of rum extract.

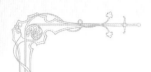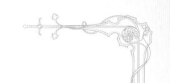

Vengeful · Spaniard's Sangria

SERVES 4

Inigo Montoya's quest to avenge his father, Domingo Montoya, is one of the most gripping side-plots in film history with a seriously satisfying outcome. Sangria originated in Spain, and it combines red wine with fresh fruits, and sometimes contains juices, spices, and other spirits. The word *sangria* means "blood" in Spanish, due to the blood-red color of the drink, which is quite appropriate for our favorite Spaniard with a blood oath to avenge his father. Just make sure you're not too drunk to buy the brandy!

INGREDIENTS

1 lemon, cut into thin slices

1 lime, cut into thin slices

1 orange, cut into thin slices

½ cup (100 g) granulated sugar, or to taste

4 cinnamon sticks

1½ cups (355 ml) brandy, chilled

1 (750 ml) bottle dry red wine, chilled

1 cup (235 ml) orange juice, chilled

1. Add the lemon, lime, and orange to a punch bowl. Add the sugar, cinnamon sticks, and the brandy. Chill in the refrigerator for at least 2 hours.

2. When ready to serve, lightly crush the fruit with a wooden spoon. Stir in the wine and orange juice. Adjust sweetness to taste.

3. Let the sangria mingle for about 10 minutes, then add a cinnamon stick and some fruit into each serving glass and pour the sangria on top. Sangria, like vengeance, is best served cold.

GARNISH: Cinnamon stick and citrus slices

SERVING VESSEL: Sangria glass, chalice, goblet, or wine glass

PAIRINGS: "Prepare To Die" Fiery Spanish Croquetas (page 55) or The Capo Ferro Technique (page 92)

VIRGINIZE: Omit the brandy. Replace the wine with 1 cup (235 ml) of apple juice and 1 cup (235 ml) of grape juice plus 1½ cups (355 ml) sparkling water. Add some berries of your choice.

"Mostly Dead" Corpse Reviver

SERVES 1

Before Westley is revived by the Miracle Max's Chocolate-Covered Miracle Pill (page 125), Max uses an ancient contraption called a bellows to pump a strong gust of air into Westley's lungs so he can tell him why his life is worth living. Think of this drink as the bellows. You can toast to "true love" or, alternatively, "to blave!"

INGREDIENTS

1 oz (30 ml) London Dry Gin

1 oz (30 ml) Swedish Punsch (substitute Cocchi Americano or a dry vermouth)

1 oz (30 ml) orange liqueur

1 oz (30 ml) lemon juice

Splash of absinthe

Lemon peel, for garnish

1. This cocktail benefits from a chilled serving glass, so pop your chosen glassware into the freezer for at least 30 minutes before mixing.

2. Fill a cocktail shaker with ice. Add the gin, Punsch, orange liqueur, lemon juice, and absinthe. Shake well.

3. Pour into the chilled serving glass, and garnish with the lemon peel.

GARNISH: Lemon peel

SERVING VESSEL: Goblet, chalice, delmonico, or coupe glass

PAIRINGS: MLT: Mutton, Lettuce, and Tomato (page 80) or Miracle Max's Chocolate-Covered Miracle Pill (page 125)

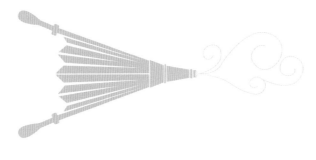

"Cliffs of Insanity" Shot

The Cliffs of Insanity consist of a sheer rock face jutting out of the ocean. The shooting location for these scenes was the Cliffs of Moher on the coast of County Clare in Ireland, which inspires the Irish Cream in this drink. As for "insanity," absinthe (in its early forms) was rumored to have caused hallucinations and even psychosis. Once the syrup is added, the drink will look like steep cliffs reaching for the clouds. This one is meant to be downed in one swig, but whatever you do, don't look down!

INGREDIENTS

1½ oz (45 ml) peach schnapps

½ oz (15 ml) Baileys™ Irish Cream

1–2 teaspoons (5–10 ml) absinthe

Splashes of green apple syrup

1. This is a layered shot so we're not mixing. It helps if you have everything pre-measured rather than pouring directly from the bottle.

2. Pour the peach schnapps into the shot glass. Take a spoon and place the tip of the spoon very close to the schnapps. Carefully and slowly pour in Irish Cream over the back of the spoon and into the glass.

3. Repeat the spoon method to layer the absinthe on top of the Irish Cream. Then, add a couple splashes of green apple syrup.

4. Watch the insanity for a moment before downing the shot in one swig.

SERVING VESSEL: 3-ounce shooter, grappa glass, or a tall 2½- to 3-ounce shot glass

PAIRINGS: Swordmasters' Fon-Duel (page 68)

The Brut Squad

For plausible deniability in his scheme to start a war with Guilder, Humperdinck has The Chief Enforcer of Florin, Yellin, form a "Brute Squad" to clear out the Thieves' Forest. Fezzik joins the Brute Squad, which leads to him being reunited with Inigo. This is a PUNCH (get it?) made with BRUT champagne (do ya get it?) meant to be enjoyed with the whole SQUAD (you get it, right?). It'd be flavored with BLACK and BLUE berries and BLOOD oranges . . . . Fair warning, the hangover could be brutal.

INGREDIENTS

10 oz (283 g) frozen blackberries

5 oz (142 g) frozen blueberries

6 oz (175 ml) Grand Marnier®
    or Cointreau

2 oz (60 ml) calvados or apple brandy

1 blood orange, thinly sliced

1 bottle (750 ml) Brut champagne, chilled

2–3 tablespoons (40–60 g) blueberry
    and/or blackberry preserves

1–2 oz (30–60 ml) lime juice

6 oz (175 ml) seltzer or ginger ale

Fresh blackberries, blueberries,
    and blood orange slices, for garnish

1. In a large punch bowl, gently muddle the berries.

2. Add the orange liqueur, brandy, orange slices, champagne, lime juice, preserves, and soda. Gently stir and let the flavors mingle for about 10 minutes.

3. To serve, use a ladle and pour the punch into ice-filled glasses.

GARNISH: Fresh blackberries, blueberries, and blood orange slices

SERVING VESSEL: Punch bowl with punch cups, tumblers, goblets, or chalices

PAIRINGS: Gentle Giant's Gargantuan Gougères (page 58) or Hippopotamic Land Mass Lollipops (page 89)

VIRGINIZE: Replace the champagne with ginger ale, the brandy with 1 to 2 ounces (15 to 30 ml) of apple cider vinegar (trust me here!) and the orange liqueur with orange juice.

"The Sea · After a Storm" Dark and Stormy

SERVES 1

After rescuing Buttercup, while still in disguise as the Man in Black, Westley is jealous and hurt by Buttercup's betrothal to Humperdinck and he antagonizes her relentlessly. At one point, he prods Buttercup about her lost lover and she describes him as "Poor and perfect with eyes like the sea after a storm." This drink is a take on a Dark 'N Stormy™ a cocktail made with dark rum and ginger beer. It was invented in Bermuda, known as the shipwreck capital of the world. I made a few tweaks on the original recipe to get that sea-after-storm color.

INGREDIENTS

Small pinch of activated charcoal, a drop of squid ink, or a drop of black food coloring (optional)

2 oz (60 ml) black spiced rum

½ oz (15 ml) blue curaçao

4 oz (120 ml) ginger beer

Juice of ½ a lime

Lime wedge, for garnish

1. If you want a very black color to your rum, add the rum and a tiny bit of activated charcoal, squid ink, or black food coloring to a cocktail shaker with some ice. Shake for a few seconds to combine.

2. Add the blue curaçao to the glass, then fill with ice. Add the ginger beer and lime juice.

3. Take a spoon and place the tip of the spoon very close to the ginger beer. Slowly pour in rum over the back of the spoon and into the glass. Garnish with a lime wedge.

4. Admire the stormy hues before giving it all a stir with a straw before you drink.

GARNISH: Lime wedge
SERVING VESSEL: A sling, hurricane (small), highball, or zombie glass
PAIRINGS: The Pirate Ship *Revenge* Salmagundi (page 95) or "Life is Pain" Pandemain (page 49)
VIRGINIZE: To replace the rum, mix 2 tablespoons (40 g) of blackstrap molasses thoroughly with 2 ounces (60 ml) of additional lime juice. If you want it to be very black, add activated charcoal, squid ink, or black food coloring. Add the molasses mixture to the glass first, then pour in the ginger beer, add a drop of the blue food coloring, and gently stir it to disperse.

Four White Horses

In true fairy-tale fashion, our story closes with the four heroes escaping on four white horses and riding off into adventures unknown. An alternative ending to the film had Fred Savage's character go to his window to see Westley, Buttercup, Inigo, and Fezzik riding off into the night. Personally, I like the version we ended up with better. This drink contains four "white" components that will have you riding off into the night.

INGREDIENTS

2 oz (60 ml) white rum

2 oz (60 ml) cream or whole milk

½ oz (15 ml) white chocolate liqueur

½ oz (15 ml) cream of coconut

1.   Fill a cocktail shaker with ice.

2.   Add the rum, cream, white chocolate liqueur, and cream of coconut to the shaker. Shake well.

3.   Strain into the serving vessel.

SERVING VESSEL: Julep cup, mug, coupe, tumbler, or cocktail glass

PAIRINGS: Hello Lady(fingers)! (page 136)

VIRGINIZE: Replace liqueur with white chocolate sauce and the rum with coconut nut milk mixed with a couple of drops of rum extract.

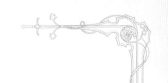

Not a · Witch's Brew

Valerie had relatively few lines in the film, but they made an impression—thanks in no small part to Carol Kane's comedic prowess. Although Valerie is adamant that she's not a witch, it's clear she knows a thing or two and could probably whip up a good potion or elixir any day of the week. Like this chocolate elixir! We know Max and Val have a penchant for chocolate, and cocoa actually has properties which can reduce inflammation, ease a cough, and soothe a sore throat. Low and slow cooking develops a very rich flavored hot cocoa and if you think about it, crock pots are basically electric cauldrons.

INGREDIENTS

FOR THE BREW

1½ cups (262 g) semisweet chocolate chips
¼ cup (22 g) cocoa powder
½ cup (100 g) granulated sugar
2 teaspoons (10 ml) vanilla extract or
    vanilla bean paste
Pinch of kosher salt
1 cinnamon stick (optional)
1 cup (235 ml) heavy cream
    or evaporated milk
6 cups (1.4 L) whole milk

FOR TOPPING

1 cup (235 ml) heavy whipping cream,
    chilled
2 tablespoons (26 g) granulated sugar
½ teaspoon vanilla extract or
    vanilla bean paste
Cocoa powder

1. To make the brew, place the chocolate chips, cocoa, sugar, vanilla, salt, cinnamon stick (if using), cream, and milk in a large slow cooker or a medium saucepan. Stir to combine.

2. If using a slow cooker, cook on low for 5 hours or on high for 3 hours, whisking every 30 to 45 minutes to make sure the chocolate isn't burning on the bottom. If using a saucepan, simmer over low heat for 20 minutes, stirring occasionally, until the chocolate has completely melted and the ingredients have completely melded.

3.   To make the topping, when it's near serving time, pour the heavy whipping cream, sugar, and vanilla in a cold mixing bowl. Whisk on high speed for about 1 minute, until stiff peaks form.

4.   Divide the brew into six mugs, top with whipped cream, and sprinkle with cocoa powder. If you are serving less than six, let the excess come down to room temperature before storing in the refrigerator.

FROM THE PAGES

During the part of the book where Max is negotiating with Inigo,
Valerie is brewing up some hot chocolate. In fact, one of the reasons
Miracle Max agrees to take the job (aside from humiliating Humperdinck, of course)
is because he and Val are almost out of cocoa powder!

Are you just ladling
around with me or what?

Soups
and Stews

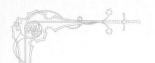

Fezzik's Restorative Stew

SERVES 6 TO 8

Fezzik finds Inigo in a sorry state when the two are reunited in the Thieves' Quarter. To nurse his friend back to health, he dunks Inigo's head alternately in hot and cold water, and spoon-feeds him what appears to be a rich stew. Here we have a hearty beef stew with almost an entire bottle of red wine for the base. What a fantastic way to finish your wine stock and remove Inigo's temptation to drink it! Plus, hair of the dog, amirite?

INGREDIENTS

3 lb. (1.4 kg) beef chuck, cut into
 2-inch (5-cm) cubes
Salt and ground black pepper
6 oz (170 g) thick-cut bacon, lardons,
 or pancetta, diced
1 yellow onion, chopped
3 carrots, peeled and roughly chopped
4 cloves garlic, minced
2 teaspoons (11 g) tomato paste
2 tablespoons (16 g) all-purpose flour
2 teaspoons (4 g) allspice

¾ bottle (560 ml) red wine
1 cup (235 ml) beef broth
2 bay leaves
2 sprigs of fresh thyme
3 russet potatoes, peeled and
 coarsely chopped
1 tablespoon (15 ml) extra-virgin olive oil
¼ cup (60 ml) water
15 pearl onions, peeled
Pinch of granulated sugar
Chopped fresh Italian parsley (optional)

1. Preheat the oven to 350°F (175°C). Season the beef with salt and pepper. Set aside for 30 minutes to 1 hour, until room temperature.

2. In a large Dutch oven, cook the bacon over medium heat until brown and crispy. Set the bacon aside on a paper towel. Keep the fat in the pot. Increase the heat to medium-high until the bacon fat starts to smoke and sizzle. Add beef cubes in a single layer with space between each cube. Cook until brown, rotating to brown all sides. When done, set them aside on a plate. Repeat with the remaining cubes; this might take two or three rounds.

3. Reduce the heat to medium. Stir in the onion and carrots, season with salt and pepper, and cook until softened. Stir in the garlic and cook for 1 minute, then add in the tomato paste and cook for 1 minute. Stir in the flour and allspice. Cook for 1 minute, stirring occasionally.

4. Add the wine, broth, bay leaves, and thyme, scraping up the browned bits on the bottom of the pot. Add the beef and half the bacon back to the pot. Cover and cook in the oven for 45 minutes. Take the stew out and give it all a stir. Taste and adjust the seasonings. Add the potatoes and transfer the pot back to the oven. Cook for 45 minutes.

5. While that's becoming more delicious, heat a small or medium skillet over high heat. Add the olive oil, pearl onions, water, and sugar. Season with salt and pepper. Bring to a simmer, reduce the heat to medium and cover. Cook for 15 minutes. Uncover, raise the heat to high, and sauté until the onions are tender and have good caramelization.

6. Remove the stew from the oven after 45 minutes. The beef should be very tender, but give it another 10 or 20 minutes if you prefer it more tender. Scatter the onions and the remaining bacon over the top of the stew. Sprinkle parsley (if desired).

FROM THE PAGES

In the book, Fezzik makes this stew with roast beef
and something that may be a potato.

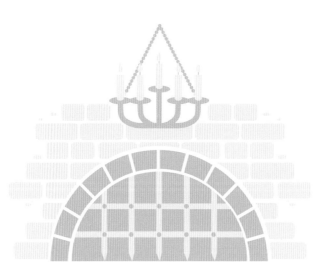

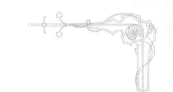

Florinese "Mawidge" Soup

Known in the script only as "Impressive Clergyman," Peter Cook delivered a very solemn speech in the most absurd manner possible. This recipe is a take on *minestra maritata* or "married soup." It is known as Italian Wedding Soup outside of Italy, named so because it's the perfect "mawidge" of flavors. When serving, tell your guests that "mawidge" is what bwings them togewer today.

INGREDIENTS

FOR THE MEATBALLS

16 oz (454 g) Italian sausage
    and/or ground beef
½ cup (60 g) bread crumbs
½ cup (40 g) finely shredded Parmesan
2 cloves garlic, minced
1 tablespoon (3 g) minced fresh chives
½ tablespoon (3 g) finely chopped
    fresh, flat-leaf parsley
Red pepper flakes
1 large egg
Salt and ground black pepper
1 tablespoon (15 ml) extra-virgin olive oil

FOR THE SOUP

1 tablespoon (15 ml) extra-virgin olive oil
3 carrots, diced
1 large yellow onion, diced
3 stalks of celery, diced
5 cloves garlic, minced
Zest of 1 lemon
4–6 cups (1–1.4 L) chicken broth
1 tablespoon (4 g) chopped fresh oregano
Salt and ground black pepper
1 cup (235 ml) dry *acini de pepe*
    or ditalini pasta
6 oz (170 g) fresh baby spinach
    or chopped escarole
½ cup (120 ml) heavy cream (optional)
Pinch of red pepper flakes (optional)
Finely shredded Parmesan and/or fontina

1. To make the meatballs, add all the meatball ingredients except the olive oil to a large mixing bowl. Use your hands to thoroughly combine. Shape the mixture into meatballs, about 1 inch (2.5 cm) in diameter, and transfer to a large plate.

2. Heat the olive oil in a large, nonstick skillet over medium-high heat. Add the meatballs and cook for about 5 minutes, turning occasionally, until brown. You may need to do this in batches to prevent overcrowding. Transfer the meatballs to a paper towel–lined plate. The meatballs won't be cooked through; they'll finish cooking in the soup.

3. To make the soup, heat the olive oil in a large pot over medium-high heat. Add carrots, onions, and celery. Sauté for 7 minutes, until the veggies soften. Add the garlic and sauté for 1 minute.

4. Pour in the broth. Add the oregano, and season with salt and pepper to taste. Bring the mixture to a boil. Add the pasta and meatballs, and reduce the heat to medium-low.

5. Cover and cook for about 20 minutes, stirring occasionally, until the pasta is tender and meatballs have cooked through. Add the spinach, cream, and red pepper flakes (if using) during the last few minutes of cooking. Adjust the seasonings to taste. Serve hot with a sprinkle of Parmesan.

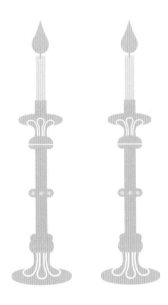

"Unemployed in Greenland" Suaasat

When Fezzik expresses misgivings at the idea of murdering Buttercup, Vizzini threatens to send him back where he found him: unemployed in Greenland. Being unemployed in Greenland sounds like a terrible fate, but it probably won't be all bad for Fezzik . . . at least he'd have this humble stew to comfort him! Suaasat is the national dish of Greenland. It's a simple and unassuming dish, traditionally made with seal meat, but sometimes other game meats are used. This stew calls for inexpensive ingredients, so it won't break the bank even if you're between jobs.

INGREDIENTS

2–3 lb. (907 g to 1.4 kg) lamb leg or beef short ribs (If you have access to game meat you can also use caribou, venison, or elk.)

Sea salt and ground black pepper

2 white onions, chopped

3 carrots, chopped

5 cups (1.2 L) water

8–10 red potatoes, chopped

½ cup (100 g) pearl barley, soaked overnight

½ cup (80 g) wild rice

½ cup (13 g) dried porcini mushrooms

1 teaspoon dried rosemary

1 teaspoon dried sage

1 teaspoon dried thyme

2 bay leaves

1 tablespoon (21 g) whole-grain mustard

1. Season the meat liberally with salt and pepper, and let it sit at room temperature for about 30 minutes.

2. In a large stockpot or Dutch oven, brown the meat on all sides over medium-high heat. Depending on the size of your pot and the type of meat you are using, you may need to do this in batches to prevent overcrowding. Remove the meat and set aside.

3. In the same pot, add the onions and carrots. Sauté until the onions are translucent and the carrots are just beginning to soften. Use a wooden spoon to stir and try to scrape up the brown bits leftover from browning the meat.

4. Add the meat back to the pot, along with the remaining ingredients. Bring to a boil.

5. Turn the heat to low and let it simmer for 2 hours, until the meat, rice, and barley are tender. Taste and adjust the seasonings as it cooks.

Farm Boy Stew

SERVES 6 TO 8

Initially Buttercup is oblivious to Westley's devotion and oblivious to her own feelings for him. She calls Westley "Farm boy" and takes great joy in ordering him around. This stew is loosely based on an old farmer's stew called coq au vin, originally made using rooster meat and red wine. This version uses chicken and white wine, with fresh cream and goat cheese to give some extra farmstead flare. While you put this together, enjoy imagining Buttercup ordering Westley around to fetch and prep the ingredients.

INGREDIENTS

1 cup (80 g) chopped lardons, pancetta, or thick-sliced bacon

8 pieces bone-in chicken

Salt and ground black pepper

1 yellow onion, finely chopped

3 carrots, chopped

6 cloves garlic, thinly sliced

1 cup (70 g) halved cremini mushrooms

1 tablespoon (15 ml) extra-virgin olive oil or butter, if needed

2 bay leaves

4 sprigs of fresh thyme

1 cup (235 ml) cream

⅔ bottle (500 ml) dry white wine

Crumbled goat cheese

Chopped fresh, flat-leaf parsley

1. In a Dutch oven, fry the lardons over medium-high heat until crispy. Once done, remove on a paper towel–lined plate and set aside.

2. Season the chicken with salt and pepper, and brown it in the leftover bacon fat over medium-high heat. Set aside.

3. Pour a small amount of the wine into the pot and scrape up the browned bits from the bottom of the pot. Add the onion and carrots. Cook over low heat for 5 to 7 minutes, then add the garlic when the onion is tender and translucent. Cook for 1 minute longer. Set aside.

4. Add the mushrooms to the Dutch oven and cook them for 5 minutes over medium-high heat. You may need to add some oil to prevent burning.

5. Return the chicken, onion, garlic, and lardons to the pan. Add the bay leaves and thyme, then pour in the wine. Bring to a boil, then turn the heat to low, cover it, and let it simmer for 20 minutes. Uncover and cook for another 20 minutes. Add the cream and simmer for 10 minutes.

6. Remove the thyme stems and serve with goat cheese and a sprinkle of parsley.

Grandfather's Matzo Ball Soup

SERVES 6 TO 8

The Princess Bride opens and closes with a grandfather, played beautifully by the late Peter Falk. He is reading a book to his sick grandson. It's a special story that has been passed down through the family for generations. A good story is obviously panacea for the body and soul, but there's another cold-buster that's often cherished within families: chicken soup. The healing powers of chicken soup are ancient and well-known. Maimonides, a twelfth century Jewish philosopher and physician, said that chicken soup could cure all manner of illnesses, which is one of the many reasons that chicken soup eventually earned the title "Jewish Penicillin." Even a retired Miracle Man would tell you: a good story and some chicken soup are just the thing to beat a winter cold.

INGREDIENTS

FOR THE MATZO BALLS

4 eggs, whisked

¼ cup (60 ml) schmaltz (sub vegetable or canola oil)

1 teaspoon baking powder

¼ cup (60 ml) chicken broth

1 cup (116 g) matzo meal

½ teaspoon garlic powder

½ teaspoon onion powder

Pinch of powdered ginger (optional)

1 tablespoon (4 g) finely chopped fresh, flat-leaf parsley

1 tablespoon (4 g) finely chopped fresh dill fronds

Kosher salt and ground black pepper

FOR THE SOUP

1 tablespoon (15 ml) schmaltz or unsalted butter

1 large white onion, finely diced

2–3 carrots, peeled, halved lengthwise and sliced

2 stalks of celery, sliced

4 cloves garlic, minced

2x Buttercup's Perfect (Chicken) Breasts (page 78) or 2½ cups (350 g) cooked chicken, shredded

6–8 cups (1.4–1.9 L) chicken stock

2 tablespoons (8 g) chopped fresh dill fronds

Garlic and onion powder

Salt and ground black pepper

2 tablespoons (8 g) chopped fresh, flat-leaf parsley

1. To make the matzo balls, combine all the matzo ingredients in a large mixing bowl. Gently mix with a whisk or spoon. Cover and refrigerate for at least 3 hours, until chilled. This can be stored overnight.

2. To make the soup, add the schmaltz to a Dutch oven or large saucepan over medium heat. Add the onion, carrots, and celery to the pot and cook for 4 to 5 minutes, or until softened. Add the garlic and cook for 30 seconds. Add the chicken, stock, dill, garlic powder, onion powder, salt, and pepper. Bring to a simmer.

3. Wet your hands and take some of the matzo mixture and mold it into the size and shape of a Ping-Pong™ ball. Drop the balls into the soup. Cover the pot and simmer for 25 to 30 minutes, or until the balls are puffed and vegetables are tender.

4. Sprinkle parsley, then serve.

FROM THE PAGES

If you're wondering why Matzo Ball specifically, Goldman himself is Jewish.
In the novel, he is attempting to bond with his son by sharing his favorite book,
The Princess Bride: S. Morgenstern's Classic Tale of True Love and High Adventure,
which his father read to him when he was a child. He also specifically notes
that the fictional author S. Morgenstern is Jewish as well
and that Max and Valerie are based on Morgenstern's parents!

*Do you always begin
meals this way?*

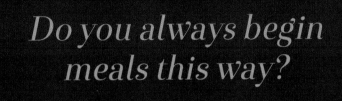

Appetizers and Accompaniments

"Not a Lot of Money in Revenge" Beggar's Purses

SERVES 4 TO 6

We first hear Inigo's tale of vengeance and woe atop the Cliffs of Insanity, in the ruins where the sword fight would soon take place, whilst he and the Man in Black have their pre-battle get-to-know-you chat. Inigo tells the Man in Black about his life's purpose and how after years of searching he's still been unable to locate the six-fingered man who murdered his beloved father. He explains that this isn't exactly the most lucrative lifestyle, so he works for Vizzini to pay the bills. These tasty morsels are often called "beggar's purses" because of their unique shape, which is similar to a coin purse.

INGREDIENTS

⅓ cup (27 g) chopped pancetta, bacon, or smoked salmon

6 oz (170 g) goat cheese or cream cheese, softened

1 tablespoon (3 g) chopped fresh chives

1 tablespoon (3–5 g) finely chopped fresh herbs, such as thyme, parsley, or dill

Zest of 1 lemon

Salt and ground black pepper

6 sheets of phyllo dough

½ cup (112 g) unsalted butter, melted

Whole chives or narrow strips of green onions

1. Preheat the oven to 400°F (200°C). Line a baking sheet with parchment. If using pancetta or bacon, fry it in a medium-size skillet over medium heat, until crisp and the fat has rendered. Then let it drain and cool to room temperature on a paper towel–lined plate. If using smoked salmon, skip the frying and move on to the next step.

2. In a small bowl, mix the goat cheese, chives, herbs, lemon zest, and pancetta. Season to taste with salt and pepper.

3. Unroll the phyllo dough onto a dry surface. Remove one sheet of phyllo dough and place it on a dry surface. Brush the entire sheet with melted butter. Top with another sheet of phyllo and brush it with melted butter. Repeat with one more sheet of phyllo. Cut the stack into four equal rectangles. Do this step again with the other three sheets.

4. Place 3 tablespoons (45 to 60 g) of filling onto the center of each piece of dough. Gather the sides of the dough into a pouch and form a purse, pinching it together. Tie a chive around the dough.

5. Place the purse on the baking sheet and lightly brush with melted butter. Bake for 8 to 10 minutes until the phyllo purse tops are golden brown and crispy.

6. Remove from the oven and let cool. Serve warm or at room temperature.

"Life is Pain" Pandemain

MAKES 2

Pain is the French word for bread, and bread is a frequent prop in the film. It's there during the Battle of Wits. It's there when Fezzik nurses Inigo back to health. It's even in the Pit of Despair. This recipe is for *pandemain*, a crusty white bread made for nobility throughout the Medieval and the Renaissance era, first referenced in Chaucer's *Canterbury Tales*. Plus it rhymes with pain, which would make Fezzik happy. To the pain!

INGREDIENTS

2 tablespoons (26 g) granulated sugar, divided

1 package (21 g) active dry yeast

¼ cup (60 ml) water, warm but not hot

2 cups (475 ml) whole milk, scalded

1 teaspoon kosher salt

1 tablespoon (15 ml) extra-virgin olive oil or grapeseed oil

6 cups (750 g) unbleached, all-purpose flour, sifted

2 tablespoons (28 g) salted butter, melted

1. In a small bowl, add 1 tablespoon (13 g) of sugar to the warm water. Add the packet of yeast and give it a gentle stir. Let the yeast dissolve for 5 to 10 minutes.

2. In the meantime, combine the hot milk, remaining sugar, salt, and oil. Let cool until lukewarm.

3. Stir in ¼ of the flour and mix well with a stand mixer. You can use a hand mixer or even just your hands, but you may have a tougher go of it.

4. Add the yeast mixture and continue mixing. Add a little at a time, enough of the remaining flour to make a stiff dough. Use the dough hook on your mixer to knead the dough for 7 minutes, or until smooth. Or, use your hands to knead for 10 to 12 minutes until the dough is smooth and elastic.

5. Shape the dough into a ball and place it in a lightly greased bowl. Cover with plastic wrap and let the dough rise at room temperature until it has doubled in size. Punch down, then let it rise again until doubled.

6. Preheat the oven to 400°F (200°C). Cut the dough into two portions and shape each into a smooth ball. Cover and let rest for 10 minutes, then shape into round loaves. Place the loaves on greased pans. With a sharp knife, slash an X or a cross on the tops, and once again let it rise until doubled.

7. Bake for 35 minutes, or until the crust is golden and the internal temperature is 200°F (93°C).

8. Remove from the oven, brush the tops with melted butter and let the loaves rest in the pan for 10 minutes before transferring to a rack to cool to a desired serving temperature. Slice and serve!

TIP

You may need more or less flour depending on the humidity of your home. During kneading, the dough should be a little sticky but pull away from the sides of the bowl, leaving the bowl mostly clean. Also, keep in mind that the colder your house is, the longer the bread will take to rise.

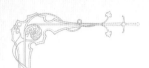

Arancini à la Vizzini

Vizzini is a man of dizzying intellect, quite possibly the smartest man who ever lived (by his own estimation). During the Battle of Wits, he admonishes Westley for falling for one of the two classic blunders: going against a Sicilian when death is on the line. The other blunder being "never get involved in a land war in Asia." Arancini is a classic Sicilian appetizer, fried balls of creamy risotto with various flavors and fillings. This recipe has a few twists to incorporate both of the classic blunders.

INGREDIENTS

2 ½ cups (570 ml) chicken broth

½ oz (14 g) dried porcini mushrooms

1 tablespoon (15 ml) extra-virgin olive oil

1 white onion, finely chopped

4 cloves garlic, minced

1 cup (200 g) sushi rice

½ cup (120 ml) sake or other rice wine

½ cup (65 g) frozen green peas

10 oz (283 g) shiitake mushrooms, finely chopped

Sea salt and ground black pepper

Dash of shichimi togarashi (optional)

½ cup (50 g) finely grated Parmesan cheese, plus more for serving

1 egg, whisked

1 large egg, plus more if needed

1 tablespoon (15 ml) whole milk, plus more if needed

4 oz (113 g) mozzarella cheese, cut into 1-inch (2.5-cm) cubes

½ cup (64 g) all-purpose flour, plus more if needed

1 cup (50 g) ground panko flakes or bread crumbs, plus more if needed

1 cup (236 ml) vegetable oil, for deep frying

Fresh, flat-leaf parsley, chopped

Marinara sauce, warmed

1. Bring the chicken broth to a simmer in a heavy medium-size saucepan. Add the porcini mushrooms. Set aside until the mushrooms are tender, about 5 minutes.

2. Heat the olive oil in a large saucepan over medium heat. Add the onion and sauté for 1 minute. Add the garlic and mushrooms, and sauté for 1 minute until onions are translucent. Stir in the rice and cook for another 2 minutes, stirring continuously.

3. Add the sake and continue to stir until the liquid has completely evaporated. Then, add the chicken broth ⅓ cup (80 ml) at a time, stirring and cooking until the liquid has evaporated before adding more.

4. After the chicken stock has all been added, and the liquid has completely evaporated, stir in the peas. Season with salt, pepper, and shichimi togarashi (if using). Remove from the heat, and stir in the Parmesan cheese.

5. Transfer the risotto to a separate bowl, and allow it to cool almost to room temperature before stirring in the beaten egg.

6. In a separate, smaller bowl, whisk the other egg with the milk. Roll 2 tablespoons (about 40 g) of the risotto into a ball. Press a piece of the mozzarella cheese into the center, and roll to enclose.

7. Lightly coat the ball with flour, dip into the milk mixture, then roll it in the ground panko to coat. Repeat until you have used all the risotto. You may need additional eggs, milk, flour, and panko.

8. Preheat the oven to 200°F (93°C). Heat the vegetable oil in a deep fryer or a large, thick-bottomed saucepan to 350°F (175°C). Fry the balls in small batches until evenly golden, turning as needed. Be sure not to crowd the fryer.

9. Drain on paper towels. Keep the balls warm in the oven while the rest are frying.

10. Sprinkle with additional Parmesan and parsley. Serve with your favorite marinara sauce.

"Prepare To Die" Fiery Spanish Croquetas

Being a Spaniard, it's entirely possible that the morning after a brandy binge Inigo would have partaken in some croquettes (or *croquetas* in Spanish). Luscious fried dumplings filled with creamy béchamel, it's no wonder croquettes are one of the most popular hangover foods in Spain. Croquettes are generally quite mild, but this recipe makes them fiery like Inigo's burning need for revenge. Served with chorizo and a spicy mojo sauce. Alert your taste buds, "prepare to die!"

INGREDIENTS

FOR THE CROQUETTES

¼ cup (55 g) unsalted butter
¼ cup (59 ml) extra-virgin olive oil
1 cup (125 g) all-purpose flour
1 Spanish onion, finely chopped
1 teaspoon smoked paprika
1 teaspoon Aleppo pepper, or to taste
1 teaspoon garlic powder
1 teaspoon nutmeg
¼ teaspoon cayenne or 1 teaspoon
    red pepper flakes, or to taste
1 teaspoon salt, or to taste
1 teaspoon ground black pepper,
    or to taste
7 oz (198 g) picante (hot) Spanish chorizo,
    diced into small pieces (see note)
All-purpose flour
4 cups (940 ml) whole milk at
    room temperature
2 eggs, whisked, or more if needed
Bread crumbs
Vegetable oil or any high-smoke-point oil

FOR THE MOJO SAUCE

2 large red bell peppers, de-seeded
1–2 red chili peppers, such as Fresno
4–5 cloves garlic, minced
½ tablespoon (4 g) cumin
2 teaspoons (5 g) paprika
Pinch of cayenne or red pepper flakes
    (optional)
Salt
3 tablespoons (45 ml) extra-virgin
    olive oil

1. To make the croquettes, begin the béchamel by melting the butter and warming the oil in a medium-size saucepan over medium-high heat. Add the onion and sauté for 3 minutes, until it just starts to color. Add smoked paprika, Aleppo pepper, garlic powder, nutmeg, and cayenne (if using). Season with salt and pepper. Stir to combine. Add the chorizo and sauté for 1 minute.

2. Add the flour a little bit at a time, stirring continuously to prevent burning, until the flour turns a golden color. When the flour is completely incorporated and the mixture has the golden color, slowly add the milk, a little at a time, stirring continuously. Don't add more until the previous amount is fully incorporated. It will take about 15 to 20 minutes to add it all. Remove from the heat and let cool to room temperature.

3. Grease the sides of a large bowl with butter and put the croquette dough inside. Cover the mixture with plastic wrap and refrigerate at least 4 hours, but preferably overnight.

4. When you're ready to fry the croquettes, take the béchamel out of the fridge. Shape it into small logs. You can use your hands or two spoons to shape them.

5. Sprinkle some flour onto a plate and roll the logs in it. Dip the flour-covered béchamel logs into the whisked eggs. You can whisk in more eggs as needed, if you run out. After the logs have been dipped in the eggs, roll each log in the bread crumbs until fully coated. Set aside. Repeat until all the logs have been breaded.

6. Heat the oil in a deep fryer or a large thick-bottomed saucepan to 350°F (175°C). Fry the logs in small batches until evenly golden, turning as needed, around 3 to 5 minutes on each side. Do not get tempted to crowd the fryer or saucepan. Remove the croquettes from the fryer and place on a paper towel to drain the excess oil. Repeat until all the croquettes have been fried.

7. While the croquettes cool, make the mojo! Using a food processor or blender, add all ingredients except the olive oil. Blend until smooth. You can also use an immersion blender or even a mortar and pestle (if you want to go old school).

8. To serve, spear the croquettes with cocktail swords. Use the swords to dip the croquettes into the mojo sauce before eating!

TIP

Spanish chorizo is hard; it's similar in texture and form to salami.
Mexican-style chorizo, which is soft and oily, won't work here.

Gentle Giant's Gargantuan Gougères

André the Giant, being a French native, had a penchant for French cuisine. In Cary Elwes's book, *As You Wish: Inconceivable Tales from the Making of The Princess Bride*, Elwes fondly recalls the occasion when André brought back wine and various other delicacies from France to a grateful crew who had been shooting in a remote part of England. *Gougères* are French pastry bites, made of a savory pâte à choux dough mixed with cheese. Generally, they are quite small, but this recipe will make them more Fezzik-sized. You can hold them in your hand like large rocks, but don't throw them at anyone because that wouldn't be very sportsmanlike.

INGREDIENTS

FOR THE GOUGÈRES
1 cup (235 ml) whole milk
1 cup (235 ml) water
6 tablespoons (84 g) salted butter,
 cut into pieces
1 teaspoon salt, or more to taste
1½ cups (188 g) plus 1 tablespoon (8 g)
 all-purpose flour
½ teaspoon piment d'Espelette or
 a pinch of cayenne pepper (optional)
Pinch of nutmeg
4 large eggs
2 cups (240 g) shredded Comté or
 Gruyère cheese, divided
Sea salt and ground black pepper

FOR THE FILLING (OPTIONAL)
11 oz (312 g) chèvre, room temperature
6 oz (170 g) cream cheese,
 room temperature
½ cup (120 ml) heavy whipping cream
2 teaspoons (4 g) lemon zest
2 tablespoons (8 g) chopped fresh parsley
2 tablespoons (6 g) chopped fresh chives
2 cloves garlic, minced
Salt and ground black pepper

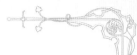

1. Preheat the oven to 400°F (200°C). Line two baking sheets with parchment paper.

2. To make the gougères, add the milk, water, butter, and salt to a large saucepan. Bring to a boil over medium-high heat. Add the flour, piment d'Espelette, and nutmeg, and mix vigorously with a wooden spoon until the flour is thoroughly incorporated. Reduce the heat to low, stirring constantly for about 3 to 5 minutes.

3. Remove the saucepan from the heat and let stand at room temperature for about 5 minutes, stirring occasionally, until the dough cools slightly. Using a hand mixer, beat in the eggs one at a time, thoroughly incorporating each egg. The dough may break initially when adding the eggs but will come together with more mixing. Stir in 1½ cups (180 g) of the cheese (reserving the rest for sprinkling).

4. Place mounds of dough (about 3 tablespoons each) onto the baking sheets, 2 inches (5 cm) apart. Sprinkle each mound with cheese and top with salt and pepper.

5. Bake for 15 minutes at 400°F (200°C) then reduce the temperature to 350°F (175°C) and bake for 30 minutes, until the gougères are puffed and browned. Turn off the oven, open the door, and let the gougères rest in the oven for about 30 minutes. They can be served like this, slightly warm, or at room temperature, but move ahead if you want to add filling.

6. To make the filling, using either a stand mixer or hand mixer, whip the chèvre and cream cheese together for 2 to 3 minutes, then add the lemon zest, parsley, chives, and garlic. Continue to whip for 2 to 3 minutes until everything is well incorporated.

7. In a separate mixing bowl, whip the heavy cream until stiff peaks form. Add the whipped cream to the chèvre mixture and mix for 2 to 3 minutes until well incorporated. Season with salt and pepper to taste. Spoon the chèvre mixture into a piping bag with a small round attachment. Pierce a small hole into the bottom or side of the cooled gougères and use the piping bag to fill with the whipped chèvre mixture. Serve immediately!

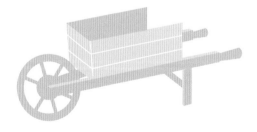

Six-Fingered Man Skewers (Rugen's Flammkuchen)

Count Rugen is Humperdinck's best friend and sidekick. He's a very diabolical and insidious presence in the film, harboring a twisted fascination with pain and inflicting it upon others. Skewers seemed highly appropriate given his well-deserved fate at the end of the film. This recipe makes exactly six, one for each of that SOB's fingers.

INGREDIENTS

1 tablespoon (14 g) unsalted butter

1 large yellow onion, thinly sliced

1 teaspoon brown sugar

Salt and ground black pepper

¼ cup (56 g) crème fraîche and/or sour cream

½ teaspoon nutmeg (optional)

14 oz (397 g) pizza dough (homemade or store bought)

¾ cup (90 g) grated Gruyère or other alpine cheese

6 strips of bacon

1. Melt the butter in a medium skillet. Add the onions and sauté over low heat for 15 to 20 minutes, stirring frequently, until onions are considerably shrunk. Near the end, stir in the sugar and season with salt and pepper.

2. In a small bowl, mix the crème fraîche and nutmeg. Season to taste with salt and pepper.

3. Preheat the oven to 375°F (190°C). Roll out the dough and use a pizza cutter to cut it into twelve strips. On six of the strips, spread some of the sour cream mixture along the center. On top of that, layer on the cheese and the onions.

4. Take the other strips and lay them on top of the strips with the toppings. Use your hands to pinch the dough together around the edges to seal the filling inside. Small gaps and holes are okay.

5. Weave the filled strips securely onto the skewers, then wrap the bacon strips around them in a spiral pattern.

6. Line a baking sheet with aluminum foil and place a wire rack on top. Grease or spray the rack to prevent sticking.

7. Place the skewers on the rack and bake for 20 to 25 minutes, until both the bacon and the dough have cooked through.

FROM THE PAGES

Christopher Guest, the actor who played Count Rugen, also starred in *This is Spinal Tap,* Rob Reiner's directorial debut. That film convinced author William Goldman that Rob was the right director to bring his story to life!

"Battle of Wits" Brie and Apple Crostini

SERVES 6 TO 8

When the Man in Black approaches Vizzini holding Buttercup hostage, Vizzini has set up a nice little spread with some apples, some crusty bread, and a big hunk of white-rinded cheese. When Vizzini had the time to set all that up and where he was hiding those things is unclear, although my guess would be they were hidden in those puffy sleeves . . . . If the situation didn't call for hostilities, the three of them might have had a lovely picnic. This dish can be considered a fan-made "alternative ending" to the Battle of Wits.

INGREDIENTS

FOR THE RED WINE DRIZZLE
1 cup (235 ml) red wine
¼ cup (85 g) honey
Pinch of sea salt

FOR THE CROSTINI
1 baguette
1 tablespoon (15 ml) extra-virgin olive oil
7 oz (198 g) Brie, sliced
2 Honeycrisp or Pink Lady apples, thinly sliced
½ cup (60 g) chopped candied walnuts, pecans, or pistachios

1. Add the wine, honey, and salt to a large pan over medium heat. Simmer until the liquid is reduced to approximately ¼ cup (60 ml). Set aside.

2. Preheat the oven to 350°F (175°C). Line a baking sheet with parchment paper. Using a serrated knife, slice the baguette crosswise on a slight diagonal into ½-inch (1-cm)-thick slices. Transfer the slices to the prepared baking sheet and brush them with olive oil.

3. Top each piece of bread with 1 to 2 slices of Brie. Place in the oven for about 5 minutes, or until the bread turns golden brown at the edges and the Brie is melty.

4. Add one or two apple slices on top of each crostini. Drizzle each crostini with the red wine sauce that was set aside earlier and sprinkle with candied nuts.

The National Dish of Florin

Florin is the fictional kingdom in which most of the story takes place. But what sort of place is Florin, and, more importantly, what do people eat there? This recipe is a take on a Danish dish called "Burning Love," which is a sort of true love and an inferior form of "twu wuv." Burning love is topped with caramelized onions and bacon. If you're really not a fan of rutabagas, toss the rutabagas at the screen during the "booooo!" scene (assuming your television is insured against root vegetable related damages) and use turnips or potatoes instead.

INGREDIENTS

FOR THE MASH
2 lb. (907 g) rutabaga, peeled
1 teaspoon kosher salt
1 tablespoon (13 g) granulated sugar
⅓ cup (75 g) unsalted butter
½ cup (115 g) sour cream
Pinch of nutmeg (optional)
Salt and ground black pepper

FOR THE TOPPING
1 lb. (454 g) bacon, diced
1 large yellow or red onion, sliced
Chopped fresh chives and/or
   flat-leaf parsley
Pickled beets (optional)

1. To make the mash, cut the peeled rutabagas into 1- to 2-inch (2.5- to 5-cm) chunks. Place the rutabagas in a large saucepan and cover with water. Add the salt and sugar. Bring to a boil over medium-high heat. Reduce the heat to low, cover, and let it simmer for about 30 minutes or until tender.

2. To make the topping, fry the bacon in a large skillet over medium-high heat until done to your liking. Set the bacon aside but keep the fat in the pan. Reduce the heat to low, and add the onions to the pan. Cook for 15 to 20 minutes, or longer for caramelization. Discard or keep any remaining fat in the pan at your discretion.

3. Drain the cooked rutabagas and let them dry in a colander for 5 minutes. Mash the rutabagas with the butter, then mix in the sour cream and nutmeg (if using). Season with salt and pepper to taste.

4. Portion out the servings of mashed rutabaga. Create a well in the middle of each serving and spoon some onions into the well, then top with the bacon. Garnish with chives and serve with pickled beets on the side (if desired).

Swordmasters' Fon-Duel

The sword fight between the mysterious Man in Black and Inigo Montoya is no doubt one of the most thrilling in film history. Cary Elwes and Mandy Patinkin studied fencing and trained diligently so they could do all the fighting themselves without doubles. To commemorate this incredible feat, I concocted these two fondues. The Man in Black's fondue can be made with either black truffle or black garlic and fontina cheese. Inigo's fondue is flavored with Manchego, smoked paprika, and brandy. For an extra challenge, try using your nondominant hand to skewer and dip, but don't hurt yourself if engaging in any skewer duels!

INIGO'S FONDUE

1 clove garlic, peeled and cut in half
1 tablespoon (8 g) cornstarch
2 cups (240 g) grated Comté or
    Gruyère cheese
2 cups (200 g) grated Manchego cheese

½ cup (120 ml) dry white wine or
    chicken broth
1–2 teaspoons (3–5 g) smoked paprika
1 tablespoon (15 ml) brandy (optional)

MAN IN BLACK'S FONDUE

1 clove garlic, peeled and cut in half
1 tablespoon (8 g) cornstarch
2 cups (240 g) grated Gruyère or
    Emmentaler cheese
2 cups (220 g) grated fontina cheese
½ cup (120 ml) dry white wine or
    chicken broth

1–2 teaspoons (5–10 ml) black truffle oil
    or 1 tablespoon (10 g) minced
    black garlic
¼ of a black truffle, shaved, or ground
    black pepper (optional)

SUGGESTIONS FOR DIPPERS

"Life is Pain" Pandemain (page 49) or
    French bread, cubed
Buttercup's Perfect (Chicken) Breasts
    (page 78) or cooked chicken, cubed
Roasted baby potatoes

Sliced apples
Cherry tomatoes
Steamed or roasted veggies
Cornichons, rinsed and patted dry
Spanish chorizo

1. Make each fondue separately in a medium saucepan before transferring them to the serving vessel(s). Cut the garlic cloves in half and rub each saucepan with the cut side.

2. Thoroughly mix the cornstarch with the two grated cheeses in a large mixing bowl. Set aside.

3. Heat the wine over medium heat until you begin to see bubbles rise to the surface. Do not boil. Add the cheeses by small handfuls slowly, stirring continuously in a figure-eight motion.

4. Once the fondue reaches a hot and melted—but not boiling—consistency, stir in the flavorings. For Inigo's fondue, add smoked paprika and brandy (if using). For the mysterious Man in Black's fondue, add shaved black truffle and black truffle oil.

5. Rub each of your serving destination(s) with garlic. Transfer the fondue to the serving vessel(s) and keep warm. Continue to stir occasionally until it's serving time, which should be as soon as possible. Serve with skewers and an assortment of dippers.

TIP

Much like sword fighting with your nondominant hand, making two fondues at once can be a little tricky. The process for these two is pretty much the same, but you'll need to keep both the fondues warm for serving. Ideally, you can use a fondue set or a small crockpot. Or if you need to, you can use a hotplate, or a pot stand with some tea candles underneath, and a small saucepan over that. Any combination of these will work.

Have You the Wings?

SERVES 3 TO 5

Mawidge may be what brings people together, and chicken wings are often found whenever people gather. Taking inspiration from a few different chicken dishes from the Middle Ages, these wings are flavored with spices and honey and topped with fried almonds. Think of them as hot wings, Florin style! And instead of watching the football game on TV, imagine you're spectating a joust or a duel. Or perhaps a very strange royal wedding?

INGREDIENTS

FOR THE WINGS
1 tablespoon (15 g) kosher salt
1 tablespoon (14 g) baking powder
1 tablespoon (6 g) ground black pepper
1 tablespoon (7 g) French four spice
1 tablespoon (7 g) paprika
3 lb. (1.4 kg) chicken wings
    (drums and flats)

FOR THE GLAZE
½ cup (112 g) salted butter
1 tablespoon (7 g) French four spice
1 tablespoon (6 g) ground black pepper
1 tablespoon (7 g) paprika
1 tablespoon (6 g) orange zest
6 tablespoons (120 g) honey, warmed
2 tablespoons (28 ml) orange juice

FOR THE TOPPING
2 tablespoons (28 g) salted butter
½ cup (56 g) sliced almonds

1. Mix all spices for the chicken wings in a small bowl. In a separate large mixing bowl, add the chicken wing pieces. Sprinkle in the spice mixture slowly while tossing wings to coat evenly on all sides. Cover and place in the refrigerator for at least 4 hours or overnight. Remove from the fridge and let it rest for about 1 hour.

2. Set an oven rack or broiler rack to a level 6 to 7 inches (15 to 18 cm) from the broiler and preheat the oven broiler to about 500°F (260°C). Grease a baking sheet or cover it with aluminum foil or parchment paper. Lay chicken wings skin-side down (bottom side facing up) on the prepared baking sheet.

3. To make the glaze, melt the butter in a microwave or saucepan. Add the spices and zest. Stir well, then stir in the honey and orange juice. Mix until well incorporated. If the honey doesn't completely mix with the melted butter, you may need to heat it up.

4. To make the topping, melt the butter in a small skillet over medium heat. Add almond slices. Cook until lightly browned and toasted, stirring frequently. Remove from the heat when toasted. It's easy to burn these so watch carefully.

5. Place chicken wings under the broiler for 15 minutes. Remove the chicken wings and flip them over skin-side up. Return to the broiler for 15 minutes. Check occasionally to prevent burning. Remove from the oven and place the wings in a medium-size, clean mixing bowl.

6. Pour the glaze mixture over the wings while tossing to coat all sides. Add the almond topping and toss again.

Prepare to dine!

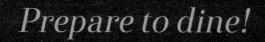

Main Courses

The Albino's Pre-Torture Nourishment

SERVES 4 TO 6

In the Pit of Despair, the Albino walks in carrying a plate of food and drink for Westley. I have freeze-framed and scanned this scene many times trying to figure out what's on the plate. And pork tenderloin is my best guess. This roasted pork tenderloin with apples and a bright, herbaceous sauce could even make you hale and hearty enough to withstand The Machine.

INGREDIENTS

FOR THE ROAST

1 (2 lb. or 907 g) pork tenderloin (or 2 lb. [907 g] chicken breasts for kosher)

1 teaspoon salt, or more to taste

½ teaspoon ground black pepper, or more to taste

6 cloves garlic, minced

1 tablespoon (2 g) finely chopped fresh rosemary

2 tablespoons (30 ml) extra-virgin olive oil

1 tablespoon (15 ml) apple cider vinegar

2 Honeycrisp, Pink Lady, or Fuji apples, cored and quartered

1 yellow onion, cut into eighths

3 tablespoons (42 g) unsalted butter, cut into small pieces

2 sprigs of fresh rosemary

2 sprigs of fresh thyme

2 sprigs of fresh sage

¼ cup (85 g) honey

FOR THE SAUCE

1 Braeburn or Granny Smith apple, cored and quartered

1 tablespoon (6 g) lemon zest

3 tablespoons (45 ml) lemon juice, or more if needed

5 cloves garlic, minced

1 teaspoon finely chopped fresh sage

1 teaspoon finely chopped fresh, flat-leaf parsley

1 teaspoon finely chopped fresh mint

½ teaspoon finely chopped fresh rosemary

¼ cup (59 ml) extra-virgin olive oil, or more if needed

Salt and ground black pepper

1. To make the roast, preheat the oven to 400°F (200°C). Score the meat in a crisscross pattern.

2. In a small dish, add the salt, pepper, and garlic. Crush it with the side of a knife to create a paste. Mix the chopped rosemary into the paste. Rub the garlic-rosemary paste evenly over all sides of the meat, pressing it into the scored parts. Set aside at room temperature for 30 minutes.

3. Heat the oil in a medium-large, cast-iron skillet over medium-high heat, add the pork and sear on all sides until it's deep golden brown, about 5 minutes per side. Once you have browned all sides, set the tenderloin aside on a plate. Deglaze the pan with the apple cider vinegar, then turn the stove off.

4. Scatter the apples, onion, butter, rosemary, and sage around the pan. Place the tenderloin on top of the onion, apples, and herbs, and pour in any accumulated juices from the plate. Drizzle everything with honey.

5. Roast the pork for about 25 minutes, until a thermometer inserted into the thickest part reads 145°F (63°C). If using chicken breasts, the internal temperature should read 165°F (74°C).

6. In the meantime, make the sauce. Place all the sauce ingredients in a blender and pulse until it's around the same consistency as chimichurri. You may need to add more olive oil and lemon juice to achieve this. Adjust the seasonings to taste.

7. Let the meat rest for 15 to 20 minutes before slicing. Slice crosswise into ¾-inch (2-cm)-thick slices. Serve on top of the onions, apples, and pan sauce, and drizzle the herb sauce on top.

FROM THE PAGES

The book does not specifically mention what kind of food the Albino brings Westley but Westley does note that the food was hot and nourishing and was given along with good wine and brandy.

Buttercup's Perfect (Chicken) Breasts

SERVES 2

When Buttercup attempts to plunge a dagger through her broken heart, Westley stops her by lamenting the loss of her perfect breasts. There are a lot of ways to cook chicken breasts, but the simplest, most elegant way is poaching. Poached chicken breast is soft and delicate, one could even say . . . supple. Look, I'm trying to keep this PG but you get the idea. A poached chicken breast, when done right, is absolute perfection.

INGREDIENTS

2 skinless boneless chicken breasts

2 large cloves garlic, smashed

1 bay leaf

1 sprig of fresh thyme

1 sprig of fresh rosemary

1 sprig of fresh, flat-leaf parsley

1 teaspoon peppercorns

1–2 shallots, peeled and quartered

Kosher salt

4–6 cups (940 ml to 1.4 L) chicken broth
(may vary)

1. Place everything but the chicken broth in a medium saucepan or small stockpot. Generally, you want the breasts in the center of the pot, parallel to each other but not touching. Arrange all the herbs and aromatics evenly around them. Add enough chicken broth to cover the breasts by about ½ inch (1 cm).

2. Clip a candy thermometer to the side of the pot. Heat over medium-high heat until the temperature of the stock reaches 170°F (77°C). Cook for about 20 to 24 minutes, adjusting the heat to keep the liquid between 170°F (77°C) and 180°F (82°C) until an instant-read thermometer inserted into the thickest part of chicken breast registers 165°F (74°C).

3. Remove the chicken breasts from the liquid using a slotted spoon or tongs. Let them rest for 5 to 10 minutes before serving.

· MLT: ·
Mutton, Lettuce, Tomato
SERVES 4 TO 6

Like many of Miracle Max's lines in the film, the MLT line was completely improvised by Billy Crystal. While filming the Miracle Max sequences, director Rob Reiner had to walk off the set so as to not ruin takes by laughing out loud and Mandy Patinkin has said that the only injury he sustained during filming was a bruised rib from holding back laughter. Mutton is the culinary term for sheep meat. It was extremely popular in the late Medieval and early Renaissance period throughout Europe. It's an inherently non-lean cut of meat and a "lean" cut of mutton, like Max so passionately describes, would actually taste like lamb. This sandwich has it all: lean "mutton," crispy red lettuce and, of course, those perky heirloom tomatoes. Better than true love? You decide.

INGREDIENTS

FOR THE LAMB
1 leg of lamb, butterflied and trimmed
4 teaspoons (20 g) kosher salt, or to taste
6 cloves garlic, minced
½ cup (48 g) finely chopped fresh mint
¼ cup (7 g) chopped fresh rosemary
3 tablespoons (45 ml) extra-virgin
 olive oil

FOR THE SANDWICH
1 "Life is Pain" Pandemain (page 49)
 or bread of your choice, sliced
1 head baby red butter lettuce
Extra-virgin olive oil (optional)
Red wine vinegar (optional)
¼ cup (60 g) mayonnaise
1 teaspoon lemon juice
1 clove garlic, minced
1 ripe tomato, sliced
1 sweet onion, sliced very thin (optional)
Salt and ground black pepper (optional)

1. To make the lamb, make shallow diagonal slices in the thicker parts of the lamb and gently press the slices open like pages in a book. Then, lightly score the meat in a 1-inch (2.5-cm) crosshatch.

2. Oil a wire rack and set it over a rimmed baking sheet. Place the lamb on the rack.

3. In a small dish, add the salt, garlic, mint, and rosemary. Stir in the olive oil to make a paste. Rub the garlic-herb mixture over the prepared lamb, working the mixture into all the crevices. Let the lamb rest for 1 hour for it to come to room temperature.

4. Preheat the oven to 425°F (220°C). Transfer the baking sheet with the lamb still on the wire rack and roast it for 25 to 35 minutes, depending on desired doneness. For medium-rare an instant-read thermometer will register 125° to 130°F (52° to 55°C). For medium, it's 140° to 145°F (60° to 63°C). Let the lamb rest until it's room temperature before slicing. Once at room temperature, cut the lamb into thin slices, against the grain whenever possible.

5. To make the sandwich(es), toast the bread slices lightly if you like. Drizzle the lettuce with olive oil and red wine vinegar. In a small dish, mix the mayonnaise, lemon juice, garlic, and a pinch of salt. Let it settle for a minute.

6. Spread the mayonnaise mixture on two slices of bread. Add a piece or two of lettuce and a slice or two of the tomato onto the mayo side of one of the bread pieces. Season the tomato with salt and pepper. Add a few slices of your lamb, followed by the onion. Top it off with the other bread slice, mayo side down.

7. Cut the sandwich in half before serving. Repeat this step for more sandwiches!

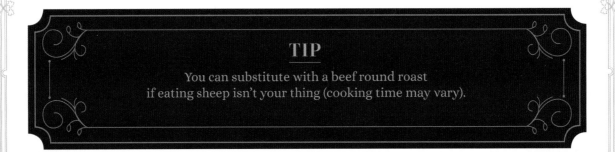

TIP

You can substitute with a beef round roast
if eating sheep isn't your thing (cooking time may vary).

Roasted R.O.U.S.

The final terror Westley and Buttercup encounter in the Fire Swamp are the Rodents Of Unusual Size (R.O.U.S.). And if a person was stuck in the Fire Swamp long enough (or inexplicably built a summer home there) they might eventually find themselves roasting a R.O.U.S. over an open flame spurt. Sculpting a monstrous rodent out of meat is oddly satisfying and makes this recipe a fun activity for the whole family!

INGREDIENTS

FOR THE MAC 'N' CHEESE
2 cups (210 g) elbow macaroni
1 tablespoon (14 g) butter
¾ cup (175 ml) heavy whipping cream
2 eggs, lightly beaten
4 oz (113 g) cream cheese
½ teaspoon coarse or medium grind
    black pepper
½ teaspoon sea salt
½ teaspoon onion powder
2 cups (240 g) grated sharp Cheddar
1 cup (120 g) mild Cheddar

FOR THE MEATLOAF
3 lb. (1.4 kg) ground beef, turkey,
    and/or pork
2 cups (230 g) bread crumbs
4 eggs, lightly beaten
1 white onions, chopped very fine
4–6 cloves garlic, minced
3 tablespoons (45 ml)
    Worcestershire sauce
Salt and ground black pepper
Other seasonings (your preference
    and to taste)

FOR THE SAUCE
½ cup (120 g) ketchup
½ cup (75 g) unpacked brown sugar
2 tablespoons (22 g) mustard
2 tablespoons (30 ml)
    Worcestershire sauce
1 packet French onion soup mix

FOR THE FACE
2 whole black olives
1–2 small red potatoes
6–8 pieces uncooked capellini
    or spaghetti
6 whole thin cloves garlic

1. To make the mac 'n' cheese, fill a medium saucepan with enough water to cover the pasta by about 2 inches (5 cm) and add some salt. Bring to a boil. Add the pasta and cook for 10 minutes, or until the pasta is soft but chewy. Drain the pasta and place it in a mixing bowl. Add the butter and toss, to add flavor and to prevent it from sticking together.

2. Using a whisk, mix the cream and eggs until well blended. Add to a medium saucepan and turn the heat to low. When the mixture is hot but not boiling add the cream cheese, salt, pepper, and onion powder, and stir until melted and incorporated. Add the sharp Cheddar and stir until melted and smooth. Continue to cook until the sauce reduces a bit, stirring occasionally. Pour sauce over cooked macaroni and stir until mixed thoroughly. Set aside.

3. To make the sauce, combine all ingredients in a small bowl. Set aside.

4. Preheat the oven to 375°F (190°C). To make the meatloaf, grease a large roasting tray. Add all the meatloaf ingredients to a large mixing bowl, and, using your hands, mix thoroughly.

5. Take a little less than half of the meatloaf and shape it like a large, flat rodent. On its "body," form a shallow groove or well for the mac 'n' cheese. Drizzle some sauce into the groove. Spoon the mac 'n' cheese into the well. Since you'll be adding a second layer of meat, try to estimate the height of the rodent when you add the second layer of meat. Fit as much pasta as you can without overflowing the well, you will likely have some excess pasta. Drizzle some sauce on top, then top with the mild Cheddar.

6. Take the rest of the meat mixture and flatten it out into an oval-ish shape; it doesn't have to be perfect. Place the oval on top of the macaroni. Use your hands to seal the top part of the meatloaf with the bottom part and mold the body of the R.O.U.S around the mac 'n' cheese. It helps to have a visual reference, so pop on the Fire Swamp scene for ambience.

7. Once you've created the rodent shape, add the face: a screengrab for reference helps here. Use a knife to slice two thin rounds out of the red potato to act as the ears. Slice off the end of a smaller red potato to act as the nose, carving in two holes for nostrils. Slice up some garlic for the fangs. Break the noodles in half and use them for the whiskers. Add two black olives for the beady eyes, sticking them most of the way into the meat. This meatloaf holds its shape pretty well; if you're satisfied with how it looks uncooked, it won't change too much when you cook it.

8. Brush the entire meatloaf with the remaining sauce and cook in the oven for 1 hour. When serving to guests, it makes for a better presentation to serve slices from the body, leaving the head for last!

Shrieking Eel Pie

In one of the more intense scenes, Buttercup is surrounded by bloodthirsty eels who, according to Vizzini, shriek when they are about to dine on human flesh. But what if Buttercup turned the tables and ate the eels? In locations where eels are plentiful, they often become part of the local diet, prized for their succulent meaty flavor, and they were commonly cooked into pies throughout Medieval Europe. Perhaps that fisherman really was out for a pleasure cruise through eel-infested waters after all! Mashed potatoes are the traditional side for this dish. You can also use The National Dish of Florin (page 66).

INGREDIENTS

FOR THE CRUST

2 cups (250 g) all-purpose flour

1 teaspoon salt

⅔ cup (150 g) lard or cold butter

5 tablespoons (75 ml) ice water, or as needed

1 (17.3-oz or 490-g) packet frozen premade puff pastry

1 egg, lightly beaten

FOR THE FILLING

¼ cup (60 ml) Worcestershire sauce

6 garlic cloves, minced

2 shallots, thinly sliced

1 lb. (454 g) cooked eel (unagi), chopped (substitute cooked trout, catfish, or Japanese eggplant)

½ lb. (226 g) baby bella mushrooms, chopped

½ cup (120 ml) cooking sherry

½ teaspoon nutmeg

6 yolks from medium-boiled eggs

Juice from ½ lemon

Salt and ground black pepper

FOR THE PARSLEY SAUCE (OPTIONAL)

¼ cup (55 g) unsalted butter

¼ cup (32 g) all-purpose flour

1¾ cups (410 ml) chicken broth

½ cup (30 g) chopped fresh, flat-leaf parsley

2 cloves garlic, minced

2 teaspoons (10 ml) malt vinegar

Salt

TIP

Japanese eggplant
makes a wonderful
veggie substitution
for eel.

1. Before you begin, combine the garlic and the Worcestershire sauce for the filling in a small bowl. Set aside.

2. To make the crust, combine the flour and the salt in a medium mixing bowl. Work in the lard until the mixture resembles coarse crumbs. Sprinkle in the ice water, a tablespoon (15 ml) at a time, until the pastry holds together. Shape the dough into a ball, cover with plastic wrap and chill it in the fridge for 30 to 40 minutes.

3. Bring out the pie dough and let it warm up slightly, just enough so it can be rolled out. Roll it out on a lightly floured surface until it's about ⅛-inch (3-cm) thick. Grease four 4-ounce (118-ml) ramekins with butter and line them with the crust, trimming off any excess.

4. In a medium saucepan, sauté the shallots over medium heat until translucent and just beginning to brown, then add the chopped eel and mushrooms. Cook until the eel starts to brown, then add the sherry, nutmeg, Worcestershire sauce, and garlic. Season to taste with salt and pepper. Cook for 5 to 7 minutes. Drain the excess liquid, but leave a little behind. Stir in a little flour or cornstarch to thicken the liquid into a gravy-like consistency. Taste and adjust seasoning. Set aside and let it cool down for 10 minutes.

5. Preheat the oven to 425°F (220°C). Roll out the puff pastry to a ¼-inch (6-mm)-thick sheet and use a knife to cut tops for each pie—estimate about 1 inch (2.5 cm) bigger than your ramekins.

6. Distribute the filling evenly among the ramekins, then top with the crumbled egg yolks. Sprinkle each with the lemon juice, then drape the puff pastry tops over the pies. Trim any excess puff pastry and crimp the edges with your fingers to seal. You can use any excess dough to carve out little eels and place them on top of the pies. Brush the pies with egg wash.

7. Add about ½ inch (1 cm) of lukewarm water to a roasting pan, then place the ramekins in it. Put this in the oven at 425°F (220°C) for about 15 minutes. Lower the heat to 325°F (165°C) and cook for another 25 to 30 minutes, until the puff pastry is golden brown and flaky.

8. To make the parsley sauce (if using), melt the butter in a small saucepan over a medium heat and whisk in the flour to make a paste. Gradually stir in the broth, stirring regularly and bringing it all to a simmer, then stir in the parsley, garlic, malt vinegar, and salt. Keep stirring until the sauce is thickened and smooth. Remove from the heat and set aside.

9. Remove the pies from the oven and let settle for 5 to 10 minutes before serving. If you are using the parsley sauce, pour it generously over the pies.

· Hippopotamic · Land Mass Lollipops

SERVES 2 TO 4

Meat lollipops are usually made with chicken legs, but for a giant like Fezzik, turkey legs are the only appropriate size. After all, it's not Fezzik's fault that he's the biggest and strongest. He doesn't even exercise! These giant meat sticks can be used as dumbbells (if you want to get big and strong like Fezzik), and they have a succulent sweet and smoky flavor that will satisfy the giant in you. Feel free to adjust the spice levels in the rub to suit your tastes.

INGREDIENTS

FOR THE LOLLIPOPS
2 turkey legs
10–12 thin strips of bacon
    or turkey bacon
Pomegranate molasses, maple syrup,
    or honey (optional)
Dry rub (see below)

FOR THE RUB
2 teaspoons (10 g) kosher salt
1 tablespoon (10 g) unpacked
    dark brown sugar
1 teaspoon garlic powder
1 teaspoon cumin
½ teaspoon allspice
½ teaspoon dried oregano
¼ teaspoon Aleppo pepper
¼ teaspoon black pepper
¼ teaspoon turmeric
¼ teaspoon smoked paprika

1. To make the rub, combine the ingredients in a small bowl.

2. Generously season the meat with three-quarters of the rub and let sit at room temperature for 30 minutes. Wrap the meat with the bacon and use toothpicks to secure it. Use the remaining rub to season the bacon.

3. Wrap the exposed bone with aluminum foil and tie the two turkey legs together at the top of the bone using twine, this will help them to stand with bones upright for a more even cook.

4. If you are smoking the turkey legs, smoke for 20 to 25 minutes at 450°F (230°C) until golden brown outside, then for another 30 to 40 minutes at 325°F (165°C) until the internal temperature reaches 160°F (71°C).

5. If you are roasting them, roast for 20 to 25 minutes at 450°F (230°C) until golden brown outside, then for another 20 to 25 minutes at 325°F (165°C) until the internal temperature reaches 160°F (71°C). Cooking times may vary a bit depending on the size of the turkey legs.

6. Brush with the pomegranate molasses (if using) 10 minutes before cooking is complete. Cut the twine before serving.

TIP

To make the lollipops, you'll need to french the turkey legs to get a clean bone handle. Your butcher might be able to do this for you which will save time, but it's totally possible to do it yourself: use a paring knife to slice around the circumference of the leg just below where the meat begins to swell at the ankle. This will expose the bone along with some tendons. Scrape the skin and cartilage off toward the end of the bone, making sure the knife is always moving away from you. Use some paper towels to rub and pull away all the scraped skin from the bone. Use a pair of clean pliers and grip the end of each tendon and pull firmly to remove them. Some meat might come off with them, but you can use your knife to carefully separate the meat from the tendon as you pull. Use your paring knife to clear away anything remaining in the crevices of the bone and gently push the meat up the bone to make a rounder shape. You should now have a clean handle to grip and a tendon-free round of meat to bite into once cooked, like a giant lollipop! Repeat this process for the second turkey leg.

The Capo Farro Technique

SERVES 6 TO 8

During their chatty duel, the Man in Black and Inigo admire each other's skill and reference specific techniques. The techniques discussed are actually real fencing techniques from the sixteenth and seventeenth century. One of these is the Capo Ferro technique, named after Ridolfo Capo Ferro, a seventeenth century Italian fencing master. For this dish I combined Italian caponata (a sort of relish consisting of chopped eggplant and various other vegetables) with farro (a grain that's popular in Italy). It is easy to make this vegan by using vegetable broth and skipping the cheese topping. If you're an omnivore, you can add meat, like Buttercup's Perfect (Chicken) Breasts (page 78).

INGREDIENTS

FOR THE FARRO
¼ cup (59 ml) extra-virgin olive oil
1 stalks celery, chopped
1 carrot, chopped
1 yellow onion, chopped
5 cloves garlic, chopped
½ lb. (226 g) Italian farro
2–3 cups (475–705 ml) chicken
    or vegetable broth
2 bay leaves
Salt and ground black pepper

FOR THE CAPONATA
1 medium eggplant
½ cup (118 ml) extra-virgin olive oil,
    plus more as needed
1 stalks celery, diced
1 yellow onion, diced
4 cloves garlic, minced

1 (14.5-oz or 411-g) can plum tomatoes,
    crushed
½ cup (75 g) golden raisins,
    softened in warm water
1–2 tablespoons (20–40 g) honey
¼ cup (36 g) capers
¼ cup (32 g) kalamata olives,
    pitted and sliced
¼ cup (35 g) pine nuts, toasted
2 tablespoons (28 ml) red wine vinegar
1–2 teaspoons (2–4 g) red pepper flakes
1–2 tablespoons (4–8 g) chopped fresh,
    flat-leaf Italian parsley
1–2 tablespoons (4–8 g) chopped fresh
    oregano
Salt and ground black pepper
Burrata or chèvre cheese (optional)

1. To prepare the eggplant, slice it into ½-inch (1-cm)-thick disks. Lay them out on a sheet pan and salt generously. Let sit for 40 to 45 minutes to pull out moisture.

2. To make the farro, heat the oil in a large saucepan. Add the vegetables and sweat until soft. Add farro and stir for 1 minute. Add the chicken broth and bay leaves, and bring to a boil. Reduce to a simmer and cook until tender, about 25 to 30 minutes. Season with salt and pepper to taste. Set aside.

3. To make the caponata, rinse and pat the eggplant dry with a paper towel, then dice it. In a large sauté pan, heat the olive oil over medium-high heat and brown the eggplant for 5 to 6 minutes. Remove the eggplant from the pan and set it aside.

4. Add the celery, onion, garlic and, if necessary, more olive oil. Cook for 5 minutes, until onions are completely softened and have begun to brown. Add the tomatoes and cook until the excess moisture has begun to evaporate. Add the raisins, honey, capers, olives, pine nuts, vinegar, red pepper flakes, and cooked eggplant. Stir for 2 minutes, then remove from the heat. Add the chopped herbs and season to taste.

5. To serve, add the farro on the serving plate(s) then spoon the caponata on top. Top with burrata (if using). If you are feeding a large party, you can serve this in a casserole dish by layering the farro, followed by the caponata. If you're using, add the burrata on top of the caponata.

The Pirate Ship· Revenge Salmagundi

SERVES 6 TO 8

Salmagundi is a hodgepodge salad thought to have been popular among pirates in the seventeenth century. It was sort of like pirate charcuterie. Due to the length of sea voyages, most ingredients were foods with low perishability: cured meats, hard cheeses, olives, and other preserves. Chickens were often kept on board for eggs (and eventually eaten), so eggs and chicken were also common ingredients. Whenever fresh fruits or vegetables were available, they'd be added too. It's likely Westley occasionally dined on salmagundi during his years aboard *Revenge*, perhaps before bedtime when Ryan would wish him goodnight.

INGREDIENTS

FOR THE DRESSING

¼ cup (12 g) minced fresh chives

4 cloves garlic

¼ cup (60 ml) apple cider vinegar, or more if needed

2 tablespoons (28 ml) lime juice

½ cup (24 g) chopped fresh herbs, such as mint, basil, thyme, or dill

½ cup (118 ml) extra-virgin olive oil, or more if needed

2 tablespoons (40 g) honey

¼ teaspoon cayenne (optional)

2–4 slices of jalapeño (optional)

Salt and ground black pepper

FOR THE SALMAGUNDI

1 cup (110–150 g) whole new potatoes

1 tablespoon (15 ml) olive oil

Sea salt and ground black pepper

Radicchio or red-leaf lettuce

1 Buttercup's Perfect (Chicken) Breasts (page 78), sliced

3 medium-boiled eggs, peeled and halved

1 cup (180 g) baby heirloom tomatoes, halved

Grapes (on the vine)

6–8 oz (170–226 g) prosciutto or serrano ham

Anchovies and/or sardines (optional)

1 cup (128 g) pitted mixed olives

1 cup (100 g) haricot verts, green beans, and/or asparagus, blanched

6 oz (170 g) hard cheese of your choice, thinly sliced

2 shallots, sliced

TIP

This is a versatile dish that's easy to make vegetarian or even vegan. You can nix the ingredients you can't eat and add grilled Halloumi, nuts, roasted chickpeas, vegan/vegetarian proteins of your choice, or any other ingredient you like.

1. To make the dressing, add all ingredients into a blender and blend until smooth. You may need to add more olive oil and vinegar to get the right consistency for a dressing. Adjust the seasonings to taste. Set aside until serving time. It can be stored in the fridge, but give it time to come to room temperature before serving because the olive oil will solidify at low temperature.

2. To make the salmagundi, preheat the oven to 250°F (120°C).

3. Place the potatoes in a medium mixing bowl and toss with olive oil, salt, and pepper. Spread the potatoes in a single layer on a parchment-lined baking sheet. Roast for 20 to 30 minutes, or until the potatoes can be easily pierced by a fork.

4. Cover a large serving platter with radicchio, then arrange the rest of the items, aside from the shallots, on top of that. The ingredients should be separate but touching. Garnish with the sliced shallots.

5. Add the dressing to a dressing pitcher and place it on the serving platter. Serve with a set of tongs so guests can pick what they want and put it on their plates.

FROM THE PAGES

There's a good reason for the spicy vinaigrette: when Westley is recounting his journey of becoming the Dread Pirate Roberts, he mentions that the ship's cook didn't know the difference between table salt and cayenne pepper. Whether intentional on Goldman's part or not, there's some basis for this in historical fact! It wasn't uncommon for cooks on ships to season food more aggressively to distract from the fact that some ingredients weren't entirely fresh.

Humperdinck's Crown Roast

SERVES 12 TO 14

Much like Humperdinck himself, this dish looks elegant and a bit fussy but it's actually quite simple. Really, any "wart-hog faced buffoon" can make it! It's a showstopper that would look spectacular adorning any castle feast, and since it feeds a crowd, you might want to save it for special occasions. I chose pork because Westley calls Humperdinck a "pig" more than once throughout the film. If pork is a deal-breaker for you, this can also be done with standing beef rib roasts or racks of lamb (cooking time may vary).

INGREDIENTS

FOR THE ROAST
7–8 lb. (3.2–3.6 kg) crown roast of pork (12–14 ribs), room temperature (see note)
Salt and ground black pepper
5 cloves garlic, peeled and halved lengthwise
2–3 sprigs of fresh thyme
2–3 sprigs of fresh rosemary
1 yellow onion, peeled and cut into eighths
1 large orange, sliced (Keep the peel on!)

FOR THE RUB
¼ cup (59 ml) extra-virgin olive oil
6 cloves garlic, minced
2 teaspoons (1 g) chopped fresh rosemary
2 teaspoons (1 g) fresh thyme
4 teaspoons (20 g) salt
2 teaspoons (4 g) ground black pepper
Zest of 2 oranges

1. Preheat the oven to 450°F (230°C).

2. To make the rub, combine all the rub ingredients in a small bowl. Set aside.

3. To make the roast, season the cavity of the pork with salt and pepper and stuff it with the garlic, sprigs of rosemary, thyme, onion, and orange slices. This is just to impart flavor. Wrap the ends of the ribs with small pieces of aluminum foil to prevent burning.

4. Place the roast on a rack in a roasting pan and use your hands to coat the surface of the meat with the rub. Pour ½ inch (1 cm) of water in the bottom of the pan and place the pork in the oven.

5. Roast for 15 minutes, then reduce the oven temperature to 325°F (165°C). Continue roasting until a thermometer inserted in the thickest part of the meat registers at least 145°F (63°C). Total cooking time should be around 2 hours for a 7- to 8-pound (3.2- to 3.6-kg) roast.

6. Allow the roast to rest for at least 20 minutes before serving. To serve, carve the roast by slicing between the rib bones to separate into individual chops.

NOTE: DIY Crown Roast Cut: You'll need 2 racks of pork loin chops, lamb racks, or beef rib roasts. If the ribs are not frenched, start by frenching each rib by trimming and scraping away the meat, fat, and sinew from the exposed end of the ribs so that a section of the bones is bare. Remove the skin that covers the bottom of the rib. Score the rib-side near the cap and on the backside of the bones to allow the rib roast to flex and bend. Lay the two roasts end to end and tie them together with a butcher's twine by the rib bones. Bend the ribs until they form a circular crown and tie the other side of the bones together. To hold the crown-shape while cooking, wrap butcher's twine around the entire roast twice and tie into a tight double knot.

FROM THE PAGES

In the book, Humperdinck holds a feast featuring "Essence of Brandied Pig," but things go terribly wrong when they try to light the pigs on fire. If you like, heat ¼ cup (80 g) of apricot preserves in a saucepan, remove from the heat and add ¼ cup (60 ml) of brandy to the heated mixture. Ignite with a lighter and pour the mixture over the crown roast.

The Machine's Excruciating Tourtière

SERVES 6 TO 8

Westley is taken down to the Pit of Despair and subjected to torturous experiments at the six-fingered hands of Count Rugen, who has invented a truly diabolical torture contraption called The Machine. The Machine works by sucking years of one's life away. Sounding an awful lot like "torture", the *tourtière* bears a striking resemblance to a Medieval meat pie with much of the same contents and spices. Like The Machine, this rich pie might just knock a year or two off your life, but unlike The Machine, it'll be an enjoyable experience.

INGREDIENTS

FOR THE CRUST

3 cups (375 g) all-purpose flour

1 teaspoon salt

1 cup (225 g) unsalted butter, cold

6 tablespoons (90 ml) ice water

1 large egg, whisked

FOR THE FILLING

3 golden potatoes, peeled and quartered

1 teaspoon dried thyme

1 teaspoon dried sage

1 teaspoon ground mustard

½ teaspoon ground cinnamon

½ teaspoon ground ginger

¼ teaspoon ground nutmeg

½ teaspoon ground allspice

1 teaspoon onion powder

1 teaspoon garlic powder

Salt and ground black pepper

1 tablespoon (14 g) butter

1 large onion, finely chopped

4 cloves garlic, crushed

¼ cup (30 g) finely diced celery

1 lb. (454 g) ground beef

1 lb. (454 g) ground pork or turkey

1. To make the crust, place the flour, salt, and cold butter slices in the bowl of a food processor or a mixer. Pulse until the butter is pea-size. Drizzle the ice water into the flour mixture. Pulse on and off for about 10 seconds, until the mixture is crumbly and holds together when you pinch a piece off. Keep adding water, a little at a time, until the dough starts to come together. Transfer the mixture to a lightly floured work surface. Mold the dough into a ball and wrap in plastic wrap. Refrigerate until chilled, at least 1 hour.

2. To make the filling, add the potatoes to a medium saucepan and cover with water. Add a teaspoon of salt. Bring to a boil over high heat, then reduce the heat to medium-low. Simmer for about 15 minutes, until cooked through. Carefully remove the potatoes from the water and transfer to a bowl, but save the cooking liquid. Mash the potatoes with a potato masher.

3. In a small bowl, mix the thyme, sage, mustard, cinnamon, ginger, nutmeg, allspice, onion powder, and garlic powder. Season with salt and pepper to taste.

4. Melt a tablespoon (14 g) of butter in a large skillet over medium heat. Add the onion and a pinch of salt. Cook and stir for 8 to 10 minutes, until they begin to brown. Stir in the garlic, celery, and the mixed spices until the onion mixture is evenly coated with the spices, then add the ground beef and ground pork. Stir to combine.

5. Drain some of the excess fat. Add about ¾ cup (175 ml) of the potato cooking liquid to the skillet. Continue to stir, for about 25 minutes, until the meat is browned, tender, and most of the liquid has evaporated. Stir in the mashed potatoes and adjust seasonings to taste. Remove from the heat and cool to room temperature.

6. Preheat the oven to 375°F (190°C) with a rack in the center. Separate the chilled dough for the crust into 2 pieces, one a little larger than the other. On a lightly floured work surface, roll the larger piece out into a 12-inch (30-cm) disc.

7. Place the dough in a lightly greased 9-inch (23-cm) springform pan or a 9-inch (23-cm) deep dish pie plate and press it into the bottom and sides so there are no gaps. Roll the top crust out into a 11-inch (28-cm) disc. Fill the bottom crust with the meat mixture and smooth out the surface. Place top crust onto the pie and press lightly around the edges to seal. Trim any excess dough from the crust. Crimp the edges of the crust and add slits to the top crust to vent. If you wish, use molds to create gears out of the excess dough and place those on the top crust. Brush the entire exposed surface of the pie with egg wash.

8. Bake on the center rack until well browned, about 1 hour. Check on the pie at around 45 minutes, you may need to wrap the edges loosely in aluminum foil if they're cooking too fast compared to the center. Let the pie cool to almost room temperature before slicing and serving.

I'll eat you both apart!
I'll bake you both together!

Cakes, Pies, and Tarts

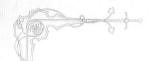

· Princess · Buttercups

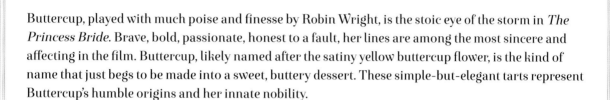

Buttercup, played with much poise and finesse by Robin Wright, is the stoic eye of the storm in *The Princess Bride*. Brave, bold, passionate, honest to a fault, her lines are among the most sincere and affecting in the film. Buttercup, likely named after the satiny yellow buttercup flower, is the kind of name that just begs to be made into a sweet, buttery dessert. These simple-but-elegant tarts represent Buttercup's humble origins and her innate nobility.

INGREDIENTS

FOR THE CRUST
2¾ cups (346 g) all-purpose flour
1 tablespoon (10 g) unpacked
    light brown sugar
5 tablespoons (69 g) unsalted butter,
    chilled
¼ cup (55 g) lard or shortening
1 teaspoon orange zest
¼ teaspoon salt
⅓ cup (80 ml) ice water

FOR THE FILLING
¾ cup (113 g) unpacked light brown sugar
¼ cup (85 g) golden syrup, honey,
    or maple syrup
¼ cup (55 g) unsalted butter, melted
2 large eggs
½ teaspoon vanilla extract
½ teaspoon orange flower water
    (optional)
¼ teaspoon salt
Pinch of nutmeg (optional)

FOR THE WHIPPED CREAM
1 cup (235 ml) heavy whipping cream,
    chilled
¼ cup (85 g) honey (orange blossom
    is ideal)
1 teaspoon orange blossom water
Icing crowns, gold crown sprinkles,
    or gold crown cupcake toppers
    (optional)

1. To make the dough, add the flour, butter, lard, orange zest, and salt to a large mixing bowl. Rub the fats into the flour by pinching and mixing it with your fingers until the mixture resembles coarse bread crumbs. Add the ice water a little at a time, just enough to make the dough come together. Knead the dough a few times, then shape it into a disc and wrap it tightly in plastic wrap. Chill it in the fridge for at least 1 hour.

2. Preheat the oven to 200°F (93°C) then start on the filling. Add all the filling ingredients to a mixing bowl. Whisk together until smooth and well-combined. Set aside.

3. Roll out the chilled dough to a ⅛-inch (3-mm) thickness on a lightly floured surface. Cut out 4-inch (10-cm) circles, then re-roll the scraps to get more rounds; this should make about 12.

4. Line 12 to 14 silicone molds or a 12-hole muffin pan with the pastry circles, making sure to get the pastry into the bottom corners of the pan. Fill each pastry shell three-quarters full with the filling. Do not be tempted to overfill the shells as this will cause overflow and burning during baking.

5. Bake at 200°F (93°C) for 15 minutes, then turn the heat up to 350°F (175°C) and bake for another 10 to 15 minutes. Keep a sharp eye on the tarts near the end of the baking time, make sure none are overflowing. When the crust is a pale golden brown around the edges and the filling is browned, remove them from the oven.

6. Let the tarts cool in the pan for about 5 minutes, then remove them and place on a wire rack to cool completely.

7. To make the whipped cream, pour the heavy cream into a chilled stainless-steel mixing bowl. Use the wire whisk attachment on a hand mixer to whip the cream on medium speed until it begins to thicken slightly. Add the honey and orange blossom water. Whip the cream on medium-high speed until stiff peaks form.

8. Spoon or pipe the whipped cream onto the cooled tarts and top with icing gold crowns, sprinkles, or cupcake toppers. Serve immediately!

Flaming Fezzik Flambé

Using only Fezzik, a wheelbarrow, and the "Holocaust Cloak" obtained from Miracle Max, our trio of heroes storm the castle in style and flames. Crêpes are ideal because they have a cloak-like quality and taste wonderful flambéed. I know the flambé technique is intimidating, but it's not nearly as terrifying as the Dread Pirate Roberts screaming that he's here for your sooooooul.

INGREDIENTS

FOR THE CHOCOLATE CRÊPES
¾ cup (94 g) all-purpose flour
¼ cup (22 g) cocoa powder
¼ cup (38 g) unpacked brown sugar
½ teaspoon salt
1½ cups (355 ml) whole milk
3 large eggs, gently whisked
3½ tablespoons (49 g) unsalted butter, melted
2 teaspoons (10 ml) vanilla extract
Additional butter for cooking

FOR THE ORANGE BUTTER
6 tablespoons (84 g) unsalted butter, melted
¼ cup (50 g) plus 2 tablespoons (26 g) granulated sugar
Zest of 1 orange
⅓ cup (80 ml) fresh orange juice
¼ cup (60 ml) Grand Marnier® or Cointreau
2 tablespoons (30 ml) cognac or brandy

1. To make the crêpes, add the flour, cocoa powder, brown sugar, and salt to a large mixing bowl. Whisk to combine. While whisking, add about ½ cup (120 ml) of the milk to form a smooth paste. Add the eggs, butter, and vanilla, and continue to whisk. Whisk in the rest of the milk until smooth. Let the batter rest for 15 minutes.

2. Heat butter in a nonstick skillet. Add 3 to 4 tablespoons (45 to 60 ml) of the batter and tilt the skillet to distribute the batter evenly, pouring any excess batter back into the bowl. If there are any holes in the batter, just spoon a little extra batter to cover the spot. The first crêpe may not come out perfect; this is usually called the test crêpe.

3. Cook the crêpe over medium-high heat for about 45 seconds, until the edges of the crêpe start to curl. Flip the crêpe and cook for another 10 seconds. Flip the crêpe out onto a clean baking sheet. Repeat to make twelve crêpes, buttering the skillet as necessary. Set the crêpes aside.

4. To make the orange butter, blend the butter with the sugar and orange zest using a hand mixer on low. Gradually add the orange juice until incorporated.

5. Preheat a broiler to 450°F (230°C) with a rack in the center. Butter a large, rimmed baking sheet, and sprinkle it with some sugar.

6. In the center of each crêpe, place 2 rounded teaspoons (10 g) of the orange butter. Fold the crêpes in half and again in half to form triangles.

7. Arrange the crêpes on the prepared baking sheet, pointing them in the same direction, overlapping slightly. Sprinkle with the remaining sugar and broil until they begin to caramelize, about 2 minutes. Transfer the crêpes to a heatproof serving dish.

8. In a small saucepan, heat the Grand Marnier and cognac. Ignite carefully with a long lighter or a long-handled match and pour the flaming mixture over the crêpes. Tilt the platter and, with a spoon, carefully baste the crêpes in the flaming Grand Marnier mixture until the flames subside. Serve immediately.

"As You Wish" Appeltaart

SERVES 8

What does apple pie have to do with the beloved "as you wish" line? Hear me out. As Grandfather is saying that "as you wish" really means "I love you", Buttercup asks Westley to fetch a pitcher that's clearly within arm's reach just so he'll get closer to her and look into her eyes... During this romantic, pivotal point in the film, Buttercup is working a dough and there are apples on the worktable. Go ahead, watch it if you don't believe me. I'll wait. You see? It's settled. I've opted to make a Dutch-style apple pie, also known as *appeltaart*. Trust me, this warm, intoxicating dessert tastes an awful lot like true love.

INGREDIENTS

FOR THE CRUST

3 cups (375 g) all-purpose flour
½ cup (100 g) granulated sugar
½ cup (75 g) unpacked light brown sugar
½ teaspoon salt
Zest of 1 lemon
2½ sticks (280 g) unsalted butter, chilled
1 egg, whisked
1 tablespoon (15 ml) ice water,
     or as needed

FOR THE FILLING

6 Pink Lady or Honeycrisp apples,
     cored and sliced or chopped
½ cup (75 g) raisins or currants
     (optional)
½ cup (100 g) granulated sugar
2 teaspoons (5 g) ground cinnamon
Pinch of ground ginger (optional)

Pinch of ground nutmeg (optional)
Pinch of ground clove (optional)
Pinch of mace (optional)
Pinch of ground cardamom (optional)
2 teaspoons (10 ml) lemon juice
2 tablespoons (16 g) all-purpose flour

FINISHING TOUCHES

¼ cup (30 g) bread crumbs
1 egg, whisked

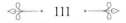

1. Preheat the oven to 325°F (165°C) and grease a 9-inch (23-cm) springform pan.

2. To make the crust, combine the flour, sugars, salt, and lemon zest in a large mixing bowl. With the mixer running, add the butter and then the egg. Mix until it forms coarse, wet crumbs. Place the dough on a lightly floured surface and knead, adding the ice water as needed for the dough to come together.

3. Roll out two-thirds of the dough into a large 16-inch (41-cm) round (reserve the rest for the top of the pie). Press the dough into the buttered springform pan and work the dough up the sides.

4. To make the filling, add the apples, raisins (if using), sugar, spices, and lemon juice to a large mixing bowl and toss. Sprinkle with the flour and mix it in.

5. Sprinkle the bread crumbs on the bottom of the tart shell, coating it evenly, then pour the apple mixture on top.

6. Roll out the remaining dough into a round. You can slice it with a pizza cutter or a knife to make a lattice design. To go all out, you can also carve out the letters of *As You Wish* and put them on top. You may need to fold the sides of the dough over the top of the pie if they're a bit too high. Once you're done with the top of the pie, brush the top with the egg wash and sprinkle on some granulated sugar.

7. Bake for 1 hour. Check on the pie; you want the crust to be crisp and golden, the apples tender and the juices bubbling. If it doesn't look quite done, cook for 15 minutes until done. You may need to loosely cover the edges with tinfoil at this juncture to prevent the sides from burning.

8. Once it's perfect, let it cool completely in the pan before releasing it for serving.

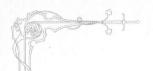

· Princess · Bridal Cake

SERVES 12 TO 15

Humperdinck and Buttercup's wedding may have been a farce but it sure was impressive and I've no doubt there was an equally magnificent feast waiting after the event. Perhaps there's more than one reason Humperdinck wanted to skip to the end of the ceremony and it's the same reason many of us get impatient during weddings: Cake! Inspired by the *Prinsesstårta* or Swedish Princess Cake, this classic cake is elegant enough for a royal affair and has a design that matches Buttercup's gorgeous bridal dress.

INGREDIENTS

FOR THE FILLINGS
20 oz (591 ml) whole milk
1 teaspoon almond extract (optional)
1 teaspoon vanilla extract
6 egg yolks
½ cup (100 g) caster sugar
¼ cup (32 g) cornstarch
¼ cup (55 g) unsalted butter
2 cups (640 g) blueberry preserves
2½ cups (570 ml) heavy whipping cream
2 tablespoons (26 g) granulated sugar

FOR THE CAKE
4 large eggs
¾ cup (150 g) superfine/caster sugar
1 teaspoon almond extract (optional)
1 teaspoon vanilla extract
⅓ cup (43 g) cornstarch, sifted
¾ cup (94 g) all-purpose flour

1 teaspoon baking powder
½ teaspoon kosher salt
¼ cup (55 g) unsalted butter, melted but
　　cooled to room temperature

FOR DECORATING
1 lb. (454 g) marzipan
Blue food coloring gel (don't use liquid)
Confectioners' sugar
A Doily or lace fondant impression mat
　　(optional)
Royal icing (optional)
White sugar pearls (optional)
Pearl lustre spray (optional)

1. To make the pastry cream, pour the milk, almond extract (if using), and vanilla into a medium saucepan. Place over low heat until simmering lightly. Remove from the heat.

2. In a large bowl, whisk together the egg yolks, sugar, and cornstarch until they're creamy and smooth. Slowly stir the warm milk into the egg mixture.

3. Once combined, pour the mixture back into the pan and bring to high heat but do not boil. Reduce the heat to low and simmer for about 5 minutes, whisking regularly, until the mixture has thickened considerably.

4. Remove the milk mixture from the heat and beat in the butter until incorporated. Transfer over to a mixing bowl and cover with plastic wrap to prevent the surface from drying out. Let that cool down in the fridge.

5. To make the cake, preheat the oven to 350°F (175°C). Grease and line the base of an 8-inch (20-cm) springform cake pan with parchment paper.

6. Use an electric mixer, fitted with a whisk attachment, to beat the eggs and sugar for about 5 to 7 minutes until very thick, pale, and fluffy. Add the almond (if using) and vanilla.

7. In a separate bowl, sift together the flour, cornstarch, salt, and baking powder, fold this into the egg-sugar mixture with a spatula. Fold in the melted butter and stir briefly to combine.

8. Pour the batter into the prepared pan and bake for 25 to 30 minutes, or until a toothpick comes out clean. Let the cake cool in the pan for about 5 minutes before turning it out onto a rack to cool completely.

9. Meanwhile, make the decorations. Unpack the marzipan. Start with just a tiny drop of the blue food coloring and knead it into the marzipan dough until the color is uniform, adding more coloring as needed.

10. Shape the marzipan into a disk. Place the disk between two 18-inch (45-cm) sheets of waxed paper. Working from the middle, use a rolling pin to roll out the disk into a 16-inch (41-cm) circle of even thickness.

11. In a large mixing bowl, combine the heavy whipping cream and granulated sugar and whip together using an electric mixer until stiff peaks form. Fold in one-third of the pastry cream into the whipped cream mixture.

12. Once the cake is completely cooled, use a serrated knife to cut the cake horizontally into two layers. Place the bottom piece on the serving plate. Spread half the preserves onto the top of the bottom piece, then spread the other two-thirds of the pastry cream on top of the jam layer, then add another layer of the remaining jam. Top with the other cake layer.

13. Frost the sides of the cake with the whipped cream in a 1-inch (2.5-cm) layer. Spoon the remaining whipped cream on top of the cake and shape it into a round dome using an icing smoother, spatula, or a butter knife.

14. Remove the top level of waxed paper from the marzipan. Place the doily or impression mat in the center of the marzipan disk and place the waxed paper back on top. Use a rolling pin to gently roll over the doily to create an imprint. Don't roll too hard or you'll break the marzipan.

15. Remove the doily and the waxed paper and drape the marzipan disk over the cake with the doily imprint centered. Gently press the marzipan down over the cake with the imprint facing up and gently smooth down the sides with your hands. Trim any excess with a knife or tuck it under the cake.

16. Finishing touches! Gently rub the confectioners' sugar into the marzipan with your fingers to fill in the doily imprint. Very lightly wipe away the excess sugar with your hands or a dry cloth.

17. Once the imprint stands out against the color of the marzipan, use the royal icing to stick the sugar pearls in aesthetically pleasing spots to compliment the lace doily design.

18. This cake is best served ASAP because it can lose its shape over time but it can be chilled in the fridge for up to an hour, maybe two, before serving. The leftovers will refrigerate fine for a day or two.

Have Fun · Storming the Chastletes!

Max and Valerie send Inigo, Fezzik and a mostly dead Westley on their way to storm a castle like grandparents waving off their grandchildren to go play in the park. Chastletes were very elaborate Medieval pies made to look like castles. Although this recipe simplifies the chastletes considerably, it will result in pies shaped like castle turrets, complete with bricks and battlements, filled with luscious frangipane and topped with poached pears. Have fun eating the castle!

INGREDIENTS

FOR THE POACHED PEARS

2 cups (475 ml) dry red wine,
    pomegranate juice, or red grape juice
⅓ cup (66 g) granulated sugar
    (less if using juice for the liquid)
1 teaspoon vanilla bean paste
    or vanilla extract
2 cinnamon sticks
2 whole cloves
2 whole allspice
2–3 firm pears, peeled, pitted and halved
    (substitute: apples or plums)

FOR THE CRUST

3 cups (375 g) all-purpose flour
½ cup (100 g) granulated sugar
½ teaspoon salt

Zest of 1 lemon
2½ sticks (280 g) unsalted butter, chilled
2 eggs, whisked
1 tablespoon (30 ml) ice water,
    or as needed

FOR THE FRANGIPANE

¾ cup (168 g) unsalted butter, softened
¾ cup (150 g) granulated sugar
1½ cups (156 g) almond meal
3 tablespoons (24 g) all-purpose flour
2 large eggs
1–2 teaspoons (5–10 ml) almond extract

FOR THE OPTIONAL TOPPER

Sliced almonds

1. To make the poached pears, add the wine, vanilla, and spices to a medium saucepan and bring to a boil over medium-high heat. Add the pears and reduce the heat to low. Simmer for 30 to 40 minutes, rotating the pears periodically. The pears are done when they have a nice deep burgundy hue and are soft but not mushy.

2. In the meantime, make the dough. In a large mixing bowl, combine the flour, sugar, salt, and lemon zest. With a mixer running, add the butter and then half of the whisked egg until it forms coarse crumbs. Place the dough on a lightly floured surface and knead together, adding the ice water as needed for the dough to come together.

3. Preheat the oven to 350°F (175°C).

4. Take 3 to 4 clean, empty soup cans (labels removed) and wrap them tightly in parchment paper, folding and tucking the bottom and wrapping any excess at the top inside the can. Then, turn the cans upside down. Take some of the dough—how much depends on the size of the cans—and roll it out ½ inch (1 cm) thick. Drape the dough over the can and with your hands mold it onto the sides as evenly as possible. Get a sharp knife and cut around the bottom so the dough is even, then cut out the battlements. Once the battlements are cut, use your hands to shape them up and get rid of any jagged edges. Use the knife to cut shallow bricks-like shapes in a crisscross pattern across the pie. Repeat this until you run out of dough, generally you'll get three to four pies. Brush each with egg wash.

5. Place the dough-lined cans bottoms up on a baking sheet and bake at 350°F (175°C) for 20 minutes. When done, remove from the oven and let cool for 15 minutes, then flip the cans over and carefully remove them from the crusts. The crusts should be solid enough to stand on their own now. Let them come down to room temperature.

6. To make the frangipane, combine all ingredients in a medium mixing bowl. Use a hand mixer to mix until thoroughly combined. Add the frangipane to the cooled crusts and top them with slices of poached pears.

7. Bake the pies for 30 minutes. Check the pies and if a toothpick inserted comes out clean, they are done. If not, bake for another 10 minutes. You may need to cover them loosely with foil to prevent the tops of the battlements from burning.

8. Once done, let cool to room temperature before serving. Garnish with sliced almonds, if desired.

Skip to the end . . .

Desserts
and Candies

Clever Sicilian's "Inconceivable!" Dessert

It's a toss-up between "inconceivable!" or "as you wish" as the most quoted line from *The Princess Bride*, a film that is filled to the brim with quotable lines. Wallace Shawn, knowing he was director Rob Reiner's second choice for the role after Danny DeVito, was actually extremely nervous about being fired because he couldn't speak in a Sicilian accent. *The Princess Bride* without Wallace Shawn? Inconceivable! Frying gelato at high temperatures without melting it? INCONCEIVABLE! This dish is a fusion of a tempura-fried ice cream and Sicilian *brioche con gelato*. Aristotle, Plato, Socrates, and all those other morons could NEVER conceive.

INGREDIENTS

FOR THE FRIED GELATO

2 pints (946 ml) of your favorite gelato

12 oz (340 g) brioche, castella, or
   pound cake, sliced into
   2-inch (5-cm)-thick slices

Canola oil, for frying

1 cup (125 g) all-purpose flour

1 large egg

1 cup (235 ml) cold water

1–2 cups (50–100 g) panko bread crumbs,
   or more as needed

FOR TOPPINGS

Confectioners' sugar

Whipped cream

Red and green glazed cherries
   or maraschino cherries

Chocolate sauce

Chopped pistachios

1. To make the fried gelato, scoop out 6 balls of gelato onto a parchment paper–lined baking sheet and freeze uncovered for at least 2 hours, or until firm.

2. Line up two or three slices of brioche side by side on plastic wrap. Top them with another sheet of plastic wrap and flatten them with a rolling pin. Be careful not to flatten so much that they crumble. Get the gelato balls out of the freezer and wrap them in the brioche. Repeat until all the ice cream balls are securely wrapped and fully enclosed. Freeze the wrapped balls for at least 2 hours, or until firm.

3. In a deep fryer or thick-bottomed saucepan, heat the canola oil to 400°F (200°C). Use a candy thermometer to keep track of the temperature if you're using a saucepan.

4. Mix the flour, egg, and water to create a batter. Coat the wrapped ice cream balls in the batter and roll the balls in panko. Best to do this one ball at a time.

5. Carefully lower the batter-coated ice cream ball into the oil and cook for 15 to 30 seconds, until golden brown. Don't fry for too long because the ice cream will melt. Remove from the oil and pat dry with a paper towel. Repeat for the remaining balls.

6. If you used brioche, use a sieve to dust the gelato balls with confectioners' sugar; skip this if you used cake. Add whipped cream around the perimeter of the ball and dot with the glazed cherries. Drizzle chocolate sauce over everything and sprinkle with pistachios. Serve immediately!

Miracle Max's Chocolate-Covered Miracle Pill

As Max and Valerie finish making the pill that will revive Westley, Val coats it with chocolate, informing an incredulous Inigo that the chocolate coating will help it go down easier. Our little chocolate-coated pills are filled with a decadent espresso cream that will take you all the way from mostly dead to slightly alive. Truffle-making takes patience so be sure not to rush through the process because what happens when you rush a Miracle Man? That's right. Remember not to go swimming for at least an hour after eating!

INGREDIENTS

32 oz (907 g) semisweet chocolate, finely chopped

1 cup (235 ml) heavy whipping cream

1 tablespoon (6 g) espresso powder and/ or cocoa powder, or to taste

1 teaspoon cinnamon (optional)

6 tablespoons (84 g) unsalted butter, room temperature

1. Add half of the chocolate to a heatproof bowl. In a small saucepan, bring the cream to a boil over medium heat. Once it starts to boil, remove it from the heat and whisk in the espresso powder and cinnamon.

2. Pour the espresso cream over the chopped chocolate. Allow the mixture to sit for 2 to 3 minutes, or until the chocolate has mostly melted, then whisk until smooth. Stir in the butter, then whisk until mixture is smooth and shiny.

3. Cool the mixture to room temperature, then cover the bowl with plastic wrap. Refrigerate for 2 hours, or until it's firm enough to scoop.

4. Line two large baking sheets with parchment paper. Scoop about a tablespoon of the truffle filling and quickly roll it between your hands to form a pill shape. Transfer to the prepared baking sheet, and repeat until you've used all the chocolate-espresso mixture. Refrigerate for 30 minutes.

5. In the meantime, begin tempering the chocolate coating. A double boiler will make this step easier. If you don't have one, fill a medium saucepan one-third full with water and bring it to a gentle simmer over medium heat. Place a large stainless-steel bowl on top of the pan, making sure it is not directly touching the simmering water.

6. Reduce the heat to low and add two-thirds of the remaining chocolate to the bowl. Place a candy thermometer into the chocolate and let it melt, stirring frequently with a silicone spatula. The temperature of the chocolate should never exceed 120°F (49°C).

7. Once the chocolate has completely melted, remove the bowl from the heat but keep the water simmering. Stir in the remaining chocolate a little bit at a time, making sure what you add has completely melted before adding any more.

8. Set aside and allow the chocolate to cool to 80°F (27°C). Once the chocolate has reached 80°F, place it back over the simmering water and reheat to around 90°F (32°C), then remove the bowl.

9. Using a candy dipper or a fork, dip each refrigerated truffle in the chocolate, allowing excess chocolate to drip back into the bowl before transferring it back to the parchment-lined baking sheet. You may need to drip some additional coating to cover any holes that happen when removing the fork.

10. Allow the chocolate coating to completely set before serving in about 1 hour.

Anybody Want a Peanut (Buttercup?)

Fezzik can't resist a good rhyme and Inigo is happy to challenge him, much to Vizzini's vexation. The peanut line is among one of the most quoted lines from the film (which is really saying something!) so I wanted to make something extra special to commemorate it. Rich dark chocolate ganache and a creamy peanut butter filling make this dessert so deliciously decadent that you may find yourself speaking in rhyming couplets. I'll go first! It really is very sweet, eating it will be a treat!

INGREDIENTS

FOR THE CRUST
¼ cup (55 g) unsalted butter
5 oz (142 g) semisweet chocolate, chopped
40 (9 oz or 255 g) chocolate cookie wafers

FOR THE PEANUT BUTTER FILLING
8 oz (226 g) cream cheese,
    room temperature
1 cup (260 g) smooth peanut butter
¾ cup (150 g) granulated sugar
2 teaspoons (10 ml) vanilla extract
    or vanilla bean paste
1 cup (235 ml) heavy whipping cream,
    chilled

FOR THE TOPPING
5 oz (142 g) semisweet chocolate, chopped
½ cup (120 ml) heavy whipping cream
¼ cup (36 g) roasted peanuts, halved

1. To make the crust, preheat the oven to 375°F (190°C).

2. Add the cookie wafers to a dry blender or food processor. Pulse until they resemble fine crumbs.

3. Melt the butter in a microwave-safe bowl. While the butter is hot, add the chocolate chips and stir until melted. You may need to microwave it for 30 more seconds to completely melt the chocolate.

4. Add the cookie crumbs and stir until combined. Press the cookie crumbs evenly over the bottom and sides of either a 10-inch (25 cm) tart pan with a removable bottom or a 10-inch (25-cm) springform pan. Bake the crust for 10 to 12 minutes, then let it cool.

5. Meanwhile, make the peanut butter filling. Using an electric mixer and a large bowl, beat the cream cheese with the peanut butter, sugar, and vanilla on medium speed for about 2 minutes, until well blended.

6. In another large bowl, whip the cream until stiff peaks form. Add half of the whipped cream to the peanut butter mixture. Beat on low speed to combine. Add the rest of the whipped cream and fold in until evenly combined.

7. Spoon the filling into the crust, smoothing down the surface with a rubber spatula. Refrigerate for 1 hour.

8. To make the topping, combine the chocolate with the heavy cream in a medium microwave-safe bowl. Microwave at high power in 20-second intervals, until the chocolate is melted and the cream is hot. Stir until smooth and well-combined, then let it cool to barely warm, stirring occasionally.

9. Spread the chocolate topping over the chilled peanut butter filling.

10. To garnish, create little buttercup flowers out of halved peanuts by arranging them into circles using the peanuts as petals. Chill uncovered in the refrigerator for 3 hours.

11. To serve, carefully remove the rim from the pan by gently pressing upward on the bottom while holding the rim in place. If using a springform pan, run a knife around the edges to loosen it, then release the tart from the springform ring. Serve chilled.

Man in Black's "No One to Be Trifled With" Trifle

Before the Man in Black reveals himself as Westley, Buttercup asks him who he is and he replies, "No one to be trifled with." The word "trifle" is actually used three times in the script (yes, I counted). Of course, trifle in this context means a thing of little value or importance. But it's also a dessert, dating at least as far back as 1585, with layers of cake, custard, fruit, and often flavored with liqueurs. This black forest trifle can be made into individual servings or in one impressive presentation.

INGREDIENTS

FOR THE CUSTARD
1 cup (235 ml) heavy whipping cream
1 cup (235 ml) whole milk
2 teaspoons (10 ml) vanilla extract
    or vanilla bean paste
4 egg yolks
1½ tablespoons (12 g) cornstarch
¼ cup (50 g) granulated sugar

FOR THE TRIFLE
1 (15-oz or 425-g) can pitted black
    cherries or dark cherries in syrup
2 cups (310 g) pitted fresh or frozen
    black cherries
3 tablespoons (45 ml) cherry liqueur
    or cherry juice
3 tablespoons (45 ml) spiced rum
    or 1 teaspoon rum extract (optional)
1½ cups (355 ml) heavy whipping cream
1 cup (224 g) crème fraîche or sour cream
30–40 brownie bites

FOR THE DÉCOR
2 sheets of thick, quality paper (optional)
Chocolate shavings (optional)
Whole black cherries (optional)
Black mask cupcake toppers (optional)

1. To make the custard, combine the milk, heavy cream, and vanilla in a medium saucepan over medium heat. Stir continuously for 5 to 6 minutes, then remove from the heat when the mixture is hot but not boiling.

2. In a large heatproof bowl, whisk together the egg yolks, cornstarch, and sugar until well blended.

3. Slowly pour the hot cream mixture into the egg yolk mixture, whisking constantly to prevent the eggs from scrambling. Return this mixture back to the saucepan and set over low heat. Stir for 8 to 10 minutes, or until the custard has thickened and easily coats the spoon. Do not bring custard to a boil as it will curdle. Once thickened, allow the custard to cool to room temperature, cover with plastic wrap and place in the fridge for at least one hour, up to overnight.

4. To make the trifle, drain the canned cherries and reserve half a cup (120 ml) of the syrup. Add the canned cherries and the pitted cherries to a mixing bowl. Stir together and set aside. Mix half the reserved syrup with the cherry liqueur and set aside. Mix the other half of the syrup with the rum (if using) and stir that into the mixed cherry mixture.

5. Add the heavy cream and the crème fraîche to a large mixing bowl. Whip with a hand mixer until soft peaks form. Bring out the custard you made earlier and stir a large spoonful of the whipped cream into the custard to loosen the consistency.

6. Scatter about half of the brownie bites over the base of a large, glass trifle dish or into separate clear dessert cups. Drizzle half of the cherry liqueur mixture evenly over the brownies.

7. Cover the brownies with half of the mixed cherries, then spread over it half of the custard and half of the whipped cream. Repeat with a second layer of the remaining brownies, liqueur syrup, cherries, and custard. Finish with the whipped cream.

8. To decorate, you can simply sprinkle on some dark chocolate shavings and add some black cherries on top. To add some swashbuckling flare, make a paper cutout of the Man in Black's mask: from the center of the paper cut out a large, rounded upside down 'B'-ish shape. From the other sheet of paper, cut out two smaller ovals to use for the mask's eye holes. It may take a few tries to get the sizing correct. Place the paper with the B-shape on top of the trifle and place the two ovals within the B-shape to make the eyes. Now, sprinkle the chocolate shaving generously over the cutout, then remove the paper. Voilà!

9. If you are serving the trifle in individual dessert cups, I recommend black masquerade cupcake toppers. These can be found on many online retailers, or you can DIY with black construction paper, glue, and toothpicks.

10. Loosely cover the top of the trifle(s) with plastic wrap and chill for at least 1 hour and up to 24 hours before serving.

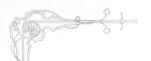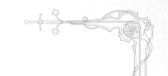

Lightning Sand Parfait

 SERVES 4 TO 6

Lightning sand is the second of the three terrors which Westley and Buttercup encounter in the Fire Swamp. I'm sure I speak for many people born after 1980-ish when I say that *The Princess Bride* is one of the major contributors to our belief that quicksand would be a big problem in life. "But what would it taste like?" is a question you have probably never asked yourself. Well, I'm happy to offer the unsolicited answer to that question with this recipe.

INGREDIENTS

4 graham crackers

25 vanilla wafers

2 chocolate creme-filled
   sandwich cookies

8 oz (226 g) cream cheese, softened

¼ cup (56 g) crème fraîche or sour cream

1½ teaspoons vanilla bean paste
   or vanilla extract

½ cup (100 g) caster/superfine sugar

1 cup (235 ml) heavy whipping cream

1. In a food processor, add the graham crackers and vanilla wafers. Combine until very fine and sand-like. Place the sandwich cookies in a ziplock bag and use a pastry roller to crush them into fine crumbs.

2. In a large bowl using a hand mixer or stand mixer with the paddle attachment, beat the cream cheese, crème fraîche, vanilla, and half the sugar on medium speed until completely smooth and creamy.

3. In a medium bowl, whisk the heavy cream and remaining sugar until medium peaks form. Gently fold in half of the whipped cream into the cream cheese mixture. Reserve the other half.

4. Divide your cream cheese mixture among four to six clear dessert cups. Add a layer of the whipped cream. On top of that, add your sand.

5. Sprinkle the sandwich crumbs around the perimeter of the sand to imitate what it looked like in the movie with dark swamp soil surrounding fine sand.

FROM THE PAGES

In the book the Fire Swamp actually has snow sand, which, Goldman notes, is distinct from lightning sand. Snow sand is dry and powdery and suffocates those unfortunate enough to wander into it, whereas lightning sand is wet and drowns its victims. This variance in moisture and texture is represented well by a parfait!

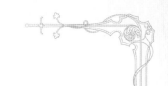

Hello · Lady(fingers)!

When Fezzik brings the four white horses to aid in the final escape, he notices Buttercup in the window, with a huge smile and a little wave, he says "Hello, Lady!" The sweetness of that moment and the way Fezzik and Buttercup smile at each other really warms the heart. The friendship between André the Giant and Robin Wright was adorable behind the scenes as well. Robin has said that when she got cold while filming in chilly weather, André would place one of his immense hands over her head to keep her warm. It's friendship worth commemorating and this ladyfinger dessert, which has French origins like André, resembles Buttercup's iconic red dress.

INGREDIENTS

FOR THE CAKE
Unsalted butter
¼ cup (60 ml) raspberry or strawberry
    liqueur, such as Chambord®
    or crème de fraise
20–25 ladyfinger cookies
⅔ cup (160 ml) water, room temperature
2 envelopes (½ oz or 14 g total)
    unflavored gelatin
½ cup (100 g) granulated sugar,
    or more to taste
2 cups (500 g) frozen raspberries or
    strawberries, thawed
3 tablespoons (45 ml) fresh lemon juice
Zest of 1 lemon
2 cups (475 ml) heavy whipping cream

FOR THE TOPPING
1 cup (235 ml) heavy whipping cream
2 tablespoons (26 g) caster/superfine sugar
1–2 cups (125–250 g) fresh raspberries
    or strawberries, stems removed
Sprigs of fresh mint (optional)
Ribbon (optional)

1. To make the cake, grease a 9-inch (23-cm) springform cake pan with butter. Sprinkle the raspberry liqueur along the un-sugared sides of the ladyfinger cookies. Arrange a layer of the cookies around the sides of the pan, liqueur sides facing inward; you want the dry sides facing outward for presentation. Line the bottom with the remaining cookies, you may need to cut them up into smaller pieces to fit. Set this aside.

2. In a small saucepan, mix the water and gelatin. Let it sit for a couple of minutes. Heat the gelatin mixture over low heat, stirring occasionally, until the gelatin is completely dissolved. Remove from the heat and add the sugar, raspberries, lemon juice, and lemon zest. Beat with a whisk until foamy. Chill in the fridge for 10 to 20 minutes until the mixture thickens a bit.

3. Use a hand mixer on high to whip the cream until stiff peaks form, then carefully fold the raspberry mixture into the whipped cream. Taste and adjust sweetness. Pour the entire mixture into the pan prepared with the ladyfingers, smoothing it with a spatula. Refrigerate for approximately 4 hours until it's firm and set, then release it from the pan.

4. To make the topping, whip the whipping cream and sugar on high speed until stiff peaks form. Spread the whipped cream over the top of the cake. Decorate the top with fresh raspberries and dot with sprigs of fresh mint. You can also line the bottom of the cake with additional raspberries. If desired, tie a ribbon or twine around the cake for presentation and remove it before slicing.

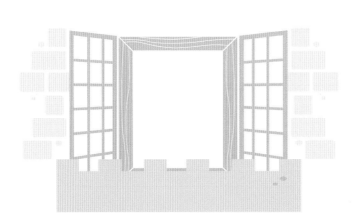

Oh, You Mean · THIS Gate Key (Lime Posset)!

SERVES 4 TO 6

Adding citrus juice to cream causes it to curdle, much like Yellin's blood when Inigo tells Fezzik to rip his arms off. This results in a creamy custard called a *posset*. Originating in the fifteenth century, possets are deliciously smooth, sweet, slightly tangy, and pairs perfectly with shortbread cookies. This recipe will make more cookies than strictly necessary to allow for some inevitable accidents, breaks, and mysterious disappearances.

INGREDIENTS

FOR THE POSSET
2 cups (475 ml) heavy cream
¾ cup (150 g) granulated sugar
5 tablespoons (75 ml) key lime juice
Zest of 1 key lime

FOR THE COOKIES
¾ cup (168 g) salted butter, softened
½ cup (60 g) confectioners' sugar
1½ tablespoons (25 ml) key lime juice
2 teaspoons (4 g) key lime zest
1½ cups (188 g) all-purpose flour
Key-shaped cookie cutters (optional)

FOR THE EXTRA DÉCOR (OPTIONAL)
Slices of key lime
Key lime zest

1. To make the posset, bring the cream and sugar to a boil over medium-high heat, stirring occasionally, until the sugar has dissolved. Reduce the heat to medium and boil for 3 to 4 minutes, stirring constantly. Remove from the heat, and stir in the lime juice and zest. Let cool for about 10 minutes, then pour the mixture into serving glasses. Cover with plastic wrap and chill for at least 2 hours and up to 24 hours in the fridge, or until the posset has set.

2. To make the cookies, mix the butter, confectioners' sugar, lime juice, and zest in a large mixing bowl. Sift in the flour a little at a time, stirring between each addition. Once the dough starts to come together, move to a floured surface and knead into a compact ball.

3. On a lightly floured surface, roll out the cookie dough to about ¼-inch (6-mm) thickness. If it's too cold to roll, let it rest for about 10 minutes before trying again. Use a key-shaped cookie cutter to cut out the cookies. You can also use a knife to cut them yourself, key shapes are pretty simple, especially with a template or even just a reference! Place the cookies on a parchment paper–lined cookie sheet and refrigerate for 1 hour.

4. Preheat the oven to 350°F (175°C). Bake for approximately 12 minutes and let cool to room temperature.

5. Remove the possets from the fridge. If desired, top with thin lime slices and sprinkle with zest before adding the key cookies on top. Serve!

FROM THE PAGES

The posset is closely related to the syllabub, a whipped cream dessert made with wine or liquor. In the book, Buttercup says some harsh words to Westley in anger and later tells him she didn't mean a single "syllabub," which Westley finds highly endearing. To make the lime posset into a syllabub, skip the heating steps and replace half of the lime juice with a sweet white wine. Whip the ingredients together until light and fluffy, then set in the fridge for at least an hour.

Kissing Book Kisses

At first, Fred Savage's character is very resistant to the love part of this love story, preferring to skip over the yucky grown-up stuff like kissing. But *The Princess Bride* is the greatest love story ever told, and by the end of the film he is fully invested in Westley and Buttercup's romance. Meringue kisses are pure, with an appearance like fluffy white clouds, even a kid wouldn't want to skip these kisses.

INGREDIENTS

4 large egg whites, room temperature
¼ teaspoon cream of tartar
¼ teaspoon kosher salt
¾ cup (150 g) superfine sugar

½ teaspoon vanilla extract or rose water
Drops of gel food coloring (optional)
Sugar pearls, sprinkles or
    other decorations (optional)

1. Preheat the oven to 200°F (93°C). You're not so much baking these as drying them out. Line a baking sheet with parchment paper.

2. Place the egg whites in a large mixing bowl. Add the cream of tartar and salt. With a hand mixer, whip the whites on medium speed until foamy and just beginning to turn white.

3. While continuing to whip, very slowly add the sugar about ¼ teaspoon at a time. Once all the sugar has been added, switch the mixer to high speed and whip until the meringue is shiny and very stiff.

4. Fold in the vanilla and the food coloring (if using).

5. Transfer the meringue to a piping bag fitted with a French star tip. Pipe 1-inch (2.5-cm) diameter kisses onto a parchment-lined baking sheet. Top with decorations of your choice (if using).

6. Bake the meringues in the oven for 2 hours, or until light and crisp. Do not brown.

Cherry Pits of Despair

SERVES 4 TO 6

The Pit of Despair: a dank, cavernous dungeon where Count Rugen conducts his torturous experiments and the Albino prepares the victims. And apparently where Humperdinck occasionally stops by to watch them work—whenever he's not too busy murdering his wife and framing Guilder. The Pit of Despair is truly the pits, but this dessert is actually quite pleasant. If you elect to keep the cherry pits in, they impart a subtle almond flavor but removing them while you eat will add just the right amount of annoyance and discomfort for you to get a taste of despair. Just make sure you don't swallow or bite into them, that would be cause for ultimate suffering!

INGREDIENTS

Unsalted butter
1½ cups (207–231 g) fresh or frozen
    black cherries, with or without pits
4 large eggs
½ cup (100 g) granulated sugar
1 cup (235 ml) whole milk or cream
½ teaspoon vanilla extract or
    vanilla bean paste

½ tablespoon (8 ml) amaretto
    or ½ teaspoon almond extract
¾ cup (94 g) all-purpose flour
½ teaspoon salt
Confectioners' sugar

1. Preheat the oven to 350°F (175°C). Grease a 9-inch (23-cm) round cake pan with butter. Spread the cherries out in an even layer in the bottom of the pan.

2. In a mixing bowl, add the eggs and sugar. Use a hand mixer to blend until the eggs are very frothy. Add the milk, vanilla, amaretto, flour, and salt. Blend until combined. Slowly pour the batter over the cherries in the pan.

3. Bake for about 35 minutes, until golden and a toothpick inserted in the middle comes out clean.

4. Let it cool to room temperature, then use a sieve to dust with confectioners' sugar.

5. Serve in slices. Make sure to let your guests know if you kept in the cherry pits!

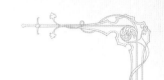

Twu Wuv Twuffles

MAKES 15 TO 20

True love is at the heart of *The Princess Bride*, and many of the characters deliver admirable monologues about it—perhaps none quite so memorably as the Impressive Clergyman while officiating Buttercup and Humperdinck's wedding. Although his message may be somewhat undermined by his unusual pronunciation, he's absolutely right: you should tweasuwe your wuv! With a striking appearance and flavors of raspberry and rose, these truffles are perfect for romantic gestures. Gift them to your twu wuv for any occasion!

INGREDIENTS

FOR THE FILLING

2 oz (57 g) freeze-dried raspberries

10 oz (283 g) white chocolate, chopped

⅓ cup (80 ml) heavy whipping cream

¼ cup (55 g) unsalted butter,
    room temperature

1 tablespoon (15 ml) rose water

FOR THE COATING

10 oz (283 g) white chocolate melting
    wafers or candy melts

Freeze-dried raspberries, powdered

1. To make the filling, use a food processor or blender to pulse the raspberries into fine crumbs.

2. Add the white chocolate, cream, and butter to a microwave-safe bowl. Heat in the medium-high setting of the microwave for intervals of 30-seconds, until the chocolate has completely melted. Stir between each interval until perfectly combined.

3. Add three-quarters of the ground raspberries and reserve the rest for the décor. Add the rosewater, and whisk until well blended. Cover with plastic wrap, making sure to press it over the surface to minimize contact with air. Allow to come to room temperature before putting the mix in the fridge to firm up for at least 4 hours and up to overnight.

4. Use a small ice cream scoop to form balls of truffle mixture. Set them on a baking tray lined with parchment paper and let them chill in the fridge for 2 hours until hardened, then let them sit at room temperature for another 15 to 30 minutes before coating.

5. Melt the candy melts in a microwave-safe bowl at low power, stirring every 30 seconds, until smooth.

6. Using a candy dipper or a fork, dip each truffle in the melted candy melts, allowing excess to drip back into the bowl before transferring it back to the parchment-lined baking sheet. You may need to drip some additional candy coating to cover any holes that happen when removing the fork.

7. Immediately sprinkle each with the remaining raspberry crumbs before coating the next truffle.

8. When all truffles are complete, allow the coating to completely set for at least 1 hour before serving.

Vegan, Vegetarian, and Kosher Replacements

EGGS

- ¼ cup (60 g) applesauce
- ¼ cup (60 g) puréed silken tofu
- ¼ cup (60 ml) buttermilk
- 1 tablespoon (11 g) chia seeds or 1 tablespoon (7 g) ground flaxseed plus 3 tablespoons (45 ml) of water
- Aquafaba or egg replacer (Follow package directions.)
- Half a medium banana, mashed (Use a browning, mushier banana if possible.)

HEAVY CREAM

- Full-fat coconut cream. If the cream is being whipped, chill a can of coconut milk overnight and use only the top solidified part. Add a pinch of cream of tartar to stabilize.

MILK

- Almond milk
- Soymilk
- Coconut milk
- Oat milk
- Hemp milk
- Macadamia milk
- Quinoa milk
- Rice milk
- Pea milk

BUTTER

- Coconut oil
- Olive oil
- Shortening
- Margarine
- Other vegan butter product

HONEY

- Agave nectar
- Maple syrup
- Brown rice syrup
- Coconut nectar

GELATIN

- Vegan jel (Use an equal amount or follow package directions.)
- Agar-agar powder (Generally use three-quarters the amount of the gelatin.)
- Xanthan gum (Use half the amount of gelatin.)

BACON

- Turkey, beef, or duck bacon, for nonvegetarian but kosher
- Equal amount mushrooms (shiitakes are ideal) plus liquid smoke or smoked paprika
- Vegan or veggie bacon products, such as coconut or tempeh bacon

Buttercup's Farmhouse Supper

After a long day of farm chores, nothing could be better than sitting down to a supper of fresh baked bread, hot stew, and apple pie for dessert. One can even hear Buttercup demanding, "Farm Boy, pass the butter." And Westley's reply: "As you wish!"

APPETIZER
"Life is Pain" Pandemain

MAIN COURSE
Farm Boy Stew

DESSERT COURSE
Princess Buttercups (sans sprinkles)
"As You Wish" Appeltaart

COCKTAIL SPECIAL
Four White Horses

DÉCOR
Linen Tablecloth
Rustic Dinnerware
Milk Can Vase
Glass Milk Bottles
Wild flowers
Woven Place Mats
Bowl of Apples
Breadbasket
Ceramic Butter Crock
Clay or Stoneware Pitcher
Decorative Hay Bale

Feast Of Insanity

Imagine climbing the Cliff of Insanity and enjoying a feast in the castle ruins where the greatest sword fight in history took place. This feast will take you there and have your guests asking, "Who are you? I must know."

APPETIZER
"Not a Lot of Money in
Revenge" Beggar's Purses

MAIN COURSE
Swordmasters' Fon-Duel
The Capo Farro Technique

DESSERT COURSE
Man in Black's "No One to Be
Trifled With" Trifle

COCKTAIL SPECIAL
"Cliffs of Insanity" Shot
Vengeful Spaniard's Sangria

DÉCOR
Moss or Green Gauze Table
Runner
Stone or Rope Place Mats
Stoneware Cups
Green and/or Stoneware
Plates
Bricks and/or Stones
A Rope
Natural Wood
Sword Skewers
Dried Moss
Decorative Swords

Storming The Castle Banquet

This sumptuous spread will have your guests feeling as if they are attending an elaborate royal banquet in Humperdinck's castle. One that might be interrupted at any moment by a giant, a Spaniard, and slightly alive pirate/farmboy.

APPETIZERS
Six-Fingered Man Skewers
(Rugen's Flammkuchen)
Flaming Fezzik Flambé

MAIN COURSE
Humperdinck's Crown Roast
The National Dish of Florin

DESSERT COURSE
Oh, You Mean THIS Key Lime
Posset
Have Fun Storming the
Chastletes!

COCKTAIL SPECIAL
Dead Pirate Robert's "No
Survivors" Bumbo "Mostly
Dead" Corpse Reviver

DÉCOR
Gold Florentine Dinnerware
Brass Candelabras
Brass Goblets
Damask Tablecloth
Embroidered Napkins
Bowls of Fresh Fruits
Castle Centerpiece
Elaborate Floral
Arrangements
Wheelbarrow Prop (optional)

True Love's Repast

True love is the greatest thing in the world, and it doesn't happen every day, so one should always treasure it. Set a romantic candlelit dinner for two that is guaranteed to net you a kiss in the Top 5.

APPETIZER
Have You the Wings?

MAIN COURSE
Florinese "Mawidge" Soup
"Life is Pain" Pandemain

DESSERT COURSE
Twu Wuv Twuffles
Kissing Book Kisses

COCKTAIL SPECIAL
"The Sea After a Storm" Dark
and Stormy

DÉCOR
Red Tablecloth
Gold or Gold-rimmed
Dinnerware
Brocade-Patterned Napkins
Roses and Baby's Breath
Rose Petals
Gold Candlesticks or Tea
Candles
Crystal Goblets or Wine
Glasses
A Chalkboard which Reads,
"As you wish!"
An Engagement Ring?

About the Author

Cassandra Reeder is an avid home cook and lifetime geek. For well over a decade, she has been helping other geeks and nerds all over the world make their fictional food fantasies come true at www.geekychef.com. In 2014, she released *The Geeky Chef Cookbook*, which, to her immense delight and gratitude, has been very well received. In 2017, she followed the success of that book with a sequel, *The Geeky Chef Strikes Back*, a collection of even more unofficial recipes from geek life, and in 2018, her collection of geeky cocktails and mocktails, *The Geeky Chef Drinks*, was published. Cassandra is always seeking new worlds and stories to bring to life though food. Cassandra currently lives in Portland, Oregon with her husband and two children.

Acknowledgments

Nicholas Reeder, thank you for taking on many of the more challenging recipes for and with me, and for distracting my little ones while I snuck away to write. I really couldn't have done this without you, big brother.

Rolanda Conversino, thank you for convincing me to take on this project and for testing so many recipes and for always cheering me on. You're the nicest, sweetest, prettiest mother of them all. Joe Conversino, thank you for all your ideas and feedback!

"Jesk" Diza, thank you for being such a supportive husband, loving father, and the most enthusiastic recipe tester. I appreciate everything you do.

Thanks to Amanda Backur for taking on a good chunk of the desserts (some of them very difficult!) and Brian for being such a good test subject. You're both the best.

Jessica Garcia, thank you for being a friend, a pal, and a confidante. I hope I made the little girl versions of us proud.

Thanks to the Bracket Battles group for the party ideas and the laughs. Duck T_____s 4ever.

Thanks to the folks at medievalcookery.com for compiling and maintaining that database.

Thanks to the guys at Milwaukie Liquor Store (it's not what you think) for all the suggestions, advice, and enthusiasm.

Huge thanks to Delia Greve and Jenna Nelson Patton for all their hard work making this cookbook happen. I feel like the three of us stormed a castle with only a wheelbarrow and a cloak!

There are no words adequate enough to thank the late and great writer William Goldman, and the entire cast and crew of *The Princess Bride*, for bringing so much comfort and happiness to me and so many others. Special thanks to Cary Elwes and Joe Layden for writing and recording the audiobook for *As You Wish: Inconceivable Tales from the Making of The Princess Bride*, which has been an incredibly fun and helpful resource.

Index